Mindfulness-based Interventions with Children and Adolescents

This book comprehensively reviews mindfulness-based interventions for specific areas of functioning in children and adolescents, with refreshing insights and perspectives. Based on a solid foundation of research and practice, it presents the nature of mindfulness, examines the psychological processes that may underlie mindfulness, and explores how to assess it.

Mindfulness is about how we can be attentive to and present for everything that happens in our daily lives. This book draws upon current research in the field in order to explore topics such as the fundamentals of teaching mindfulness to children and adolescents; assessment of mindfulness in this population; use of mindfulness in educational settings; and clinical applications in mental health, including substance abuse, hyperactivity, and intellectual and developmental disabilities. With contributions from internationally renowned clinicians and scholars, this book provides a balanced account of the strengths and weaknesses of current research and how mindfulness-based programs can be used to enhance well-being and reduce suffering.

This book will be of great interest for academics, scholars, and post-graduate students involved in the study of the mental health of children and adolescents. It will also appeal to psychologists, psychiatrists, nurses, social workers, rehabilitation therapists, and others, such as school counsellors, who provide clinical care to children and adolescents.

Nirbhay N. Singh is a clinical professor of psychiatry and health behavior at the Medical College of Georgia, Augusta University, certified behavior analyst, and developer of the Mindfulness-Based Positive Behavior Support (MBPBS) and Soles of the Feet (SoF) programs.

Subhashni D. Singh Joy is a graduate of the University of Virginia and the University of North Carolina–Chapel Hill. She has publications across a broad range of health care-related topics, including mindfulness and adolescent mental health.

The Mental Health and Well-being of Children and Adolescents

Series Editor: Garry Hornby
(University of Plymouth)

Mental health disorders in children and young people are increasing, with one in four under-16s experiencing mental health difficulties which will disrupt relationships, education and work. In addition to this, one in ten under-16s suffers from a diagnosed disorder. Access to up-to-date research and appropriate interventions minimises the mental health challenges these children and adolescents face and reduces their potentially lifelong impact.

It has been internationally recognised that the scale of mental health research is low in relation to the burden of the disorder. This research-focused series will consist of titles that consider key issues affecting young people's mental health and well-being, exploring preventative measures, promoting positive behaviour, and sharing research to develop effective and efficient treatment.

Aimed primarily at researchers and postgraduate students, this series will also be of interest to practitioners in the mental health field, such as psychologists, and some in the field of education, such as counsellors, who would like to implement research-based findings in their clinical practice.

Books in the series include:

School Bullying and Mental Health
Risks, Intervention and Prevention
Helen Cowie and Carrie-Anne Myers

Mental Health and Academic Learning in Schools
Approaches for Facilitating the Wellbeing of Children and Young People
Andrea Reupert

Mindfulness-based Interventions with Children and Adolescents
Research and Practice
Edited by Nirbhay N. Singh and Subhashni D. Singh Joy

Please visit www.routledge.com/The-Mental-Health-and-Well-being-of-Children-and-Adolescents/book-series/MHWCA.

Mindfulness-based Interventions with Children and Adolescents

Research and Practice

Edited by Nirbhay N. Singh and Subhashni D. Singh Joy

Routledge
Taylor & Francis Group
LONDON AND NEW YORK

First published 2021
by Routledge
2 Park Square, Milton Park, Abingdon, Oxon OX14 4RN

and by Routledge
52 Vanderbilt Avenue, New York, NY 10017

Routledge is an imprint of the Taylor & Francis Group, an informa business

British Library Cataloguing-in-Publication Data
A catalogue record for this book is available from the British Library

Library of Congress Cataloging-in-Publication Data
A catalog record for this book has been requested

ISBN: 978-1-138-68046-3 (hbk)
ISBN: 978-1-315-56386-2 (ebk)

Typeset in Bembo
by Apex CoVantage, LLC

Dedicated to
All children and adolescents
With skillful actions
may you decrease and eliminate suffering
and the roots of suffering

Contents

Figures

Tables

Contributors

Ajahn Amaro received a BSc Hons in psychology and physiology from the University of London. Spiritual searching led him to Thailand, where he went to Wat Pah Nanachat, a Forest Tradition monastery established for Western disciples of Thai meditation master Ajahn Chah, who ordained him as a monk in 1979. Soon afterwards he returned to England and joined Ajahn Sumedho at the newly established Chithurst Monastery. In 1983 he made an 830-mile journey on foot to Harnham Monastery in Northumberland, and in 1985 he was invited to join the community at the newly opened Amaravati Monastery. He resided for 10 years at Amaravati, making trips to California every year during the early 1990s at the invitation of Ajahn Sumedho's students who were based there. During that time at Amaravati, Ajahn Amaro helped with teaching and administration, serving as vice-abbot for the last two years. In June 1996, he established Abhayagiri Monastery in Redwood Valley, California, where he was co-abbot with Ajahn Pasanno until 2010. In July 2010 he was invited to return to Amaravati to be the successor of Ajahn Sumedho as abbot of this large monastic community. He was granted permission to be an ordination preceptor in 2011. He has presided over the ordination of nine nuns and 37 monks since that date. He has authored or coauthored about 25 books, all for free distribution. Among these are: *Finding the Missing Peace* (2011); *Roots and Currents: Collected Essays and Articles, 1991–2014* (2017); and *The Breakthrough: Buddhist Meditation as a Means of Liberation* (2016). His writings occasionally appear in the journal *Mindfulness*.

Susan Bögels is a clinical psychologist and founder of the Mindful Parenting method. She is professor of family mental health, in particular focusing on the role of mindfulness, at the University of Amsterdam and founder of UvA Minds, an academic training and treatment center for children and parents. She has published over 200 journal papers and is an Associate Editor of the journal *Mindfulness*. She is the lead author of the scholarly book *Mindful Parenting: A Guide for Mental Health Professionals* (2014) and the author of *Mindful Parenting: Finding Space to Be—In a World of To Do* (2020).

Grayson M. Butcher is a doctoral student at the University of North Texas. He received his MS from the University of North Texas in behavior analysis and is currently working toward a PhD in health services research with an emphasis in behavior analysis. His research currently focuses on stimulus control, verbal behavior, clarifying the behavioral unit of analysis, and the ways in which neuromodulatory systems contribute to selection by reinforcement. He is an author on six peer- and editor-reviewed articles and book chapters. In the future, he hopes to become a professor in order to research the behavioral unit of analysis as well as teach nonlinear contingency analysis and instructional design.

Esther I. de Bruin is Associate Professor at the University of Amsterdam, Research Institute of Child Development and Education in Amsterdam, the Netherlands. She has a PhD in child psychiatry from Erasmus University, Rotterdam, the Netherlands. She is a licensed health care psychologist and director of the outpatient academic treatment center for children, parents, and young adult, UvA Minds, Amsterdam, the Netherlands. She is an author of over 50 articles in national and international journals, coauthor of several book chapters related to mindfulness-based interventions, coauthor and developer of the Mindful2Work program for burnout-related complaints, and codeveloper of the MYmind mindfulness-based program for children with autism and their parents, and she is an Associate Editor of the journal *Mindfulness*.

Joshua C. Felver is Assistant Professor in the Department of Psychology at Syracuse University (USA) where he serves as the Director of Clinical Training in the school psychology doctoral training program. He took his PhD in school psychology and master's in special education from the University of Oregon and completed his predoctoral internship in pediatric psychology at Harvard Medical School and postdoctoral fellowship in child clinical psychology at the Alpert Medical School of Brown University. His research broadly focuses on the development, implementation, and study of mindfulness-based programming in school and community settings, with special focus on the investigation of biomechanisms underlying contemplative practices. He is a licensed and board-certified psychologist with clinical expertise in mindfulness-based programming and in the assessment and treatment of youth with social-emotional and psychiatric disabilities. He is an author of over 20 scientific publications, coauthor of the book *Mindfulness in the Classroom*, and former Associate Editor for the *Journal of Child and Family Studies* and *Mindfulness*.

Yoon-Suk Hwang obtained her doctoral degree from the University of Sydney. She was a lecturer in special education at Griffith University and research fellow at the Institute for Learning Sciences and Teacher Education, Australian Catholic University, before taking time off from formal academia to pursue spiritual interests. She is currently affiliated with the Centre for Disability Studies at the University of Sydney. Her research interests include applications of mindfulness-based training to individuals with social, emotional, behavioral, and learning difficulties, mindfulness training for teachers, and the use of mindfulness-based positive behavior support (MBPBS) as a systems-change program in agencies serving clients with different abilities. She is the lead author of the book *A Mindfulness Intervention for Children with Autism Spectrum Disorder: New Directions in Research and Practice*, and Associate Editor for *Mindfulness* and *Advances in Neurodevelopmental Disorders*.

Monica M. Jackman is an occupational therapist and owner of Little Lotus Therapy. She has a doctorate in occupational therapy from Chatham University and undergraduate and master's degrees from the University of Florida. Monica has authored book chapters on mindful engagement and the mindful engagement support model and research papers and has developed and implemented mindfulness-based training programs for caregivers, preschoolers, and school-aged children. She has presented nationally and internationally on mindfulness-based programs and interventions for children and adults. She is the developer of the OpenMind (OM) mindfulness-based social-emotional learning program.

Giulio E. Lancioni is a professor in the Department of Neuroscience and Sense Organs of the University of Bari. His research interests include, among others, the development and assessment of assistive technologies for (a) people with intellectual and developmental disabilities, (b) people with consciousness disorders, lack of speech, and pervasive motor impairments, and (c) people with neurodegenerative diseases such as Alzheimer's disease and amyotrophic lateral sclerosis. The assistive technologies are mainly used for promoting positive interaction with the environment and supporting alternative communication strategies and social and occupational skills among the aforementioned groups of people. He is the lead author of the book *Assistive Technology: Interventions for Individuals with Severe/Profound and Multiple Disabilities* and an Associate Editor of the journal *Advances in Neurodevelopmental Disorders*.

Michael E. Levin is an associate professor of Psychology at Utah State University. He received his PhD from the University of Nevada, Reno, under the mentorship of Dr. Steven Hayes and completed his clinical internship at the Brown University Clinical Psychology Training Consortium. His research focuses on delivering acceptance and commitment therapy (ACT) through online and self-guided formats for problems including college student mental health, depression, anxiety, weight management, and coping with medical conditions. He has published over 100 articles and book chapters as well as multiple books on ACT including *Innovations in Acceptance and Commitment Therapy* (Levin, Twohig & Krafft, 2020) and *ACT in Steps* (Twohig, Levin & Ong, 2020). He is the Editor-in-Chief for the *Journal of Contextual Behavioral Science*.

Renée Meppelink is currently working as a child psychologist at a mental health care center in the Netherlands, and she also works for the Sexual Assault Center. After she finished her master's in child development, she was awarded the NWO research talent grant to start her PhD at the University of Amsterdam, which she finished in 2019. Her PhD research was about the effectiveness of mindfulness training compared to the effectiveness of methylphenidate in children and adolescents with ADHD in a randomized control trial. She is an author on three articles in international journals. In her clinical work she carries on the practice of mindfulness with her patients.

Rachel E. Myers is Interim Associate Director of Undergraduate Programs in the Wellstar School of Nursing at Kennesaw State University, Georgia. She has previously held several leadership, educator, and clinical positions such as Director of Nursing, Director of Performance Improvement and Research, Director of Medical Staff Affairs, Staff Development Coordinator, Assistant Nurse Manager, and Nurse Consultant. She earned a doctoral degree in nursing from the University of South Florida. Her research interests include mindfulness-based interventions, health and wellness promotion, disease prevention, diabetes, and nursing education. She is a Qualified Mindfulness-Based Stress Reduction Teacher through the Center for Mindfulness, UMass Medical School. She is an author on over 20 articles in peer-reviewed journals and book chapters, most of which are related to mindfulness-based intervention research. She is an Associate Editor of the journal *Mindfulness*.

Sarah A. Potts is a child psychologist and Director of Behavioral Health at Partnership Health Center in Missoula, Montana. She graduated with her PhD in clinical/counseling psychology from Utah State University. She specialized in behavioral pediatrics and integrated care in her internship and fellowship at the Boys Town Center for Behavioral Health in Omaha, Nebraska. She works in an integrated behavioral health capacity with children and families and treats a variety of internalizing and externalizing behavior concerns, medical co-diagnoses, and family challenges. She specializes in evidence-based treatments such as ACT, DBT, and applied behavior interventions. Dr. Potts' research interests are focused around exploring barriers and improving access to excellent health care for all people, as well as strengthening evidence-based and cost-effective treatments as routine primary care practice.

Mary Katherine A. Schutt currently works in the Syracuse University Lerner Center for Public Health Promotion, where she is responsible for managing a national public health initiative. She received her undergraduate education in human development at the State University of New York at Oswego. She is a research assistant in the Syracuse University Mind Body Lab. Her research interests include the study of positive psychological and mindfulness interventions as they relate to compassion, authenticity, and purpose and meaning in life. She plans to pursue a doctorate in counseling psychology with a special focus on children and adolescents.

Michael P. Twohig is a licensed psychologist in the state of Utah and a professor of psychology at Utah State University. He received his BA and MS from the University of Wisconsin-Milwaukee and his PhD from the University of Nevada, Reno, and completed his clinical internship at the University of British Columbia Hospital. He is Past-President of the Association of Contextual Behavioral Science, the organization most associated with Acceptance and Commitment Therapy (ACT). His research focuses on the use of ACT across a variety of clinical presentations, with an emphasis on obsessive compulsive and related disorders. He has published over 100 peer-reviewed articles and two books: *An ACT-Enhanced Behavior Therapy Approach to the Treatment of Trichotillomania* (with Woods) and *ACT Verbatim for Depression and* Anxiety (with Hayes). His research has been funded through multiple sources including the National Institute of Mental Health.

Foreword or series editor introduction

This ground-breaking and inspiring book was completed and is being published at a time when the whole of humanity is under the negative influence of the coronavirus pandemic. The impact of this global crisis has increased stress and anxiety levels for families, which has highlighted the importance of supporting and facilitating the mental health and well-being of children and adolescents. This book focuses on mindfulness meditation, which is one of the fastest-growing therapeutic interventions in the field of adult mental health, but while its potential for application with children and adolescents has been recognized, research and development of programs on this are still in their infancy. It is this important gap that the book addresses by providing a scholarly review of relevant literature and extensive up-to-date research evidence.

It is now nearly 20 years since the need for an increased focus on children's mental health, particularly in schools, was acknowledged by the publication of the first of several books on the topic, which provides information on a wide range of mental health concerns (Atkinson & Hornby, 2002). A recent response to this realization was the creation of a series of books dedicated to addressing the mental health and well-being of children and young people. The key focus of books in this series is on evaluating the latest research and disseminating innovative interventions and programs. This book is the third in that series. The first book focused on bullying in schools (Cowie & Myers, 2018), the second book examined various approaches for promoting the mental health of children in schools (Reupert, 2020), and the current book focuses specifically on the use of mindfulness meditation for facilitating the mental health and well-being of children and young people in schools and community settings.

The book takes readers from the roots of mindfulness meditation, through an understanding of its theoretical underpinnings, to an examination of various intervention programs. It then goes on to evaluate research evidence about the effectiveness of various mindfulness-based programs that have been developed.

The book is divided into three parts. The first part discusses the origins of mindfulness meditation and provides various definitions to explain exactly what it means in practice. It then discusses how mindfulness is viewed by scholars and practitioners and addresses the issue of assessment of mindfulness in children and adolescents. The second section focuses on research evidence on the use of mindfulness-based interventions for various mental health, developmental, and behavioral issues exhibited by children and adolescents. The third section provides examples of mindfulness-based programs that have been found to be effective with children and adolescents and concludes with consideration of the role of parents and professionals in providing mindfulness-based interventions for young people.

Professionals who work with young people, their parents, and families need to be equipped with up-to-date theory and understanding of the research evidence, as well as knowledge of frameworks for providing interventions in schools (Hornby & Atkinson, 2003), in order to optimize children's mental health. This book provides professionals with knowledge and understanding related to mindfulness meditation that is needed to successfully implement mindfulness meditation with young people.

The book makes a strong case for the value of mindfulness meditation in facilitating the mental health and well-being of children and young people and provides information about evidence-based programs and useful guidelines for how to implement these effectively. It is therefore considered to be essential reading for academics and researchers who work in this field, as well as for practitioners including teachers, school leaders, counsellors, psychologists, and other professionals who work with children and young people in schools or in the community.

Emeritus Professor Garry Hornby,
University of Plymouth

References

Atkinson, M., & Hornby, G. (2002). *Mental health handbook for schools*. London, UK: RoutledgeFalmer.

Cowie, H., & Myers, C.-A. (Eds.). (2018). *School bullying and mental health: Risks, intervention and prevention*. London, UK: Routledge.

Hornby, G., & Atkinson, M. (2003). A framework for promoting mental health in schools. *Pastoral Care in Education, 21*(2), 3–9.

Reupert, A. (2020). *Mental health and academic learning in schools: Approaches for facilitating the wellbeing of children and young people*. London, UK: Routledge.

Preface

Children and adolescents are growing up in turbulent times. They are faced with not only the inevitable changes in their bodies and minds as they navigate their way through developmental stages to adulthood but also the world's rapidly changing social conditions. From a very early age they are exposed to social media that can enhance their social life, creativity, and learning and provide numerous other benefits. At the same time, social media carries serious risks that may include cyberbullying or inappropriate content that demonstrates mean, aggressive, or violent behavior or sexual language and images. In addition, children and adolescents are exposed to social injustice from an early age. Cumulatively, over time, these risk factors metabolize as mental health concerns and then as serious psychological and psychiatric problems that require professional intervention. Some children and adolescents face trauma and other adverse childhood experiences due to a large number of factors including poverty, household substance use/alcoholism, witnessing domestic violence, or having a family member shot or in jail. Others may be victims of war, forced separation from family members due to draconian immigration policies, human trafficking, and various other forms of exploitation.

Some of these children come to the attention of social and mental health services, but they rarely receive the kinds of comprehensive wraparound services that are readily available to those in privileged circumstances. The lack of universal health and mental health care means that those who need these services the most receive the least. It is with this realization that many people in human services have been investigating alternative ways of improving the lives of all children and adolescents. The search has been focused on universal programs—programs that fit within the public health model of services—that preempt the development of conditions that give rise to mental health problems. While mental health practitioners cannot overcome some systemic issues such as racial, economic, social, gender, and sexual injustices by themselves, they are in a position to provide alternative and complementary therapies that are free, portable, and effective.

Mindfulness is one of these interventions that can change the trajectory of the lives of our children and adolescents. Mindfulness meditation has caught the imagination of large parts of the world, but it has not yet seeped into the fabric of child rearing in the West. Over the last 40 years, research has increasingly shown that daily practice of a few minutes of meditation can inform and guide the use of informal mindfulness practices throughout one's day. When an individual has a disciplined daily meditation practice of about 20 minutes a day, the effects of this person's mindfulness enriches their own well-being and quality of life. Perhaps more importantly, the benefits also cascade or spill over to others around them, even those who do not meditate themselves. So how can we make this a universal program that is available freely to all?

This book offers some ways of thinking about mindfulness for children and adolescents; for parents, caregivers, and teachers; and for our society as a whole. The book begins by defining what we mean by mindfulness, one of its origins, and how it has been and continues to be seen by practitioners and academics. It presents ways by which we can measure mindfulness in children and adolescents and their pitfalls. Next is a section on what research tells us about the use of mindfulness-based interventions for various issues and conditions we may see in this population—education, attention deficit hyperactivity disorder, intellectual and developmental disorders, and mental health issues (e.g., externalizing disorders, anxiety, depression, comorbid disorders, substance use, and stress). In the final section, the book offers examples of mindfulness-based programs that researchers have reported to be effective with children and adolescents. While the field of mindfulness-based interventions for this population is still young, we are undoubtedly on the cusp of major breakthroughs that will shape its future. We present this book as a starting point for exploring the use of mindfulness in children and adolescents. Metaphorically speaking, we see this book like a little stone falling into a quiet pond, with the possibility of its ripples spreading mindfulness where it may change a few lives.

Many people have made this book possible. We are most grateful to Professor Garry Hornby, who kindly invited us to put this book together, and the folks at Routledge who produced it. Our collaborators graciously wrote their chapters and very patiently waited for the book to be edited, finalized, and printed. Of course, none of this would have been possible without the compassion and support of our family members. May all merits that accrue from this book be shared with all sentient beings.

Nirbhay N. Singh
Subhashni D. Singh Joy
Raleigh, NC

Part I

Foundations

Chapter 1

Mindfulness-based interventions with children and adolescents

Nirbhay N. Singh and Subhashni D. Singh Joy

Introduction

Victor Hugo, the French poet and novelist, once said, "You can resist an invading army; you cannot resist an idea whose time has come." We could say that the time for mindfulness has come. It took around 2,600 years for it to arrive, but it is now firmly entrenched in the consciousness of Western culture. While there is no general consensus as to what the term "mindfulness" encompasses, as Shakespeare noted, "A rose by any other name would smell as sweet." Mindfulness has been understood in different ways in different wisdom traditions across centuries to refer to how we engage with our moment-to-moment experience of emotions, sensations, perceptions, and thoughts. Western understanding of mindfulness has been heavily influenced by Buddhist philosophy, and most of the current definitions and measures come from that tradition. This is not to be understood as Buddhism being a monolithic tradition, because there is much diversity within it, as it spread throughout Asia from the days of early Buddhism (Anālayo, 2020). Furthermore, there is much diversity among current Buddhist lineages in terms of how mindfulness is understood, developed, and practiced.

One of the most commonly known definitions of mindfulness was advanced by Kabat-Zinn (1994, p. 4): "Paying attention in a particular way: on purpose, in the present moment, and nonjudgmentally." The consensus definition developed by researchers holds that mindfulness is "[a] kind of nonelaborative, nonjudgmental, present-centered awareness in which each thought, feeling, or sensation that arises in the attentional field is acknowledged and accepted as it is" (Bishop et al., 2004, p. 232). In terms of the cultivation of mindfulness through personal meditation practice or participation in a mindfulness-based intervention, it is the "moment-to-moment, non-judgmental, non-reactive attending, and the awareness, insight, and potential liberation that can arise from that intentional cultivation" (Kabat-Zinn, 2019, p. xi). Munindra noted that when mindfulness becomes second nature in our daily life, we can be mindful

> even while eating, drinking, dressing, seeing, hearing, smelling, tasting, touching, thinking. Whatever you are doing, everything should be done mindfully, dynamically, with totality, completeness, thoroughness. Then it

> becomes meditation, meaningful, purposeful. It is not thinking, but experiencing from moment to moment, living from moment to moment, without clinging, without condemning, without judging, without criticizing—choiceless awareness. . . . It should be integrated into our whole life. It is actually an education in how to see, how to hear, how to smell, how to eat, how to drink, how to walk with full awareness.
>
> (Knaster, 2010, p. 1)

Mindfulness is one of the fastest growing therapeutic interventions in adult mental health, focusing on psychological problems such as the daily hassles of life, worry, stress, anxiety, and depression, because it ameliorates the intense emotional states that give rise to these problems. Research has focused on evaluating the efficacy and effectiveness of mindfulness-based interventions (MBIs) in a wide range of clinical populations. Meta-analyses of such studies indicate that MBIs are effective in reducing psychological suffering and in enhancing personal well-being and quality of life in healthy populations (Chiesa & Serretti, 2009; Khoury et al., 2015), in people with mental health problems (Cavanagh et al., 2014), and in others with chronic somatic illnesses (Abbott et al., 2014; Zainal et al., 2013).

There is also an emerging research base on MBIs in children and adolescents, with most of the studies focused on adolescents. The first critical review provided evidence that MBIs can reduce symptoms of anxiety as well as inattention and behavioral problems (Burke, 2010). Another review from the same period suggested that sitting meditation leads to effective treatment of physiologic, psychosocial, and behavioral problems in youth aged 6 to 18 years across school, clinic, and community settings (Black et al., 2009). Research suggests that MBIs can be successfully used with adolescents who display symptoms of attention deficit hyperactivity disorder (Cairncross & Miller, 2016) or have externalizing disorders (Bögels et al., 2008). MBIs have been reported to be effective in decreasing symptoms of depression in minority children (Liehr & Diaz, 2010) and in reducing anxiety and increasing social skills in adolescents with learning disorders (Beauchemin et al., 2008). In the Sibinga et al. (2011) study with urban youth who were HIV-positive and at risk for other disorders, an MBI was effective in reducing hostility and emotional discomfort, and qualitative data suggested improvements in academic performance, interpersonal interactions, stress levels, and physical health. Meta-analyses of MBIs in schools show significant improvements in cognitive performance and resilience and nonsignificant changes in emotional problems (Zenner et al., 2014). These findings were further confirmed in updated meta-analyses that additionally showed significant improvements in the mental health of students (Carsley et al., 2018; Zoogman et al., 2015). All these research studies and meta-analyses of these studies point to the fact that MBIs for children and adolescents is a priority area for research and implementation.

This book provides a scholarly and practical examination of what we currently know about MBIs with children and adolescents. The book begins with foundational chapters on mindfulness, followed by chapters on current research in key areas in which most research has been published on this population, and finally includes practice chapters that cover research-based mindfulness programs that have had the most success with children and adolescents. The last chapter presents something a little different—how teaching mindfulness to parents, caregivers, and teachers cascades or spills over to the children and adolescents in their care.

Foundations

In the first foundational chapter (Chapter 2), Ajahn Amaro and Singh begin with a wide-ranging discussion of the definitions of mindfulness, beginning with the Buddha's own definitions of *sati*—the Pali word for what has come to be called mindfulness in English. The Buddha presented the most comprehensive account of right mindfulness in the *Satipaṭṭhānas*—known as "the four establishments of mindfulness" or more commonly as "the four foundations of mindfulness." The four foundations of mindfulness referred to in this *sutta* are the body, feelings, mind, and mind-objects. Of course, the Buddha expounded on mindfulness in other *suttas* as well, and these are covered briefly. Ajahn Amaro and Singh then present a selection of definitions offered by Buddhist practitioners, academics, and philosophers. This is followed by a discussion of the attributes of mindfulness based on the similes and metaphors the Buddha used as explanatory tools. They present a detailed account of four qualities of mindfulness that bear close examination because we can engage in mindfulness at different levels. This aspect of mindfulness is rarely mentioned in academic research on mindfulness, but without it the research is almost rudderless. This is followed by a brief discussion of the social dimensions of mindfulness. The final section touches on the emerging understanding of the mechanisms that underlie the changes seen as a result of MBIs.

The second foundational chapter (Chapter 3) is on the assessment of mindfulness in children and adolescents. Potts, Twohig, Butcher, and Levin begin with a series of concerns regarding measuring mindfulness in this population, with emphasis on age-appropriateness of rating scale items, perceived comprehension ability, ability to self-reflect, and tailoring factor structure and sophistication to the children's developmental stage. Then they examine child and adolescent measures in some detail. There is a very thoughtful section on key factors to consider when choosing an appropriate measure for a child or adolescent. In contrast to self-report rating scales, there is a section on behavioral observations of overt correlates of mindfulness that can be used for individual children across specific settings. They discuss how to assess constructs related to mindfulness, such as psychological flexibility. Finally, they cover issues and possible assessments of parental mindfulness that may affect their children in bidirectional transactions. Given that the field of mindfulness in children and adolescents is still in the nascent stages of development, this chapter presents researchers and clinicians with essential information on how to begin assessing mindfulness in this population.

Research

There has been much interest in how MBIs can be used in school settings. In the earliest review of mindfulness training with K–12 education, Meiklejohn et al. (2012) reported on early studies that indicated the potential of MBIs in improving working memory, attention, academic skills, social skills, emotional regulation, and self-esteem and in decreasing anxiety, stress, and fatigue. This was followed by special issues on mindfulness in education in *Research in Human Development* (Frank et al., 2013), *Mindfulness* (Felver & Jennings, 2016), and *Psychology in the Schools* (Renshaw & Cook, 2017) and the seminal book on the topic, *Handbook of Mindfulness in Education* (Schonert-Reichl & Roeser, 2016). In Chapter 4, Schutt and Felver synthesize current research on the use of MBIs with children and adolescents in school settings. First, they summarize extant systematic reviews and meta-analyses from 2005 to 2014 to provide a feel for where the field has been. Second, they review the research conducted in the last five years. Third, they provide recommendations for future research and guidance on implementing MBIs in school settings. Overall, Schutt and Felver conclude that MBIs are acceptable and feasible to implement in schools, are effective, and do not appear to cause any harm to the students. While acknowledging that a substantial amount of research on mindfulness in education is still preliminary and needs replication, they note several benefits for students, including reduction in psychopathology symptoms and improving psychosocial well-being, cognitive functioning, and academic outcomes.

There is a plethora of research reviews and meta-analyses of psychopharmacological treatment of attention deficit hyperactivity disorder (ADHD) in children and adolescents. Essentially, these reviews attest to the effectiveness of medication for ADHD, with low doses of medication combined with multimodal behavioral intervention being most effective and cost-efficient (Smith et al., 2019). At the same time, some children are known to decline drug treatment, poorly tolerate it, or have low long-term compliance with the drug regimen, while others may be nonresponders. In Chapter 5, de Bruin, Meppelink, and Bögels begin by discussing the core symptoms of children with ADHD, the impact of this disorder on the children's lives, the personal and emotional burdens on the families, and the economic health care costs in caring for children and adolescents with ADHD. They discuss why drug treatments are the first-line treatment and the adverse effects of such treatment on the lives of the children. They then present the argument that perhaps mindfulness may offer a safer alternative to drug treatment. This is followed by a review of meta-analyses of mindfulness research with children with ADHD and with their parents. Then follows the main part of the chapter, which reviews individual and group-based mindfulness interventions for children with ADHD and for their parents. Finally, they touch upon a specific MBI, MYmind, that has shown great potential as a research-based approach for mindfulness training of children and adolescents with ADHD and autism spectrum disorder (ASD). Given the personal, educational, and economic burdens of ADHD on children and their families, a concerted effort needs to be made to find practical non-pharmacological interventions that they can use to self-regulate their attention. This chapter provides the basis for doing so using mindfulness-based approaches.

Among children aged 3 to 17 years, about 17.8% are estimated to have a developmental disability (Zablotsky et al., 2019). This includes 2.5% with ASD and 1.2% with an intellectual disability. These children exhibit mild to profound levels of functioning due to medical, cognitive, and mental health issues. Psychopharmacological treatments were the first-line treatments for decades until it was apparent that their side effects far outweighed their benefits. Currently, behavioral interventions are the most used, particularly applied behavior analysis and positive behavior support. While very effective, these interventions are labor intensive and often stressful for the caregivers to implement. Over the last two decades, MBIs have been increasingly used to reduce the suffering of children and adolescents with intellectual and developmental disability (IDD), along with their caregivers. In Chapter 6, Singh and Hwang provide a comprehensive review of the current status of the use of MBIs with individuals with IDD. It was thought that individuals with IDD may not be able to master the art of mindfulness, but this premature cognitive commitment about their incapacity to meditate were proven to be a fallacy. The first part of the chapter reviews extant research on mindfulness programs taught directly to individuals with IDD by experienced meditation teachers or their caregivers. This research shows that individuals with IDD or ASD at the mild level of disability can learn to self-manage behaviors arising from emotional dysregulation (e.g., anger, aggression, disruption, and property destruction). The second part of the chapter provides a review of the cascading or spill over effects of mindfulness training for parents, caregivers, and teachers on the observed behavior of those individuals with IDD in their care. The third part provides a review of research on mindfulness training for parents and their children separately but in parallel sessions. Given the suffering experienced by some people with IDD and ASD and their caregivers, mindfulness offers an acceptable and effective approach to improve their well-being and quality of life.

Although the causes and conditions may be different, children and adolescents experience the same kinds of anxiety, worries, and fears as adults. When these experiences reach levels of intensity and severity that interfere with daily life, then they may need intervention for internalizing and externalizing mental health problems. Although the research literature is not very extensive, in Chapter 7, Singh and Singh Joy present a review of MBIs for these conditions.

First, they present a brief review of MBIs for externalizing behaviors, noting that the studies were not methodologically robust, but there was suggestive evidence of the effectiveness of the MBIs evaluated. Second, they review clinical trials of different MBIs for anxiety in children and adolescents. Most of these trials were pilot and feasibility studies with small samples. Even though the literature is very limited, what is available suggests that MBIs may have the potential to be beneficial in reducing anxiety in children and adolescents. Third, they present a review of six clinical trials of MBIs for depression. As with anxiety, the studies are still at the feasibility and acceptability stage but hint at the effectiveness of the MBIs that have been used in the clinical trials. Fourth, they review the effects of MBIs for adolescents with mental health and comorbid conditions. Again, the studies were not fully fledged randomized controlled trails, but some of them reported positive findings. Fifth, given the scarcity of MBI studies in this area, they briefly touch on MBIs for substance abuse. Sixth, they review MBI studies for stress and conclude that MBIs may be effective but await research using more robust methodologies. This is an area of major concern given developmental considerations, stress and anxiety, and the deterioration of social conditions in the world.

Practice

Formal and informal mindfulness practices can be taught to children and adolescents, and different MBIs have been developed and evaluated for their effects on children and adolescents. In Chapter 8, Jackman presents a sampling of programs for teaching mindfulness to children and then presents details of the OpenMind (OM) programs for preschool and kindergarten children. In Chapter 9, Singh and Singh Joy present a selection of formal mindfulness-based programs that are evidence-based for successfully teaching mindfulness to adolescents. The seven programs that are reviewed have all been shown to change critical behaviors of adolescents that positively changed the quality of their lives. In addition, Singh and Singh Joy describe three informal practices that have provided adolescents simple ways of managing their emotional arousal in difficult contexts which normally may result in anger and aggression. In Chapter 10, Singh, Lancioni, and Myers contextualize their presentation of mindfulness-based programs for parents, caregivers, and teachers within the ecological model of bidirectional transactions. For example, parent-child bidirectional interactions can be changed with the parent or the child, or with both. When parents, caregivers, and teachers learn and practice mindfulness, its effects cascade or spill over to children and adolescents in their care. This chapter presents research-based examples of mindfulness-based programs that have been shown to be effective in changing bidirectional interactions.

This book is about mindfulness in children and adolescents, how we can help them to be more mindful in their lives, and how they can use it to reduce their suffering and enhance their well-being. It is about how we can teach significant others in their lives—friends, parents, caregivers, teachers—to be more mindful in their interactions with them. While the emerging research suggests we may well be able to do this, let us not forget that in reality few evidence-based programs reach those who need them. We need to be mindful that life is short, that all of us must practice mindfulness in our daily lives, and that we must be kind, loving, and compassionate toward all sentient beings and live each day as if it is our last.

References

Abbott, R. A., Whear, R., Rodgers, L. R., Bethel, A., Thompson Coon, J., Kuyken, W., . . Dickens, C. (2014). Effectiveness of mindfulness-based stress reduction and mindfulness based cognitive therapy in vascular disease: A systematic review and meta-analysis of randomised controlled trials. *Journal of Psychosomatic Research*, *76*, 341–351.

Anālayo, B. (2020). *Introducing mindfulness: Buddhist background and practical exercises*. Cambridge, UK: Windhorse Publications.

Beauchemin, J., Hutchins, T. L., & Patterson, F. (2008). Mindfulness meditation may lessen anxiety, promote social skills, and improve academic performance among adolescents with learning disabilities. *Complementary Health Practice Review*, *13*(1), 34–45.

Bishop, S. R., Lau, M., Shapiro, S., Carlson, L., Anderson, N. D., Carmody, J., . . Devins, G. (2004). Mindfulness: A proposed operational definition. *Clinical Psychology: Science and Practice*, *11*(3), 230–241.

Black, D. S., Milam, J., & Sussman, S. (2009). Sitting-meditation interventions among youth: A review of treatment efficacy. *Pediatrics*, *124*(3), e532—e541.

Bögels, S. M., Hoogstad, B., van Dun, L., de Schutter, S., & Restifo, K. (2008). Mindfulness training for adolescents with externalizing disorders and their parents. *Behavioural and Cognitive Psychotherapy*, *36*(2), 193–209.

Burke, C. A. (2010). Mindfulness-based approaches with children and adolescents: A preliminary review of current research in an emergent field. *Journal of Child and Family Studies*, *19*(2), 133–144.

Cairncross, M., & Miller, C. J. (2016). The effectiveness of mindfulness-based therapies for ADHD: A meta-analytic review. *Journal of Attention Disorders*, *24*(5), 627–643.

Carsley, D., Khoury, B., & Heath, N. L. (2018). Effectiveness interventions for mental health in schools: A comprehensive meta-analysis. *Mindfulness*, *9*, 693–707.

Cavanagh, K., Strauss, C., Forder, L., & Jones, F. (2014). Can mindfulness and acceptance be learnt by self-help? A systematic review and meta-analysis of mindfulness and acceptance-based self-help interventions. *Clinical Psychology Review*, *34*, 118–129.

Chiesa, A., & Serretti, A. (2009). Mindfulness-based stress reduction for stress management in healthy people: A review and meta-analysis. *Journal of Alternative and Complementary Medicine*, *15*, 593–600.

Felver, J. C., & Jennings, P. A. (2016). Applications of mindfulness-based interventions in school settings: An introduction. *Mindfulness*, *7*, 1–4.

Frank, J. L., Jennings, P. A., & Greenberg, M. T. (2013). Mindfulness-based interventions in school settings: An introduction to the special issue. *Research in Human Development*, *10*, 205–210.

Kabat-Zinn, J. (1994). *Wherever you go, there you are: Mindfulness meditation in everyday life*. New York, NY: Hyperion.

Kabat-Zinn, J. (2019). Seeds of a necessary global renaissance in the making: The refining of psychology's understanding of the nature of mind, self, and embodiment through the lens of mindfulness and its origins at a key inflection point for the species. *Current Opinion in Psychology, 28*, xi–xvii.

Khoury, B., Sharma, M., Rush, S. E., & Fournier, C. (2015). Mindfulness-based stress reduction for healthy individuals: A meta-analysis. *Journal of Psychosomatic Research, 78*, 519–528.

Knaster, M. (2010). *Living this life fully: Stories and teachings of Munindra*. Boston, MA: Shambhala.

Liehr, P., & Diaz, N. (2010). A pilot study examining the effect of mindfulness on depression and anxiety for minority children. *Archives of Psychiatric Nursing, 24*(1), 69–71.

Meiklejohn, J., Phillips, C., Freedman, M. L., Griffin, M. L., Biegel, G., Roach, A., . . Saltzman, A. (2012). Integrating mindfulness training into K-12 education: Fostering the resilience of teachers and students. *Mindfulness, 3*, 291–307.

Renshaw, T. L., & Cook, C. R. (2017). Mindfulness in the schools: Historical roots, current status, and future directions. *Psychology in the Schools, 54*, 5–12.

Schonert-Reichl, K. A., & Roeser, R. W. (2016). *Handbook of mindfulness in education: Integrating theory and research into practice*. New York, NY: Springer.

Sibinga, E. M. S., Kerrigan, D., Stewart, M., Johnson, K., Magyari, T., & Ellen, J. M. (2011). Mindfulness-based stress reduction for urban youth. *Journal of Alternative and Complementary Medicine, 17*(3), 213–218.

Smith, B. H., Reid, E. K., Sajovec, P., & Namerow, L. (2019). Pharmacological treatment of attention-deficit/hyperactivity disorder. In S. M. Evans & K. M. Carpenter (Eds.), *APA handbook of psychopharmacology* (pp. 347–371). Washington, DC: American Psychological Association.

Zablotsky, B., Black, L. I., Maenner, M. J., Schieve, L. A., Danielson, M. L., Bitsko, R. H., . . Boyle, C. A. (2019). Prevalence and trends of developmental disabilities among children in the United States: 2009–2017. *Pediatrics, 144*(4), e20190811.

Zainal, N. Z., Booth, S., & Huppert, F. A. (2013). The efficacy of mindfulness-based stress reduction on mental health of breast cancer patients: A meta-analysis. *Psycho-Oncology, 22*, 1457–1465.

Zenner, C., Hermleben-Kurz, S., & Walach, H. (2014). Mindfulness-based interventions in schools: A systematic review and meta-analysis. *Frontiers in Psychology, 5*, 603.

Zoogman, S., Goldberg, S. B., Hoyt, W. T., & Miller, L. (2015). Mindfulness interventions with youth: A meta-analysis. *Mindfulness, 6*, 290–302.

Chapter 2

Mindfulness

Definitions, attributes, and mechanisms

Ajahn Amaro and Nirbhay N. Singh

Introduction

The word *mindfulness* has gathered to it a wide variety of meanings and connotations, from the distant past up to current times. This range of meanings can most easily be appreciated if we consider that mindfulness is commonly being used as shorthand for a few related yet distinct qualities. At one end of the spectrum, it can validly be employed to refer to the simple act of recollection (i.e., it comes from the same root as the Sanskrit word *smṛti*, meaning "memory," or "that which is remembered"); it also means the act of consciously paying attention. At the other end of the spectrum, one finds such statements in the scriptures as "Mindfulness is the path to the deathless" (Dhammapada [Dhp] 21), with the word "deathless" meaning total spiritual emancipation or enlightenment. This points to mindfulness as being of the most profound and liberating nature. Indeed, it is the very first on the Buddha's list of the Seven Factors of Enlightenment (*bojjhanga*) as well as being the balancing factor at the center of the Buddha's list of the Five Spiritual Faculties (*indriya*) as well as the Five Powers (*bala*).

Definitions of mindfulness

Pali is the language in which the scriptures of the Southern School of Buddhism (otherwise known as the *Theravāda*) are written; it is a close relative of Sanskrit. One of the reasons mindfulness has become such a common word today is that T.W. Rhys Davids chose it to translate the Pali word *sati* into English. Rhys Davids (1881, p. 145) wrote,

> [*S*]*ati* is literally "memory" but is used with reference to the constantly repeated phrase "mindful and thoughtful" (*sato sampajāno*); and means that activity of mind and constant presence of mind which is one of the duties most frequently inculcated on the good Buddhist.

The entry in the *Pali-English Dictionary* (Rhys Davids & Stede, 2004, p. 672) reads, "Sati (f.) [Vedic smṛti. . .] memory, recognition, consciousness. . .;

intentness of mind, wakefulness of mind, mindfulness, alertness, lucidity of mind, self-possession, conscience, self-consciousness."

The Buddha's own definitions of *sati* are many and various. Here is a succinct collection of them, showing the variety and depth of meanings of the term:

> And what, friends, is right mindfulness? Here a bhikkhu abides contemplating the body as a body, ardent, fully aware and mindful, having put away covetousness and grief for the world. He abides contemplating feelings as a feelings . . . mind as mind . . . mind-objects as mind-objects, ardent, fully aware and mindful, having put away covetousness and grief for the world. This is called right mindfulness.
>
> (Majjhima Nikāya [M] 141.30)

The four-fold framework that the Buddha is using here—the body, feelings, mind, and mind-objects—is called in Pali the four *Satipaṭṭhānas*. This latter term has been variously translated as: "frames of reference," "the establishments of mindfulness," or, most commonly and popularly, "the foundations of mindfulness," as in Nyanaponika Thera's (1962) comprehensive and much-lauded book, *The Heart of Buddhist Meditation*. The four dimensions of mindfulness referred to in the *sutta* can, in turn, be summarized as referring to the following aspects of our human experience: *Body*: Our physical body, and the bodies of others, as an object perceived through sight, sound, smell, taste, and touch. *Feelings*: The sensations of our own body (i.e., pleasant, neutral, unpleasant feelings) as well as the appreciation of the experience of such sensations in others. *Mind*: The subjective and nonjudgmental awareness of different moods and mind-states (e.g., anger/freedom from anger; agitation/freedom from agitation; contractedness/expansiveness, and so on), with the emphasis being on the subjective quality of awareness and knowing. *Mind-objects*: The changing, ephemeral, and empty nature of all aspects of the objective field of experience, coarse or subtle, wholesome or unwholesome. In this dimension of the practice of mindfulness the emphasis is on seeing all phenomena as possessing the characteristics of transiency, unsatisfactoriness, and the lack of an owner or any self-essence.

Another definitive aspect of mindfulness is its quality of attention to the present. This is most clearly characterized in the *Bhaddekaratta Sutta* ("An Auspicious Day"):

> You shouldn't chase after the past
> or place expectations on the future.
> What is past
>   is left behind.
> The future
>   is as yet unreached.
> Whatever quality is present
> you clearly see right there,
>   right there.

> Not taken in,
> unshaken,
> that's how you develop the heart.
> Ardently doing
> what should be done today,
> for—who knows?—tomorrow
> death.
> There is no bargaining
> with mortality and his mighty horde.
> Whoever lives thus ardently,
> relentlessly
> both day and night,
> has truly had an auspicious day:
> so says the Peaceful Sage.
>
> (M 131.3)

The Buddha regularly highlighted the liberating quality of such uncluttered and focused attention. In this next passage, he uses the term *appamāda* to refer to the quintessence of this quality of mindful awareness; it is closely related to *sati* but signifies its most radical, insightful aspects.

> Mindfulness is the path to the deathless,
> heedlessness is the path to death;
> the mindful never die,
> the heedless are as if dead already.
>
> (Dph 21)

The statement, "the mindful never die" might raise an eyebrow or two to those unfamiliar with the Buddha's modes of expression. It does not mean that if you are sufficiently mindful your body will live forever. Rather, it is referring to the type of psychological or "ego" death that is experienced when the mind ties itself to success, only to be grieved by disappointment or when we die socially by being unfriended on Facebook or, indeed, dying on stage through giving a poor performance. The term "the deathless" (*amata* in Pali) is one of many words the Buddha used to refer to the noumenal or transcendent dimension of experience; another is "the unconditioned." He avoided dwelling on metaphysics, preferring to keep his teachings within the range of the tangible and practical, yet he was not hesitant to point to that aspect if appropriate. However, he often used experiences that were easy to relate to when doing that kind of pointing. For example:

> Bhikkhus, I will teach you the unconditioned and the path leading to the unconditioned. . .
>
> And what, bhikkhus, is the unconditioned? The destruction of lust . . . of hatred . . . of delusion: this is called the unconditioned.
>
> And what, bhikkhus, is the path leading to the unconditioned?

> Mindfulness directed to the body: this is called the path leading to the unconditioned.
>
> (Saṃyutta Nikāya [S] 43.1)

Many notable Buddhist practitioners, academics, and others have offered their own definitions of mindfulness. All of these possess different shades of meaning and emphasis, so a variety are listed here, again, not intended to be exhaustive but rather in order to give a broad sense of the constellation of qualities that constitute mindfulness:

> Right mindfulness: . . . mindfulness and awareness in contemplating body, feelings, mind and mind-objects.
>
> (Nyanatiloka, 1952, p. 176)

> The clear and single-minded awareness of what actually happens to us and in us at the successive moments of perception.
>
> (Nyanaponika Thera, 1962, p. 5)

> Keeping one's consciousness alive to the present reality.
>
> (Hanh, 1976, p. 11)

> Mindfulness is in general connectedness, not being scatter-brained; whereas awareness is more precisely keeping oneself under constant observation, not letting one's actions (or thoughts, or feelings, etc.) pass unnoticed.
>
> (Nanavira, 1987, p. 155)

> [*Sati*] should be understood as what allows awareness of the full range and extent of *dhammas*; *sati* is an awareness of things in relation to things, and hence an awareness of their relative value. Applied to the *Satipaṭṭhānas*, presumably what this means is that *sati* is what causes the practitioner of yoga to "remember" that any feeling he may experience exists in relation to a whole variety or world of feelings that may be skillful or unskillful, with faults or faultless, relatively inferior or refined, dark or pure.
>
> (Gethin, 2001, p. 39)

> [I]n which moment-to-moment awareness of changing objects of perception is cultivated.
>
> (Epstein, 1995, p. 96)

> Giving full attention to the present, without worries about the past or future.
>
> (Thondup, 1996, p. 48)

A state of keen awareness of mental and physical phenomena as they arise within and around (oneself).

(Harvey, 2000, p. 38)

Mindfulness means awareness, openness, and acceptance of whatever arises, without attachment to pleasant, aversion to the unpleasant, or forgetfulness of natural feelings.

(Goldstein & Kornfield, 2001, p. 154)

That which "looks over" the various factors that arise in meditation is *sati*, mindfulness. . . . *Sati* is life. Whenever we don't have *sati*, when we are heedless, it's as if we are dead. If we have no *sati*, then our speech and actions have no meaning. . . *Sati* is that which watches over us while standing, walking, sitting, and lying. Even when we are no longer in *samādhi*, *sati* should be present throughout.

(Ajahn Chah, 2002, pp. 144–145)

Mindfulness is knowing, or presence of mind. What am I thinking right now? What am I doing? What am I carrying around with me?

(Ajahn Chah, 2002, p. 302)

[I]n mindfulness practice, the focus of a person's attention is opened to admit whatever enters experience, while at the same time, a stance of kindly curiosity allows the person to investigate whatever appears, without falling prey to automatic judgments or reactivity.

(Segal et al., 2002, pp. 322–323)

Awareness of present experience, with acceptance.

(Germer, 2005, p. 7)

Mindfulness is a quality of relationship to the object of awareness. Just having an experience, say hearing a sound, is not really being mindful. Knowing a sound without grasping, aversion, or delusion is being mindful.

(Salzberg, 2008, p. 135)

[*S*]*ati* . . . provides the connection between its two primary canonical meanings: as memory and as lucid awareness of present happenings.

(Bhikkhu Bodhi, 2011, p. 25)

Sati can be translated as mindfulness or awareness and can be defined as an *embodied and ethically sensitive practice of present moment recollection.*

(Stanley, 2013, p. 65)

> A particular type of social practice that leads the practitioner to an ethically minded awareness, intentionally situated in the here and now.
>
> (Nilsson & Kazemi, 2016, p. 190)

A number of criticisms have been leveled at T.W. Rhys Davids' (TWRD) choice of the word mindfulness, asserting that it is not comprehensive enough in its breadth of meaning. For example, Bhikkhu Bodhi (2006) noted, "An early translator [TWRD] cleverly drew upon the word mindfulness, which is not even in my dictionary. This has served its role admirably, but it does not preserve the connection with memory, sometimes needed to make sense of a passage." However, since it has already entered the vernacular of English conversation and scholarship, its usage in current times has begun to encompass the range of qualities listed here, even if all of those meanings were not implicit or explicit before the present development of interest. Furthermore, in notable contradiction to Bhikkhu Bodhi's comment, the current edition of the *Oxford English Dictionary* defines mindfulness as "The state or quality of being mindful; 'attention; regard'; memory; intention, purpose," and mindful as, "Taking thought or care of; heedful of; keeping remembrance of," thus indicating that the aspect of memory is, after all, well and truly included in the accepted constellation of meanings of mindfulness.

Academic research in mindfulness most commonly uses variants of a definition advanced by Kabat-Zinn (1994, p. 4), "Paying attention in a particular way: on purpose, in the present moment, and nonjudgmentally." The consensus academic definition by Bishop et al. (2004), which appears to be used less often, is, "[A] kind of nonelaborative, nonjudgmental, present-centered awareness in which each thought, feeling, or sensation that arises in the attentional field is acknowledged and accepted as it is" (p. 232). In terms of the cultivation of mindfulness, Kabat-Zinn (2019) has defined it as the "moment-to-moment, non-judgmental, non-reactive attending, and the awareness, insight, and potential liberation that can arise from that intentional cultivation" (p. xi). In terms of practice, it was probably best expressed by Munindra, who noted:

> Everything is meditation in this practice, even while eating, drinking, dressing, seeing, hearing, smelling, tasting, touching, thinking. Whatever you are doing, everything should be done mindfully, dynamically, with totality, completeness, thoroughness. Then it becomes meditation, meaningful, purposeful. It is not thinking, but experiencing from moment to moment, living from moment to moment, without clinging, without condemning, without judging, without criticizing—choiceless awareness. . . . It should be integrated into our whole life. It is actually an education in how to see, how to hear, how to smell, how to eat, how to drink, how to walk with full awareness.
>
> (Knaster, 2010, p. 1)

Attributes of mindfulness

The Buddha is well renowned as a teacher who was able to draw upon many pedagogical devices in order to help his listeners understand and retain in memory his teachings. Examples of these methods include: (1) the use of illustrative stories and parables; (2) the use of household terms versus rarified philosophical language to convey core concepts; (3) the creation a prodigious number of codified lists of related items (e.g., the Seven Factors of Enlightenment, the Five Hindrances, the Four Noble Truths, the Eightfold Path, the Three Roots of Unwholesomeness); and (4) similes to provide a graphic reference point for the principles he was expounding. In order to convey some of the key attributes of mindfulness, we present a few such images the Buddha used to illustrate his explanations.

Similes and metaphors

In this first example the Buddha uses his past experience as a warrior noble prince and his knowledge of how security would be maintained for a military outpost to show how mindfulness is most skillfully applied:

> Just as the gatekeeper in the king's frontier fortress is wise, competent, and intelligent, one who keeps out strangers and admits acquaintances, for protecting its inhabitants for warding off outsiders, so too a noble disciple is mindful, possessing supreme mindfulness and alertness, one who remembers and recollects what was done and said long ago. With mindfulness as his gatekeeper, the noble disciple abandons the unwholesome and develops the wholesome, abandons what is blameworthy and develops what is blameless and maintains himself in purity.
>
> (Aṅguttara Nikāya [A] 7.67)

> Bhikkhus, whatever a bhikkhu frequently thinks and ponders upon, that will become the inclination of his mind. If he frequently thinks and ponders upon thoughts of sensual desire, he has abandoned the thought of renunciation to cultivate the thought of sensual desire, and then his mind inclines to thoughts of sensual desire. If he frequently thinks and ponders upon thoughts of ill will . . . upon thoughts of cruelty, he has abandoned the thought of non-cruelty to cultivate the thought of cruelty, and then his mind inclines to thoughts of cruelty.
>
> Just as in the last month of the rainy season, in the autumn, when the crops thicken, a cowherd would guard his cows by constantly tapping and poking them on this side and that with a stick to check and curb them. Why is that? Because he sees that he could be flogged, imprisoned, fined, or blamed [if he let them stray into the crops]. So too I saw in unwholesome states danger, degradation, and defilement, and in wholesome states the blessing of renunciation, the aspect of cleansing.

> Bhikkhus, whatever a bhikkhu frequently thinks and ponders upon, that will become the inclination of his mind. If he frequently thinks and ponders upon thoughts of renunciation, he has abandoned the thought of sensual desire to cultivate the thought of renunciation, and then his mind inclines to thoughts of renunciation. If he frequently thinks and ponders upon thoughts of non-ill will . . . upon thoughts of non-cruelty, he has abandoned the thought of cruelty to cultivate the thought of non-cruelty, and then his mind inclines to thoughts of non-cruelty.
>
> Just as in the last month of the hot season, when all the crops have been brought inside the villages, a cowherd would guard his cows while staying at the root of a tree or out in the open, since he needs only to be mindful that the cows are there; so too, there was need for me only to be mindful that those states were there.
>
> (M 19.6–7 and 19.11–12)

In present-day terms, the principle that "whatever a person frequently thinks and ponders upon, that will become the inclination of their mind" points to some very important potentialities, some of which have been followed up in modern cognitive therapeutic models. First, that we can, to some degree, guide the direction of our thoughts—we are not helpless victims of the thinking mind. Second, that the choices that are made about what to follow and what not to follow will have a significant impact on our sense of well-being. In short: if we discern what is wholesome and beneficial, and we choose to follow that, we are going to feel better. As a matter of course the reverse is found to be true, that if we follow impulses that are unwholesome—say, self-critical, deceptive, or cruel—we are going to feel worse.

The final point that the Buddha makes here, with his engaging image of resting contentedly under the shade of a tree, is that if the mind habitually inclines toward gentle, kind and honest, respectful, compassionate thoughts, there's no need to be too cautious—the mind is not going to create too much trouble. If, however, the inclinations are toward such as self-hatred, anger, conceit, recklessness, and dishonesty—be alert! Danger and disaster are close at hand, so be extra careful.

The Simile of the Bonfire

The sluggish mind: untimely

It is a common experience in meditation, (interestingly more prevalent in people who have practiced for many years rather than in beginners) for the mind to overdo the inclination toward "calmness" and to lack the "energizing" factors. This leads to dullness, sleepiness, and "nodding" during periods of sitting meditation:

> On an occasion, bhikkhus, when the mind becomes sluggish, it is untimely to develop the enlightenment factor of tranquility, the enlightenment

> factor of concentration, and the enlightenment factor of equanimity. For what reason? Because the mind is sluggish, bhikkhus, and it is difficult to arouse it with those things.
>
> Suppose, bhikkhus, a man wants to make a small fire flare up. If he throws wet grass, wet cow dung, and wet timber into it, sprays it with water, and scatters soil over it, would he be able to make that small fire flare up?
>
> No, venerable sir.

That is to say—if one is already dull and sleepy, nodding off in the meditation, more calmness is not going to help. It is the rousing factors that are required to restore the balance.

The sluggish mind: timely

If one notices that one's head is drooping and the mind is foggy and dull, this is the time to brighten up. More energy is needed to make the period of meditation well-integrated and beneficial, so the effort is turned toward the factors that will enliven and arouse the mind. Opening the eyes for a time, inviting the posture to straighten, and sharpening the attention will all help:

> On an occasion, bhikkhus, when the mind becomes sluggish it is timely to develop the enlightenment factor of discrimination of states, the enlightenment factor of energy, and the enlightenment factor of rapture. For what reason? Because the mind is sluggish, bhikkhus, and it is easy to arouse it with those things.
>
> Suppose, bhikkhus, a man wants to make a small fire flare up. If he throws dry grass, dry cow dung, and dry timber into it, blows on it, and does not scatter soil over it, would he make that small fire flare up?'
>
> Yes, venerable sir.

Following his theme of comparing the process of mind-training to tending a bonfire, it is then easy for his students to grasp how those energizing elements will cause the system to develop in the wished-for way.

The excited mind: untimely

The opposite problem—too much restlessness in the body and busy thinking in the mind—is often found by people new to meditation practice. For some it can seem to be an impossible dream that the mind could ever be quiet or that there could be any real peace and tranquility. The Buddha continues his theme of tending a bonfire in a skillful way to describe how to work with this overabundance of energy and activity:

> On an occasion, bhikkhus, when the mind becomes excited, it is untimely to develop the enlightenment factor of discrimination of states, the

> enlightenment factor of energy, and the enlightenment factor of rapture. For what reason? Because the mind is excited, bhikkhus, and it is difficult to calm it down with those things.
> Suppose, bhikkhus, a man wants to extinguish a great bonfire. If he throws dry grass, dry cow dung, and dry timber into it, blows on it, and does not scatter soil over it, would he be able to extinguish that great bonfire?
> No, venerable sir.

Since there is already an excess of energy in the system, adding in more elements that arouse and activate the body and mind will not be helpful in establishing balance in the meditation.

The excited mind: timely

Instead, as one would expect by following the pattern that the Buddha is describing, the introduction of qualities that settle the mind and body and conduce to a state of ease and calmness will be the best way to bring about a well-integrated and beneficial period of meditation.

> On an occasion, bhikkhus, when the mind becomes excited, it is timely to develop the enlightenment factor of tranquility, the enlightenment factor of concentration, and the enlightenment factor of equanimity. For what reason? Because the mind is excited, bhikkhus, and it is easy to calm it down with those things.
> Suppose, bhikkhus, a man wants to extinguish a great bonfire. If he throws wet grass, wet cow dung, and wet timber into it, sprays it with water, and scatters soil over it, would he be able to extinguish that great bonfire?
> Yes, venerable sir.
> But mindfulness, bhikkhus, I say is always useful.
>
> (S 46.53)

The Ancient Commentary to this last line of this passage reads:

> It [mindfulness] is desirable everywhere, like salt and a versatile prime minister. Just as salt enhances the flavor of all curries, and just as a versatile prime minister accomplishes all the tasks of state, so the restraining of the excited mind and the exerting of the sluggish mind are all achieved by mindfulness, and without mindfulness this could not be done.

Once again, in present-day terms, this is telling us to know our own character and moods. Just as we don't need the same clothing in winter and summer, we need to work with the mind using different tools according to what is timely and effective for the situation. If it's 100°F outside we don't need an overcoat; if it's −20°F, we don't go out in a T-shirt. Similarly, it's important to relate to meditation and mind-training with an appreciation of the circumstances. If your mind is already dull and sleepy, or you know that you easily fall into numb and listless states, you don't need to quieten down and relax more, you need an energizing boost to enliven the system. If you know, in contrast, that you are currently feeling agitated and restless or that you are habitually prone to impatience, more energy in the mix is not going to help. In this case the calming and quieting aspects of mind are what will be most helpful. Mindfulness—like an astute and caring government minister—is what enables the recognition of what is needed, moment by moment, and directs the attention and intentions to steer things accordingly.

The Simile of the Six Animals and their Domains

A final set of images, illustrative of the way the Buddha conveyed the importance of mindfulness (and particularly mindfulness of the body) in establishing well-being, is contained in the teaching called "The Six Animals." The Buddha had a way, from time to time, of inventing startling, attention-grabbing vignettes that communicated his message in tangible and relatable ways. Such a one is the following, a somewhat bizarre scenario of tying a snake, a crocodile, a bird, a dog, a jackal, and a monkey loosely together and seeing what happens. No one in their right mind would ever do such a thing in practice, but the sheer weirdness of the idea, coupled with the easy-to-imagine chaos that would ensue if it were done, certainly gets the mind of the student onto the subject:

> Suppose bhikkhus, a man would catch six animals—with different domains and different feeding grounds—and tie them each by a strong rope. He would catch a snake, a crocodile, a bird, a dog, a jackal, and a monkey. . . . Having done so, he would tie the ropes together with a knot in the middle and release them. Then those six animals . . . would each pull in the direction of its own feeding ground and domain. The snake would pull one way, thinking, "Let me enter an anthill." The crocodile would pull another way, thinking, "Let me enter the water." The bird would pull another way, thinking, "Let me fly up into the sky." The dog would pull another way, thinking, "Let me enter a village." The jackal would pull another way, thinking, "Let me enter a charnel ground." The monkey would pull another way, thinking, "Let me enter a forest."
>
> Now when these six animals become worn out and fatigued, they would be dominated by the one among them that was the strongest; they would submit to it and come under its control. So too, bhikkhus, when a bhikkhu has not developed and cultivated mindfulness directed to the body, the eye pulls in the direction of agreeable forms and disagreeable forms are repulsive; ear . . . the nose . . . the tongue . . . the body . . . the mind pulls

> in the direction of agreeable mental phenomena and disagreeable mental phenomena are repulsive.
>
> It is in such a way that there is no restraint.
>
> Suppose bhikkhus, a man would catch six animals . . . and tie them each by a strong rope. He would catch a snake, a crocodile, a bird, a dog, a jackal, and a monkey. . . . Having done so, he would bind them to a strong post or pillar. Then those six animals with different domains and different feeding grounds would each pull in the direction of its own feeding ground and domain. . . .
>
> Now when these six animals become worn out and fatigued, they would stand close to that post or pillar, they would sit down there, they would lie down there. So too, bhikkhus, when a bhikkhu has developed and cultivated mindfulness directed to the body, the eye does not pull in the direction of agreeable forms nor are disagreeable forms repulsive; the ear . . . the nose . . . the tongue . . . the body . . . the mind does not pull in the direction of agreeable mental phenomena nor are disagreeable mental phenomena repulsive.
>
> It is in such a way that there is restraint.
>
> A strong post or pillar: this, bhikkhus, is a designation for mindfulness directed to the body.
>
> (S 35.247)

This last set of images might seem a bit remote to all except the zookeepers among us; however, the Buddha's illustration here can be very pertinent to us all today. We get distracted. If we are habitually affected in strong ways by what we see, we get dragged around by our eyes to attractive or irritating things and people. If we are a foodie, our nose and tongue will pull us into the restaurant, or coffee house, or keep us glued to the food channels. If we are a music buff, or a newshound, our ears will keep us locked into the current feeds of fresh material or old favorites. Or, if we are an intellectual, we find we are hooked on TED talks and updates from Routledge with current papers in our field. . . .

Just look around on a train or at an airport, in a university lounge, and most people have headphones on and are glued to their screen, pulled by an alligator, a snake, a bird, a dog, a jackal, or a monkey—the eyes, ears, nose, tongue, body, or mind—in effect, as the Buddha points out, by whichever "animal" is tugging hardest at the moment. Weary of the intelligence on the TED talk? Time for a muffin! Oh look, a new song just posted by Beyoncé . . . and so on.

The confused, snarling, fluttering, snapping, screeching tangled mess of the six competing and distressed animals, as depicted in this simile, is a good illustration of our inner tangled mess of emotions and reactions when our attitudes and actions are guided by habit and impulse alone. We know how unpleasant that stress-filled state is—the figuratively flying fur, feathers, claws, jaws, and scales of our competing desire systems and instinctual urges—the Buddha's advice is thus related to how to work skillfully with those chthonic, animalistic states in order to achieve a more harmonious result, actualizing well-being for the whole system.

The "firm pillar" of mindfulness of the body is a guaranteed way to ground the mind in attunement to the reality of the present. The body never wanders into abstractions, imaginary worlds, or off into the remembered past or an imagined future—it is always and only ever right here, now. It is thus like the most reliable friend who is always there to come back to. In addition, it is part of the natural order that usefully reflects the emotional states of our mind. When the attention comes back to the body we can see if we've become tense or anxious, breathless with excitement, or if there is heartache or grief, and we can feel the sensations concomitant with that emotion. Mindfulness of the body and its sensations then brings with it a balancing and integrating quality. This is the natural pacification of the six animals that the Buddha describes. With mindfulness of the body as a steady reference point, we can stay attuned to and well-integrated with the many things we need to do and the people around us.

Interpretations: a constellation of qualities

Mechanistic mindfulness. According to some common usages of the word mindfulness it is regarded as a morally neutral quality. It has been said that a squirrel jumping through the branches of a tree or a cat hunting a mouse has such mindfulness. The term, used in this way, thus also accurately includes the mindfulness required of a sniper. This points to the merely mechanistic function of paying attention in the present moment, on its own.

In classical Buddhist understanding, this quality of the simple act of paying attention to and sustaining it on an object or an action would more accurately be named "attention" (*manasikāra*) and a type of "concentration" (*samādhi*) rather than genuine mindfulness (*sammā-sati*). Or arguably, they could be ranked among the various kinds of "wrong mindfulness" (*micchā-sati*) and "wrong concentration" (*micchā-samādhi*) (Anālayo, 2003, p. 52).

As far as the Pali Canon is concerned, genuine mindfulness (*sammā-sati*) will always have an element of moral sensitivity as part of its makeup. For example, in the first three passages cited earlier (A 7.67, M 19.6–7, M 19.11–12), it is very noticeable that the Buddha incorporates an ethical dimension as an intrinsic part of his descriptions of being mindful: "With mindfulness as his gatekeeper, the noble disciple abandons the unwholesome and develops the wholesome." There is a conscious discrimination between which mind-states lead to benefit and which ones lead to harm.

If attention and concentration are taken to be the all and everything of mindfulness, this can lead to falling into a variety of errors. The practitioner can assume that they are following instructions and are using bare or non-judgmental awareness, or seeing things with the attitude of non-duality, yet in actuality can be drifting into the extremes of either self-indulgence or passivity.

The former of these errors can be summarized as the delusion that: "As long as I'm mindful, whatever I do is okay." This view has a parallel in the Antinomian heresy, the doctrine that: "by faith and the dispensation of grace a Christian is released from the obligation of adhering to any moral law" (Collins English Dictionary, 1998, p. 65).

Perhaps a more telling instance of this aspect of identifying attention and concentration alone as mindfulness is the recent account by the journalist Adee (2012). She described visiting a training facility for snipers, and after an initial unaugmented, fear-filled, and "poor performance" in the combat simulator, she is fitted with a new transcranial direct current simulator helmet, a device designed to enhance the performance of soldiers in training and on the battlefield. She wrote:

> As twenty of them run at me brandishing their guns I calmly line up my rifle, take a moment to breathe deeply, and pick off the closest one, before tranquilly assessing my next target. In what seems like next to no time, I hear a voice call out, "Okay, that's it." The lights come up in the simulation room. . . . In the sudden quiet amid the bodies around me, I was really expecting more assailants, and I'm a bit disappointed when the team begins to remove my electrodes. I look up and wonder if someone wound the clocks forward. Inexplicably, twenty minutes have just passed. "How many did I get?" I ask the assistant. She looks at me quizzically. "All of them."

Adee was certainly fully focused on her task, and indeed found it not merely enjoyable but "a near spiritual experience" because, "for the first time in my life, everything in my head finally shut up." However, from a Buddhist perspective, the mind-state she experienced was far from genuine mindfulness (*sammā-sati*). If *sati* is not *sammā*, then it is not *sati* at all, in the Buddhist sense.

The other extreme, of passivity, is the danger of becoming an abstracted or dissociated "watcher" of experience. This psychological distancing or numbing is a destructive misunderstanding of the principle of detachment. Both of these extremes can have numerous negative effects, including social conflict, alienation, and depression.

The term mindfulness is currently in common use for even this degree of mental focusing. It is impossible to simply dictate that a word not be used in the public sphere in a way that conflicts with a particular point of view; therefore, we suggest that if it is to be called a type of mindfulness, this first level can realistically be called "mechanistic mindfulness."

Ethically attuned mindfulness. Second, from the Buddhist perspective, even in its most rudimentary mode, genuine *sati* will involve an ethical element. Thus, it can be accurately stated that: If it does not involve an element of *sīla* (moral sensitivity or virtue), it cannot be said to be *sammā-sati*, genuine mindfulness (Gethin, 2004; Thānissaro, 2014a, 2014b).

It is stated in the Abhidhamma's classification of "mental factors" (*cetasikas*) that *sati* is one of the "universal beautiful mental factors" (*sobhanasādhārana*). According to the teachings of the Theravāda Buddhist school, all acts of killing, stealing, sexual misconduct, and lying will necessarily cause painful consequences for the doer—great or small, according to circumstances—irrespective of place, time, culture, or social mores (Bodhi, 2014; Gethin, 2004; Thānissaro, 2014a, 2014b). This level of mindfulness thus exhibits many of the qualities we have discussed earlier (see the section titled "Definitions of Mindfulness"), incorporating the aspects of both attention and awareness and ethical mindedness.

Of particular note in relation to ethics is the definition of mindfulness advanced by Nilsson and Kazemi (2016, p. 190): "A particular type of social practice that leads the practitioner to an ethically minded awareness, intentionally situated in the here and now." Of this definition of mindfulness, they wrote:

> [B]y advancing a new definition of mindfulness, we attempted to bridge the gap between Western and modern Buddhist forms. The inclusion of both a social and an ethical component in this new definition naturally highlights and points toward contemporary Buddhism's understanding of sati.
>
> The term *social* is meant to indicate a more engaged and all-encompassing type of mindfulness, rather than one that is primarily focused on individual self-improvement and personal enlightenment. This is more in keeping with Hahn (1976), who concludes that "true" mindfulness is always socially engaged and broadly based, focusing on the alleviation of worldly suffering and oppression.
>
> As for the ethical component, it is intended to underscore the fact that Western mindfulness cannot be ethically neutral and should call upon the practitioner to discriminate between wholesome (Pali: *kusala*) and unwholesome (Pali: *akusala*) actions, as does Buddhist sati (Kang & Whittingham, 2010; Purser & Milillo, 2015). According to Dhammika (1990), a degree of ethical judgment is necessary to properly practice mindfulness (see also Kang & Whittingham, 2010). The cultivation of ethical mindedness would enable individuals to conduct themselves with greater compassion toward others, creating a consciousness that may have a favorable impact on the productivity of the workplace as well as on society at large. Thus, individuals possessing a high level of ethical-minded awareness can be more aware of the moral dimension of their everyday actions.
>
> (p. 191)

Thus, the second level of mindfulness can be referred to as being "ethically attuned mindfulness."

Fully informed mindfulness. Sati-sampajañña means "mindfulness and clear comprehension." It is also translated as "mindfulness and full awareness" or "intuitive awareness" (Sumedho, 2007, pp. 45–60). This term describes the psychological stance wherein the object or action is fully appreciated within its context of time, place, and situation. The precursors to the current experience and its possible consequences are included. This broadening and deepening of the view intrinsically include an appreciation of the individual's attitudes and the impact any actions they are involved in will have upon themselves and others. *Sati-sampajañña*, mindfulness and full awareness, thus naturally incorporates a more refined sense of ethical and social concern, these being influential according to the degree to which full attunement to the time, place, and situation is established. In addition, the greater the development of mindfulness and full awareness is, the more the elements of kindness and compassion will be invoked, and the more apparent the appropriateness of any action will be in terms of it leading to the well-being of oneself or others. This third level can be called "fully informed mindfulness."

Holistic mindfulness. *Sati-paññā* means "mindfulness conjoined with wisdom" and is regarded as the quality that leads to spiritual liberation, the full blossoming of human well-being. The term describes the psychological standpoint wherein all experience, inner or outer, is viewed as patterns of organic change arising and passing within consciousness. This process involves the examination of all experience in a phenomenological manner. The individuals train themselves to receive the flow of experience—sight, sound, smell, taste, touch, thought, and emotion—in a completely nonreactive, unbiased way. This letting go of bias involves seeing the dependent nature and transparency of such categories as "like" or "dislike," "inside" or "outside," "mine" or "others'". In the letting go of such definitions as absolute realities, we realize that what is experienced is not "the world" as fixed and definite external reality, but it is rather "my mind's representation of the world" (S 35.68, 35.82, 35.84, 35.85). Insight meditation, *vipassanā*, is principally concerned with the development of this capacity. This fourth level can be called "holistic mindfulness."

Here is a useful simile to illustrate the relationship between these four dimensions of mindfulness: *sati*, mechanistic mindfulness, is like the hand which is able to pick up or catch an object; *sammā-sati*, ethically attuned mindfulness, dictates whether the object is appropriate to pick up or not; *sati-sampajañña*, fully informed mindfulness, is like the arm that moves the hand to the appropriate place and at the appropriate time to pick up or catch the object; and *sati-paññā*, holistic mindfulness, is like the body to which the arm is connected—it is both the life-source and the means of integration and direction for the entire system.

Currently the word mindfulness is used unsystematically to refer to all these four dimensions, so it should come as no surprise that there has been some confusion. This could be avoided if we regard the mindfulness of the sniper as comparable to that of a cat or a squirrel; it is a *kind* of mindfulness but of the most rudimentary nature. The mindfulness that discerns whether an intention is wholesome/skillful or unwholesome/unskillful gives an initial guide to relating to a situation. The mindfulness that encourages us to attune to situations skillfully and to live as a benevolent and responsible member of society is of a different order. Lastly, the mindfulness that enables us to be totally at ease and to remain emotionally balanced amid life's every vicissitude—that is the embodiment of inner security and freedom, that is of another order altogether.

A social dimension

One final consideration in the exploration of different dimensions of mindfulness is its social aspect. From the Buddhist perspective, it is understood that our well-being is deeply connected to the company we choose to keep. One of the Buddha's most well-known statements is that "Spiritual (wholesome) friendship *(kalyāṇamittatā)* is not half of the holy life, it is rather the whole of the holy life" (S 45.2)—the understanding being that when one has spiritually inclined, wholesome people as friends and companions one is going to be encouraged to develop similar noble values and qualities in oneself.

> In a comparable vein, the Buddha once stated:
>
> I don't see any other quality like spiritual friendship that does so much for a monk in training, one who has not yet attained the goal of the spiritual life [enlightenment] but who remains intent on that unsurpassed liberation from bondage. A monk who has good spiritual friends abandons what is unskillful and develops what is skillful.
>
> (Itivuttaka [Iti] 1.17)

In terms of the broader community, the Buddha provided the following description:

> What is meant by spiritual friendship? When a layperson, in whatever town or village they may dwell, spends time with others who are virtuous and who live a wholesome life. They engage them in discussions and, in turn, emulate their qualities of faith, virtue, generosity and wisdom. This is called spiritual friendship.
>
> (A 8.54)

In another discourse, the Buddha highlighted the root cause of not seeing things clearly, nescience (*avijjā*), and thereby dissatisfaction (*dukkha*), as being an absence of wise, spiritual companionship. In turn, he pointed out that it is through cultivating spiritual friendships that the development of mindfulness, and thereby well-being, is supported:

> Thus, associating with good persons leads to hearing the good Dhamma. Hearing the good Dhamma leads to faith. Faith leads to careful attention. Careful attention leads to mindfulness and clear comprehension. Mindfulness and clear comprehension lead to restraint of the sense faculties [i.e.,

> being responsive rather than reactive]. Restraint of the sense faculties leads to the three kinds of good conduct [wholesome thought, speech, and action]. The three kinds of good conduct lead to the development of the four foundations of mindfulness. The development of the four foundations of mindfulness leads to the fulfillment of the seven factors of enlightenment. The seven factors of enlightenment, becoming fulfilled lead to true knowledge and liberation. Thus, there is nutriment for true knowledge and liberation, and in this way they become fulfilled.
>
> Just as, when it is raining and the rain pours down in thick droplets on a mountaintop, the water flows down along the slope and fills the clefts, gullies, and creeks; these, becoming full, fill up the pools; these, becoming full, fill up the tarns; these, becoming full, fill up the streams; these, becoming full, fill up the rivers; and these, becoming full, fill up the great ocean; thus there is nutriment for the great ocean, and in this way it becomes full. So too, associating with good persons leads to hearing the good Dhamma. . . . The seven factors of enlightenment, becoming fulfilled lead to true knowledge and liberation.
>
> (A 10.61)

Thus, as indicated by Hanh (1976) and Nilsson and Kazemi (2016), the cultivation of mindfulness is not something that should be considered in isolation from social factors—it makes a difference who we spend time with. For those who have put time and effort into the development of mindfulness practices, it is a common experience that the presence of like-minded individuals at the training sessions and retreats has a very positive, supportive impact, facilitating the fulfillment of the quest for well-being.

Mechanisms

Clearly, there is no single authoritative definition or complete understanding of mindfulness because it is rooted in Buddhist lineages and traditions that have evolved over centuries. Thus, the concept of mindfulness should be understood in the context of practice traditions as well as in Buddhist scholarship and, more recently, within academic research, clinical applications, and personal practice. While the Buddha's emphasis was on the experiential nature of mindfulness, leading to an understanding of the nature of absolute reality and spiritual transformation, academic research has different aims. Two key aspects have been to use mindfulness-based practices as a clinical intervention and to understand how mindfulness mediates these changes. By now, we know quite a bit about how mindfulness can be used to reduce pain and suffering in clinical and nonclinical populations, reduce stress and anxiety, ameliorate compassion fatigue, and generally enhance people's quality of life. But we know little about how mindfulness meditation actually works to produce these beneficial effects.

The emphasis on the experiential nature of mindfulness has led to qualitative analyses of how people experience meditation practices and how they conceptualize the mechanisms underlying the changes that accrue from such practices. Subjective experiences of those who receive training in mindfulness-based programs, such as mindfulness-based stress reduction (Kabat-Zinn, 1990) or mindfulness-based cognitive therapy (Segal et al., 2002), can be helpful in developing explanatory models of how mindfulness works. But we have to be very careful in extrapolating from individual qualitative studies because there are questions regarding error, bias, and validity in qualitative research (Norris, 1997), and the same set of interviews can lead to somewhat different interpretations depending on the qualitative analytic methodology used (Frank et al., 2019). Our belief is that we should use insights from qualitative studies for formulating testable hypotheses regarding the explanatory models of how mindfulness works to produce personal transformation.

Several researchers have advanced models that attempt to explain the theoretical underpinnings of how mindfulness meditation works, although no single model appears sufficiently encompassing of all of the possibilities reported in current experimental research. Shapiro and Carlson (2009) proposed that mindfulness practices (defined as intention, attention, and attitude) results in *reperceiving*—a shift in perspective—which enables us to simply witness our thoughts, emotions, and judgments without identifying with them. As reperceiving strengthens through mindfulness practice, it may lead to other mechanisms kicking in that enhance the effects of mindfulness. These include: (a) self-regulation and self-management; (b) emotional, cognitive, and behavioral flexibility; (c) values clarification; and (d) exposure. In essence, as reperceiving matures, it "engenders a deep knowing and intimacy with whatever arises moment by moment" (p. 98), without attachment to the arisings, and enables us to experience the world in its unconditioned state.

Grabovac et al. (2011) developed a Buddhist psychological model of mechanisms of mindfulness based on commentaries and translations of Abhidhamma Piṭaka (Narada Maha Thera, 1987). In this model, the definition of mindfulness is presented within the *vipassana* meditation tradition as "the moment-by-moment observing of the three characteristics (impermanence, suffering, and not-self) of the meditation object." Grabovac et al. proposed a number of mechanisms that arise from their model. For example, mindfulness practices give rise to insight into the three characteristics, which decreases attachment/aversion to feelings and leads to decreased mental proliferation. In addition, acceptance/compassion play a critical role in enabling the mind to repeatedly refocus attention during meditation without engaging in self-judgment or letting other negative thoughts arise and lead to mental proliferation. Other mechanisms in this model include concentration/attentional regulation and adherence to ethical principles.

In accord with the definitions of mindfulness presented by Kabat-Zinn (1990) and Bishop et al. (2004), Hölzel et al. (2011) suggested that the practice of mindfulness meditation "encompasses focusing attention on the experience of thoughts, emotions, and body sensations, simply observing them as they arise and pass away" (p. 538). In the Hölzel et al. theoretical framework, there are four components that interact with each other to produce the effects of mindfulness meditation: attention regulation, body awareness, emotion regulation (which includes reappraisal and exposure, extinction, and reconsolidation), and change in perspective on self. Attention regulation is achieved through focused meditation practice. This practice develops executive attention by focusing on the object of meditation, such as the breath, and letting go of distractions, such as thoughts or memories that arise during meditation. Body awareness develops when the focus of attention is directed to gross and subtle bodily sensations during meditation, thus enhancing awareness of bodily states during meditation and in daily life. Mindfulness positively affects emotion regulation via at least two strategies, *reappraisal* and *extinction*. Reappraisal is a cognitive change strategy that involves reinterpreting the meaning or utility of an event or stimulus in a less self-centered light and thus generating a skillful or more adaptive emotional response to it. For example, instead of seeing an outcome as a failure, it is reappraised as a learning opportunity for a better outcome next time. Extinction is another emotion regulation strategy that may be at work. The concept of extinction is based in learning theory, which holds that consistently unreinforced responses will initially increase in frequency and then fade and disappear from a person's repertoire. Mindfulness teaches acceptance of all situations, positive or negative, without judgment. This means approaching unpleasant or aversive emotions with openness and curiosity rather than cognitive avoidance and negativity. The final linchpin of this theoretical model is the Buddhist concept of not-self—that the self is not static, unchanging, or permanent. In fact, with deep meditation comes the experience of disidentification with a sense of self and seeing the self itself as a mental construction. This change in perspective on the self enables *reperceiving* (Shapiro & Carlson, 2009; Shapiro et al., 2006) or *decentering* (Fresco et al., 2007; Safran & Segal, 1990) to take place, and thus producing some of the changes attributed to mindfulness. The essence is that cultivation of mindfulness enables us to change the nature of our relationship with our thoughts, feelings, and emotions instead of negatively responding to them and producing anxiety and stress in our lives.

Lindsay and Creswell (2017) begin their monitor and acceptance theory (MAT) with Kabat-Zinn's (1994) definition of mindfulness. The two components of MAT are: "(1) the use of attention to *monitor* one's present moment experiences, and (2) a mental attitude of *acceptance* toward momentary experience" (p. 49). Attention monitoring and acceptance are seen as the fundamental components of mindfulness and form the active mechanisms that explain the outcomes of mindfulness-based training programs. In mindfulness-based programs, participants are trained to observe and be more accepting of their present-moment experiences. Acceptance is understood to be a mental attitude that allows all experiences "to arise and pass without elaboration, evaluation, or reactivity" (pp. 49–50) and broadly includes nonreactivity, equanimity, nonjudgment, openness, nonevaluative, and elaborative constructs. Lindsay and Creswell (2017, 2019) buttress their model with current research findings from correlational, longitudinal, and intervention studies and include testable hypotheses derived from MAT.

In addition to theories rooted in cognitive and behavioral mechanisms, there are theories based on brain mechanisms. For example, Tang et al. (2015) and Tang and Leve (2016) presented a neuroscience model of mindfulness meditation, which delineates changes in brain structure that accompanies early, middle, and advanced stages of meditation practice. Vago and Silbersweig (2012) and Vago (2014) advanced the self-awareness, self-regulation, and self-transcendence (S-ART) framework for understanding the neurobiological mechanisms of mindfulness. And Zeidan (2015) has described a stage-based model of the neurobiology of mindfulness meditation. Our knowledge of the neuroscience of mindfulness is probably still somewhat rudimentary when compared to psychological models, but we suspect that an eventual synthesis of divergent and convergent theories across disciplines, together with knowledge gleaned from intervention studies, will lead to a more nuanced understanding of how mindfulness works and with whom, and how its potential can be harnessed for a world in crisis.

Abbreviations

A = *Aṅguttara Nikāya*
Dhp = *Dhammapada*
Iti = *Itivuttaka*
M = *Majjhima Nikāya*
S = *Saṃyutta Nikāya*

References

Adee, S. (2012). Zap your brain into the zone: Fast track to pure focus. *New Scientist*, 2850.

Ajahn Chah. (2002). *Food for the heart*. Somerville, MA: Wisdom.

Anālayo, B. (2003). *Satipaṭṭhāna: The direct path to realization*. Cambridge, UK: Windhorse Publications.

Bishop, S. R., Lau, M., Shapiro, S., Carlson, L., Anderson, N. D., Carmody, J., . . Devins, G. (2004). Mindfulness: A proposed operational definition. *Clinical Psychology: Science and Practice*, *11*(3), 230–241.

Bodhi, Bhikkhu. (2006). Interview with Bhikkhu Bodhi: Translator for the Buddha. *Inquiring Mind*, *22*(2).

Bodhi, Bhikkhu. (2011). What does mindfulness really mean? A canonical perspective. *Contemporary Buddhism*, *12*(1), 19–39.

Bodhi, Bhikkhu. (2014). War and peace: A Buddhist perspective. *Inquiring Mind*, *30*(2).

Collins UK. (1998). *Collins English dictionary* (4th ed.). New York, NY: HarperCollins.

Dhammika, S. (1990). *All about Buddhism: A modern introduction to an ancient spiritual tradition*. Singapore: Buddha Dhamma Mandala Society.

Epstein, R. (1995). *Thoughts without a thinker: Psychotherapy from a Buddhist perspective*. New York, NY: Basic Books.

Frank, P., Stanszus, L., Fischer, D., Kehnel, K., & Grossman, P. (2019). Cross-fertilizing qualitative perspectives on effects of a mindfulness-based intervention: An empirical comparison of four methodical approaches. *Mindfulness*, *10*, 2452–2467.

Fresco, D. M., Moore, M. T., van Dulmen, M. H., Segal, Z. V., Ma, S. H., Teasdale, J. D., & Williams, J. M. (2007). Initial psychometric properties of the Experiences Questionnaire: Validation of a self-report measure of decentering. *Behavior Therapy*, *38*, 234–246.

Germer, C. (2005). Mindfulness: What is it? What does it matter? In C. K. Germer, R. D. Siegel, & P. R. Fulton (Eds.), *Mindfulness and psychotherapy* (pp. 3–27). New York, NY: Guilford Press.

Gethin, R. (2001). *The Buddhist path to awakening*. Oxford: Oneworld Publications.

Gethin, R. (2004). Can killing a living being ever be an act of compassion? The analysis of the act of killing in the Abhidhamma and Pali commentaries. *Journal of Buddhist Ethics*, *11*, 167–202.

Goldstein, J., & Kornfield, J. (2001). *Seeking the heart of wisdom: The path of insight meditation*. Boston, MA: Shambala.

Grabovac, A. D., Lau, M. A., & Willett, B. R. (2011). Mechanisms of mindfulness: A Buddhist psychological model. *Mindfulness*, *2*, 154–166.

Hanh, Thich Nhat (1976). *Miracle of mindfulness*. Boston, MA: Beacon.

Harvey, P. (2000). *An introduction to Buddhist ethics: Foundations, values and issues*. Cambridge, UK: Cambridge University Press.

Hölzel, B. K., Lazar, S. W., Gard, T., Schuman-Olivier, Z., Vago, D. R., & Ott, U. (2011). How does mindfulness meditation work? Proposing mechanisms of action from a conceptual and neural perspective. *Perspectives on Psychological Science*, *6*, 537–559.

Kabat-Zinn, J. (1990). *Full catastrophe living: How to cope with stress, pain and illness using mindfulness meditation*. New York, NY: Delacorte.

Kabat-Zinn, J. (1994). *Wherever you go, there you are: Mindfulness meditation in everyday life*. New York, NY: Hyperion.

Kabat-Zinn, J. (2019). Seeds of a necessary global renaissance in the making: The refining of psychology's understanding of the nature of mind, self, and embodiment through the lens of mindfulness and its origins at a key inflection point for the species. *Current Opinion in Psychology*, *28*, xi–xvii.

Kang, C., & Whittingham, K. (2010). Mindfulness: A dialogue between Buddhism and clinical psychology. *Mindfulness*, *1*, 161–173.

Knaster, M. (2010). *Living this life fully: Stories and teachings of Munindra*. Boston, MA: Shambhala.

Lindsay, E. K., & Creswell, J. D. (2017). Mechanisms of mindfulness training: Monitor and acceptance. *Clinical Psychology Review*, *51*, 48–59.

Lindsay, E. K., & Creswell, J. D. (2019). Mindfulness, acceptance, and emotion regulation: Perspectives from Monitor and Acceptance Theory (MAT). *Current Opinion in Psychology*, *28*, 120–125.

Nanavira, T. (1987). *Clearing the path: Writings of Nanavira Thera (1960–1965)*. Colombo, Sri Lanka: Path Press.

Narada Maha Thera. (1987). *A manual of Abhidhamma*. Malaysia: Buddhist Missionary Society.

Nilsson, H., & Kazemi, A. (2016). Reconciling and thematizing definitions of mindfulness: The big five of mindfulness. *Review of General Psychology*, *20*(2), 183–193.

Norris, N. (1997). Error, bias and validity in qualitative research. *Educational Action Research*, *5*(1), 172–176.

Nyanaponika Thera. (1962). *The heart of Buddhist meditation*. London, UK: Rider.

Nyanatiloka. (1952). *Buddhist dictionary: Manual of Buddhist terms and doctrines*. Kandy, Sri Lanka: Buddhist Publication Society.

Purser, R. E., & Milillo, J. (2015). Mindfulness revisited: A Buddhist-based conceptualization. *Journal of Management Inquiry, 24*, 3–24.

Rhys Davids, T. W. (1881). *Buddhist sutras*. Oxford, UK: Clarendon Press.

Rhys Davids, T. W., & Stede, W. (2004). *The Pali-English dictionary*. New Delhi, India: Asian Educational Services.

Safran, J. D., & Segal, Z. V. (1990). *Interpersonal processes in cognitive therapy*. New York, NY: Basic Books.

Salzberg, S. (2008). Interview with Sharon Salzberg. In R. Shankman (Ed.), *The experience of samadhi: An in-depth exploration of Buddhist meditation* (pp. 130–135). Boston, MA: Shambala.

Segal, Z. V., Williams, J. M. G., & Teasdale, J. D. (2002). *Mindfulness-based cognitive therapy for depression: A new approach to preventing relapse*. New York, NY: Guilford Press.

Shapiro, S. L., & Carlson, L. E. (2009). *The art and science of mindfulness: Integrating mindfulness into psychology and the helping professions*. Washington, DC: American Psychological Association.

Shapiro, S. L., Carlson, L. E., Astin, J. A., & Freedman, B. (2006). Mechanisms of mindfulness. *Journal of Clinical Psychology, 62*, 373–386.

Stanley, S. (2013). From discourse to awareness: Rhetoric, mindfulness, and a psychology without foundations. *Theory & Psychology, 23*(1), 60–80.

Sumedho, Ajahn. (2007). *The sound of silence*. Somerville, MA: Wisdom.

Tang, Y.-Y., Hölzel, B. K., & Posner, M. I. (2015). The neuroscience of mindfulness meditation. *Nature Reviews Neuroscience, 16*, 213–225.

Tang, Y.-Y., & Leve, L. D. (2016). A translational neuroscience perspective on mindfulness meditation as a prevention strategy. *Translational Behavioral Medicine, 6*, 63–72.

Thānissaro, Bhikkhu. (2014a). War and peace, a Buddhist perspective: A letter to the editor from Thānissaro Bhikkhu. *Inquiring Mind, 30*(2).

Thānissaro, Bhikkhu. (2014b). War and peace, a Buddhist perspective: A postscript from Thānissaro Bhikkhu offering six observations on Ven. Bodhi's response. *Inquiring Mind, 30*(2).

Thondup, T. (1996). *The healing power of mind*. London, UK: Penguin.

Vago, D. R. (2014). Mapping modalities of self-awareness in mindfulness practice: A potential mechanism for clarifying habits of mind. *Annals of the New York Academy of Sciences, 1307*, 28–42.

Vago, D. R., & Silbersweig, D. A. (2012). Self-awareness, self-regulation, and self-transcendence (S-ART): A framework for understanding the neurobiological mechanisms of mindfulness. *Frontiers in Human Neuroscience, 6*, 296.

Zeidan, F. (2015). The neurobiology of mindfulness meditation. In K. W. Brown, J. D. Creswell, & R. M. Ryan (Eds.), *Handbook of mindfulness: Theory, research, and practice* (pp. 171–189). New York, NY: Guilford Press.

Chapter 3

Assessment of mindfulness in children and adolescents

Sarah A. Potts, Michael P. Twohig, Grayson M. Butcher, and Michael E. Levin

Introduction

Mindfulness is a multifaceted construct involving attending to one's experiences in the present moment with qualities including being accepting, nonjudgmental, flexible, and nonreactive. Mindfulness is important to measure in children and adolescents, given its pragmatic utility. However, the sophistication and complexity of this construct raises challenges for assessment with children and adolescents. Using mindfulness measures can guide treatment by considering the context of measurement in addition to individual strengths and deficits relating to specific mindfulness facets. Similarly, researching mindfulness in children and adolescents is predicated on the ability to reliably and validly assess this construct. Measuring mindfulness, like all psychological constructs, is an iterative process that involves not only a description but also doing so in a way that maximally informs empirical investigation and, eventually, clinical manipulation of its facets. This chapter seeks to examine the current status of mindfulness measures for children and adolescents, as well as identify future directions for improving measurement.

Being mindful has been shown to be beneficial in most areas of life, and this chapter focuses on the assessment of mindfulness within educational or therapeutic settings—areas that are generally part of psychology. The benefits of mindfulness and corresponding mindfulness-based interventions are now a cornerstone of empirically supported treatments for psychological disorders seen in adults (Hofmann et al., 2010). They are also commonly used in prevention and school-based interventions (Felver et al., 2016). Arguably, the use of these interventions with children and adolescents, while certainly occurring, is lagging behind their use with adult populations. In congruence, the measurement of mindfulness is also less developed than with adult populations (Greco et al., 2011b; Pallozzi et al., 2017). Nevertheless, a suitable number of mindfulness measures exist for this age group, but the diversity of measures and existing research base needs further development. The current status of the measurement of mindfulness in children and adolescents will be covered, with suggestions regarding when to use what measure and consideration of current gaps in the literature on assessing mindfulness in these age groups.

Concerns with measuring mindfulness in children and adolescents

While many questionnaires have been developed to measure mindfulness among adults (Pallozzi et al., 2017), child and adolescent mindfulness assessments have only recently become a topic of investigation (Greco et al., 2011b). There are a number of issues to consider when assessing mindfulness with children, such as age-appropriateness of items, perceived comprehension ability (e.g., abstract, concrete), limitations with regard to self-reflection, and tailoring factor structure and sophistication to respondent developmental stage. These issues will be explored in relation to mindfulness assessment prior to discussing specific measures.

Most mindfulness measures were created for use in adult populations; thus, consideration is needed when directly transferring use to children and adolescents. In particular, mindfulness measures often have specific items that are only appropriate for adults (e.g., references to older-aged tasks like driving and personal references such as suggesting noticing water on one's body in the shower). Assessing mindfulness in relation to relevant life contexts may enhance sensitivity but also requires modification given the developmental stage and abilities of the respondent (e.g., differences between mindfulness at school, when playing, when with friends, in romantic relationships). Reading level is another common issue to consider, particularly given the sophistication of some aspects of mindfulness (e.g., metacognitive skills, such as how one relates to thoughts and feelings). It is important that child and adolescent specific measures be designed with comprehensible items and instructions regarding age and reading level, since reading level and appropriateness of items often vary across ages and developmental levels. These unique considerations may require additional efforts in the development and validation of measures.

Children and adolescents are continually developing cognitively, emotionally, and academically. Therefore, one must be cognizant of various developmental issues unique to these populations beyond just reading level when developing and using mindfulness measures in younger populations. In general, self-report measures can only be useful when participants fully comprehend the items and type of responses necessary. Specific to mindfulness self-report measures, respondents must display a sense of self; they need to demonstrate the ability and awareness to reflect on their own thoughts, emotions, and behavior. In order to complete a mindfulness measure, one needs the ability for abstract thinking and taking varying self-perspectives. Development of more complex awareness begins in adolescence, and mindfulness measurement in younger populations may need to account for this difference (Keating, 2004; Pallozzi et al., 2017). Specifically, abstract and metacognitive components of mindfulness may need to be de-emphasized or assessed differently in children and adolescents than in adults.

These developmental concerns might be best highlighted with regard to the factor structure of mindfulness measures for children and adolescents. Factor structures are either multidimensional (containing multiple factors) or unidimensional (containing a single factor). This is due in part to differences in conceptualization of mindfulness, or at least in terms of what aspects are emphasized. For example, one measure for children and adolescents defines mindfulness as "a general tendency to pay attention to and have awareness of life's experiences" (Lawlor et al., 2014). This definition emphasizes present moment awareness, while de-emphasizing the central role of how one attends (e.g., with acceptance, nonreactivity, nonjudgment). In contrast, other mindfulness measures such as the Five-Facet Mindfulness Questionnaire (FFMQ; Baer et al., 2006) have multiple subscales, which often deconstruct a global definition to measure more specific facets. Separating a global definition into facets aids in measuring ways of attending to the present (e.g., describing, observing, acting with awareness) and qualities of attention (e.g., being nonjudgmental, nonreactive).

However, factors may function differently for adult and child/adolescent populations. Multidimensional measures for children routinely accompany weaker factor loadings than are seen in adult measures, making single factor measures of mindfulness generally more appropriate for children and adolescents (Pallozzi et al., 2017). A multifactor scale naturally suggests more fine-grained discriminations in assessing among aspects of mindfulness (e.g., I am good at describing my experiences, but I also tend to do things on "autopilot."). More specific discrimination might be a limitation for younger populations due to factors such as differences in working memory (Johnson et al., 2010). Similarly, some facets of mindfulness may require more advanced metacognitive skills in relation to how individuals identify internal experiences (e.g., judging one's thoughts, not reacting to urges). A unidimensional scale, which reduces some challenges inherent in particular age groups, might simplify mindfulness assessment. Examining differences between unidimensional and multidimensional scales highlights the importance of the factor structures of measures used in age groups not yet explored to ensure appropriateness of scale performance.

A final point worth noting is whether mindfulness is measured with direct or indirect assessment. Direct assessment estimates the presence of mindfulness, while indirect assessment gauges lack of mindfulness (Brown & Ryan, 2003). The indirect assessment provides greater diagnostic ability for the general population, as it is particularly appropriate for individuals who have little to no mindfulness experience (Brown, Ryan, et al., 2011). In contrast, individuals who are not familiar with mindfulness concepts may struggle with understanding some aspects of direct mindfulness assessments (e.g., whether they are "able to notice thoughts as just thoughts without reacting to them" or "accept emotions just for what they are, without defense"). The Mindful Attention

Awareness Scale (MAAS; Brown & Ryan, 2003) is written using an indirect assessment of mindfulness (e.g., uses general statements rather than specific mindfulness terminology), making it useful for large-scale screening or for those with little experience with mindfulness. While recommendations regarding these measures are provided, it is suggested to consider the unique aspects that accompany mindfulness and also the complexities of child and adolescent development, both of which are likely to be contingent upon client and setting context. For example, direct assessments may help measure progress in strength and skill building for a child who is learning mindfulness skills.

In summary, mindfulness is best conceptualized and measured differently with children and adolescents than it is with adults, and current conceptualizations seem to point to fewer, broader factors. Alternatively, the continual development of measures more sensitive to these populations may end up differentiating more facets of mindfulness. The process of psychometric assessment can be characterized as an iterative one, and the factors of mindfulness, whether they are for children, adolescents, or adults, should be understood as evolving within the broader ecology of mindfulness-based interventions.

Child and adolescent mindfulness measures

The two most empirically supported mindfulness measures for children and adolescents are the Child and Adolescent Mindfulness Measure (CAMM; Greco et al., 2011b) and the Mindful Attention and Awareness Scale-Adolescent (MAAS-A; Brown & Ryan, 2003; Brown, West, et al., 2011). The Five-Facet Mindfulness Questionnaire (FFMQ; Baer et al., 2006) is one of the most commonly used measures in adult populations but has not been adequately evaluated in children and adolescents (Pallozzi et al., 2017), and its application with adolescent populations will not be discussed in this chapter. Summary of the two suggested measures, CAMM and MAAS-A, are described, including considerations for clinical practice. Newer mindfulness measures, such as the Comprehensive Inventory of Mindfulness Experiences-Adolescents (CHIME-A; Bergomi et al., 2015; Johnson et al., 2017) and the Adolescent and Adult Mindfulness Scale (AAMS; Droutman et al., 2018) are also described.

Child and Adolescent Mindfulness Measure (CAMM)

The Child and Adolescent Mindfulness Measure (CAMM; Greco et al., 2011b) is the first mindfulness measure that was developed specifically for use with children and adolescents (specific age range: 10 to 17 years old). The CAMM assesses trait mindfulness in children and adolescents, with mindfulness defined as "acting with awareness (i.e., opposite of automatic responding)" and "accepting without judgment (i.e., a person's ability to experience the present moment without evaluating it)" (Greco et al., 2011b, p. 2). Items from the CAMM were originally based on an adult mindfulness measure (Kentucky

Inventory Mindfulness Skills [KIMS], Baer et al., 2004), which includes four subscales assessing observing, describing, acting with awareness, and accepting without judgment. However, consistent with the issues noted regarding factor structure with younger populations, the CAMM reduced the number of mindfulness factors being assessed. Items in the CAMM are reverse scored, and higher scores indicate greater trait mindfulness ability. Two example items from the CAMM are "I pay close attention to my thoughts" and "I get upset at myself for having certain thoughts." Responses are rated on a five-point scale (0 = never true, 4 = always true).

It is worth noting that factor structure research with the CAMM reflects the complexity associated with multifactor mindfulness scales in younger populations. This measure was originally developed with three factors: (1) observing; (2) lack of awareness of ongoing activity/judgmental responses to thoughts and feelings; and (3) non-accepting, avoidant stance toward unpleasant thoughts and feelings. Although original development anticipated the use of the three-factor (e.g., 25-item) version, it has not received a confirmatory factor analysis and is not recommended for use. Rather, there is research support for a 20-item multifactor CAMM measure and the strongest support for a 10-item single factor version of the CAMM, which omits observing and describing items.

Twenty-item CAMM versions have received some empirical support, although item organization within factor structure has been inconsistent across studies (e.g., Ciarrochi et al., 2011; de Bruin et al., 2014). A few two-factor structures have been tested with the following factor pairings: observing and acting with awareness (Ciarrochi et al., 2011); present moment/nonjudgmental awareness and suppression of thoughts and feelings; and nonjudgmental awareness and distractibility (de Bruin et al., 2014). Although there is some preliminary support for a CAMM two factor version, particularly in adolescent populations, confirmatory factor analyses are needed. Multiple versions (e.g., three-factor, two-factor, one-factor) have been examined in an adolescent population (N = 428, 58% female, 10–17 years old). However, at this point, the developers of the CAMM recommend a one-factor version (Greco et al., 2011a), as there is minimal distinction between factors in the two and three-factor versions and the single factor version evidences increased reliability (Kuby et al., 2015).

The CAMM 10-item, single factor version assesses lack of present moment awareness and judgmental/non-accepting responses to thoughts and feelings. This version has shown adequate internal consistency in 16 studies with children and adolescents ranging from 11 to 17 years old (Cronbach's $\alpha = 0.70$) (Pallozzi et al., 2017). A confirmatory factor analysis for the 10-item version suggested good fit (RMSEA = .07, SRMR = .06) (Greco et al., 2011a). Additional analyses indicate the 10-item CAMM has strong convergent validity (e.g., quality of life, academic competence, and social skills) and strong incremental validity (e.g., somatic complaints and internalizing and externalizing behaviors)

(Greco et al., 2011a). More research is needed on the CAMM 10-item version to determine treatment sensitivity and a cut-off score associated with clinical impairment or improved functioning.

Reading grade level of CAMM 10-item version

Pallozzi et al. (2017) assessed reading grade level (RGL) in the 10-item CAMM. This was determined by the Flesch Reading Ease Formula (Flesch-Kincaid; Flesch, 1948), a commonly accepted method for determining reading grade level (RGL, McHugh & Behar, 2009). With this method, the identified grade level is determined by assessing the number of words and number of syllables in each sentence. In general, longer sentences are indicative of higher RGLs. Using the Flesch-Kincaid method, CAMM instruction RGL is 2.6 and is 4.3 for item RGL. In terms of comprehension, the CAMM items include 80% abstract content and 20% concrete content, as measured by items that are more connected to actual or possible events (e.g., self-referencing, concrete actions, and image-evoking; Sadoski et al., 2000). The measure is estimated to take less than five minutes to complete (Goodman et al., 2017).

Mindful Attention and Awareness Scale (MAAS) and adapted versions

The Mindful Attention and Awareness Scale (MAAS; Brown & Ryan, 2003) is a 15-item unidimensional measure assessing trait mindfulness. The measure was developed with mindfulness as a single-factor and defined as the tendency to pay attention to and be aware of life experiences. The MAAS was developed for use in adult populations and has been adapted for children (MAAS-C; Lawlor et al., 2014) and adolescents (MAAS-A; Brown, West, et al., 2011). It is important to note the MAAS-A has received more psychometric testing, but the MAAS-C has not yet received a thorough psychometric evaluation. The MAAS-A, which is for adolescents 14 to 18 years old, is identical to the original MAAS with the omission of one item, which assesses awareness while driving. The MAAS-C, which is for children 9 to 13 years old, is similar to the original MAAS but contains adapted language thought to be appropriate for use with children (Lawlor et al., 2014). Interestingly, the original, adapted MAAS scale has been used in adolescent research (e.g., Black et al., 2012; Edwards et al., 2014; Lau & Hue, 2011; Marks et al., 2010; Oberle et al., 2011). Given the language and qualities of certain items (e.g., reference to awareness while driving), the original MAAS may not be appropriate for use with children and younger adolescent populations.

Items in the MAAS-C and MAAS-A are summed to obtain a total score, with higher scores indicating greater trait mindfulness ability. Two sample items from the MAAS-A are "I find it difficult to stay focused on what's happening in the present" and "I rush through activities without being really attentive to them." Responses are given on a six-point Likert scale (1 = almost always true, 6 = almost never). The MAAS-A and MAAS-C evidence moderate test-retest reliability in adolescent samples (three-month, 10-month periods, r = .35 -.52; Black et al., 2012). The MAAS-C has been validated only in one study with children (8–9 years old; Cronbach's α = 0.84; Lawlor et al., 2014). The MAAS-A has demonstrated strong internal consistency in several populations, including secondary students (Cronbach's α = 0.93), psychiatric outpatients (Cronbach's α = 0.86; Brown, West, et al., 2011), and incarcerated adolescent males (Cronbach's α = 0.91; Barnert et al., 2013). The original version of the MAAS exhibits strong predictive validity for clinical outcomes in adolescents. In comparison with other versions of mindfulness measures containing multiple factors (e.g., CAMM two- or three-factor), the single factor inherent in the MAAS-A and MAAS-C, which highlights the "presence" quality of mindfulness, has indicated the best fit for a number of adolescent samples (Brown, West, et al., 2011; Black et al., 2012; Lawlor et al., 2014).

Reading grade level of MAAS-A and MAAS-C

Using the Flesch-Kincaid method (Flesch, 1948) for determining RGL as previously described (Pallozzi et al., 2017), both the MAAS-A and MAAS-C instruction RGL is 10.0. The MAAS-A item RGL is 7 and the MAAS-C item RGL is 7.2. In regard to comprehension, the original MAAS items are characterized by 50% concrete content, which is important to consider for certain adolescent populations (Pallozzi et al., 2017). This suggests the reading level of the MAAS-A and MAAS-C is particularly appropriate for individuals between seventh and tenth grade. Although the MAAS-C content is adapted for younger populations, it still appears to have a similar reading level given the minimal differences in reading levels between the two versions. These measures are estimated to take less than five minutes to complete (Goodman et al., 2017).

Comprehensive Inventory of Mindfulness Experiences-Adolescents (CHIME-A)

The Comprehensive Inventory of Mindfulness Experiences-Adolescents (CHIME-A; Johnson et al., 2017) is a 25-item trait mindfulness measure suggested for use with adolescents between the ages of 12 and 14 years (Johnson et al., 2017). The CHIME-A is adapted from the original CHIME, which was initially developed for assessment of mindfulness in adult populations (Bergomi et al., 2015). Items on the CHIME-A are rated on a five-point rating scale (0 = never true, 4 = always true). The CHIME-A assesses mindfulness through eight subscales: awareness of internal experiences; awareness of external experiences; acting with awareness; accepting and nonjudgmental orientation; decentering and nonreactivity; openness to experiences; relativity of thoughts; and insightful understanding (Johnson et al., 2017). While the scale can be summed to obtain a total score, this is not recommended, given decreased internal consistency when combining all items. The acting with awareness subscale has been shown to have greater treatment response than other subscales. Initial Cronbach's alphas for subscales range from .65 to .77 and the total score is positively correlated with the CAMM (Johnson et al., 2017). The CHIME-A is estimated to take less than 10 minutes to complete (Goodman et al., 2017). While this measure may be particularly helpful for measuring specific components of mindfulness (e.g., awareness of internal versus external experiences), use of the total score is not recommended, and a more rigorous evaluation of this measure is warranted, such as clarifying extent of external validity.

Adolescent and Adult Mindfulness Scale (AAMS)

The Adolescent and Adult Mindfulness Scale (AAMS; Droutman et al., 2018) is a 19-item measure that was developed specifically for measuring mindfulness in both adults and adolescents (specific age range: 11 to 18 years old). Items on the AAMS are rated on a five-point rating scale (1 = rarely true, 5 = always true). Items on the AAMS measure mindfulness with the following subscales: attention and awareness; nonreactivity; nonjudgment; and self-acceptance. Initial Cronbach's alphas for subscales range from .77 to .78 and .81 for the total score (general mindfulness) for adolescent samples (Droutman et al., 2018). The total score and all subscales, except the attention and awareness subscale, are positively correlated with the CAMM (Johnson et al., 2017). Nine out of the 19 items are within the attention and awareness scale; thus, the AAMS is likely to correlate with other measures highlighting attention and awareness over other factors of mindfulness (Droutman et al., 2018). Given item count and simplicity of items, it is estimated that the AAMS would take less than 10 minutes to complete. Greater evaluation and use with adolescents are warranted given the promising initial validation data. The AAMS may be particularly helpful in measuring change in mindfulness across a long time period due to the applicability for both adolescents and adults.

Summary of Child and Adolescent Mindfulness Measurement

Adaptations to the CAMM and MAAS offer useful alternatives for measuring mindfulness in children and adolescent populations. While the MAAS-C needs additional research in determining predictive validity and test-retest in childhood populations, the CAMM and MAAS-A both evidence strong internal consistency. The MAAS-C, MAAS-A, and CAMM demonstrate strong convergent validity with a number of constructs, including negative relations with stress (Black et al., 2012; Ciesla et al., 2012; de Bruin et al., 2014), pain catastrophizing (de Bruin et al., 2014; Petter et al., 2013), substance use (Brown, Ryan, et al., 2011; Lawlor et al., 2014), aggression (Black et al., 2012) positive relations with self-control (Black et al., 2012), quality of life (de Bruin et al., 2014; Greco et al., 2011b), life satisfaction (Brown, Ryan, et al., 2011), and emotional awareness (Ciarrochi et al., 2011). It is important to note there are currently no criterion validity data for these measures among child and adolescent populations (Pallozzi et al., 2017), such that there are no established norms for those with history of mindfulness practice and those without.

The CAMM 10-item version and the MAAS-C are considered age-appropriate for child and adolescent populations, although more emphasis might be given to determining reading ability in the MAAS-A, given item similarity to the original MAAS. There are no major comprehension concerns for the MAAS adaptations, but the CAMM contains 80% abstract content, which is a consideration for use with children, who may have less abstract reasoning ability. This may present challenges in grasping item content given the variability of sophisticated awareness abilities in younger populations (Pallozzi et al., 2017).

Choosing appropriate measures

In choosing the most appropriate mindfulness measure for a child or adolescent, key factors should be considered including comprehension (e.g., abstract, concrete), age-appropriateness of content, response burden, validation, and treatment sensitivity. This section will focus on considerations proposed for the suggested child and adolescent measures: CAMM 10-item version, MAAS-C, and MAAS-A.

Summary of reading grade level

With regard to comprehension, items in the CAMM were rated using the Flesch-Kincaid method (Flesch, 1948) at an RGL between fourth and fifth grade, while the MAAS-C and MAAS-A items are considered to be an RGL between seventh and eighth grade (Pallozzi et al., 2017). The MAAS versions contain less abstract content than the CAMM (50% versus 80%; Pallozzi et al., 2017), although this difference should be considered tentative because this was analyzed using professional judgment and not a validated instrument. The CAMM 10-item version might be more appropriate for individuals at lower reading levels. However, this should be balanced with consideration that there are more abstract items, presenting a challenge for those with less sophisticated awareness abilities. It is also worth noting that fourth grade was the lowest reading level for the CAMM 10-item version, suggesting that children who are younger or who have reading difficulty may have challenges completing the measure. In summary, the CAMM 10-item version is age-appropriate for children and adolescents (e.g., lowest appropriate reading grade level is fourth). The MAAS-C and MAAS-A are also suitable for children and adolescents (e.g., lowest appropriate reading grade level is seventh).

Response burden and completion time

The MAAS-C, MAAS-A and CAMM 10-item version have low response burdens (i.e., 15-item, 14-item, and 10-item), and the response choice is low (Likert scale with five or six options). In general, a set of five or fewer response options and a completion time under 30 minutes is most acceptable for use with children and adolescents (Kuby et al., 2015). This recommendation is derived from science behind working memory, indicating that there is a positive relationship between age of children with neurotypical functioning and the ability to comprehend and respond to more complex, varied, or lengthened items (Johnson et al., 2010). Depending on child or adolescent characteristics and consideration of response burden, it may be best to deliver this measure alone and not within a larger assessment battery.

While this chapter provides a framework to apply in choosing appropriate mindfulness measures for use with children and adolescents, it not a conclusive set of considerations for all situations and settings. As with assessment tools delivered to any individual, it is always important to determine individual cognitive ability while considering applicability of the measure. It is important to consider the context in which services are provided, theoretical rationale, overall treatment goals, and the basis for measuring mindfulness.

Age and population appropriateness

The CAMM 10-item version, MAAS-C and MAAS-A have been validated for use with adolescents. The majority of research has examined the use of MAAS-C and MAAS-S with older adolescents (at least 10 years old), while the CAMM versions have been predominantly used with younger children (as young as 8 years old). The original MAAS version has been used with adolescents (11–17 years old) with externalizing symptoms (Bögels et al., 2013), and the MAAS-A has been used with older adolescents (14–18 years old) in psychiatric outpatients and incarcerated males (Barnert et al., 2013; Brown, West, et al., 2011). The CAMM has been used with adolescents with chronic illness (8–18 years old), autism spectrum disorder (11–23 years old), and general distress (13–18 years old; Petter et al., 2013).

Sensitivity to treatment

There are limited data regarding treatment sensitivity and measurement of mindfulness in interventions with children and adolescents. Preliminary research suggests the MAAS-A might be more appropriate for intervention research, given that the changes in mindfulness are associated with improvements in self-esteem, self-compassion, and depression symptoms (Pallozzi et al., 2017). Conversely, no intervention studies have found significant relationships between changes in mindfulness and outcome variables. While this may be due to intervention efficacy or methodological factors, this may also be a product of participant age. The majority of research assessing mindfulness with CAMM versions involved interventions for younger adolescents, while the majority of the studies using the MAAS versions were focusing on older adolescents.

It is worth considering what aspects of mindfulness might be most helpful to assess when selecting among measures. As noted earlier, mindfulness is multifaceted but appears to be more reliably assessed through unidimensional measures in younger populations. One might identify a measure to use based on the aspects of mindfulness that are most beneficial to assess for a given research question, assessment aim, or treatment goal. The MAAS appears to focus more on attention to the present, while the CAMM includes a greater emphasis on how one relates to present moment experiences in an accepting, nonjudgmental way. Given the limitations with current child and adolescent measures, initial efforts have been made to use other adult mindfulness measures to assess specific mindfulness facets, such as the FFMQ (nonreactivity, nonjudgment, and acting with awareness subscales; Ciesla et al., 2012) and a short form of the Freiburg Mindfulness Inventory (FMI), which characterizes mindfulness as nonjudgmental present-moment observation and openness to experience (Lau & Hue, 2011). Although one might consider these alternate measures to assess more refined aspects of mindfulness, this work should be approached with caution given the lack of validation and the high potential for issues in using adult measures with younger populations.

Behavioral observation

A vast majority of assessment measures, including those developed for mindfulness, utilize self-report questionnaires. Self-report questionnaires, however, only provide one means of investigating mindfulness and may have some limitations. Namely, measures are typically developed and normed on larger samples, with results extrapolated to individuals. There are times when the overt correlates of mindfulness (the behaviors of interest) are individual and setting specific. For example, a child may show appropriate behavior and high mindfulness in one class but poor behavior and inattentiveness in another one. Determining the variables that contribute to individualized mindful actions, especially as they differentially occur across contexts, may be of use to the child and teachers. This continual attention to—and inclusion of—environmental factors surrounding individualized and context-specific instances of mindful behavior adds the advantage of explicitly considering ways in which contextual variables aid or inhibit generalized mindful habits. Thus, an alternative—some would argue complementary—way of measuring mindfulness is referred to as a behavioral observation. Such an approach could also help overcome developmental challenges with regard to self-reflection and metacognitive skills in self-reporting mindfulness.

A behavioral observer gathers a unique kind of evidence. Instead of gathering information about individual experiences or the quality of those experiences when mindfulness is displayed, the behavioral observer asks "what behaviors, under what conditions, define mindfulness?" Goldiamond referred to this as the basic behavioral question (Andronis, 2004). This approach should not be understood as invalidating other approaches; rather, it simply limits the investigator to assessing the occurrence of a repertoire of predefined behaviors. The potential positive result of doing so is that the treatment utility of assessment is significantly augmented, as the investigators can utilize this overt, predefined understanding of mindfulness to directly target mindfulness and increase the rate, form, and/or contexts in which it occurs.

An important feature of a behavioral take on mindfulness is that it is something the person does. Thus, the observer needs to operationally define the actions that constitute mindfulness. This is a specific set of actions that the observer has predetermined to be mindful actions. Conversely, there might also be a list of actions that are the opposite of being mindful. The interesting thing is that these actions are likely to be different for each child in each setting. The operational definition should be clear enough that multiple observers could determine if the actions occurred or not. This helps reduce subjectivity in a complicated or possibly chaotic situation.

Practically speaking, defining and directly observing the overt correlates of mindfulness as it unfolds is an iterative process. What one child is doing while acting with awareness may be very different from another, while two children may demonstrate acceptance without judgment quite similarly across settings. These issues are empirical and often require continual observation and reformulation of operational definitions before a behavioral assessment can be adequately commenced. For example, it may become clear that one child tends to demonstrate acting with awareness when staring intently at a teacher, leaning forward, and crossing their hands. Another child may look away or draw diagrams while acting with awareness. The fact that the forms of these behaviors differ is not troubling—functionally, they are the same. This appears to present issues for nomothetic assessment development. Conversely, it may be the case that empirical investigation of accepting without judgment, for example, may yield a repertoire of behaviors which are formally similar (e.g., micro-reactions, emotional expressions, or nonverbal behaviors). It may initially be inconvenient to consider topographically diverse expressions as functionally equivalent, but one may find that doing so yields considerable treatment dividends.

A common way to code the occurrence of the mindful behaviors is through a partial interval coding system. In this system the observation period is broken down into blocks of time such as 30 seconds or one minute, and the rater records whether the actions occurred in those time blocks. This is a helpful system to simply get the rate of mindful actions and actions that are not mindful. The limitation is that it only tells how often actions occur and does not give information on what precipitating or consequential variables might be.

Recently, a group of researchers developed a system to observationally assess mindfulness in young children (Lemberger-Truelove et al., 2019). The Child

Observation of Mindfulness Measure (C-OMM) is a nice addition because it offers a systematic method that has data on reliability and validity to assess mindful behaviors in very young children. The participants in their validation study were 3 to 4 years of age, and the study was validated by observing behaviors across settings. Specifically, they assessed mindfulness in free play, teacher directed activities, and during meals and rated the behavior across dimensions including self-regulated attention and attention to experience.

If the observer is interested in why mindfulness is occurring or not occurring, then using a type of functional assessment might be the best option. A functional assessment is simply an objective method of monitoring what environmental events precede an action, the action, and what environment consequence(s) follow. In more applied settings, we often call this an ABC analysis (for antecedent, behavior, and consequence). The observer should remember that it makes sense to infer some private experiences (e.g., thoughts, feelings, emotions, bodily sensations) as antecedents, consequences, or just setting events (events that make it more likely). Even though thoughts or feelings are hard to see, there are certain behaviors that allow us to infer they are occurring such as looks of frustration or anger or the appearance of thinking.

Once the observer knows how often mindful actions and non-mindful actions are occurring and what events occur before and after them, the observer may start manipulating things to see if the frequency of the target actions can be altered. For example, the instructor could teach the child, "when the feelings of frustration start to occur, pay attention to where the feeling of frustration is in your body and see if you can find a place for it, then continue with the task." Continued monitoring would tell the observer something about the child's actions and what is helpful in increasing mindfulness. If the point of assessment is to empirically measure a psychological construct, then behavioral observation offers a method which is precise, consistent, and publicly verifiable (Cooper et al., 2019).

Assessing constructs related to mindfulness

Mindfulness assessments are increasingly employed to track the psychological processes and treatment outcomes involved in mindfulness and acceptance-based therapies. There are many therapies that are included under this description. One such approach is acceptance and commitment therapy (ACT), which seeks the development of a psychological flexibility—defined as "contacting the present moment as a conscious human being, fully and without needless defense—as it is and not as what it says it is—and persisting with or changing a behavior in the service of chosen values" (Hayes et al., 2012, p. 96). The Acceptance and Action Questionnaire-II (AAQ-II; Bond et al., 2011) is most frequently employed to measure psychological flexibility and has been shown to correlate with measures of mindfulness, such as the FFMQ (Baer et al., 2008). Psychological flexibility is, in turn, conceptualized as being comprised of six core psychological processes: acceptance, defusion, self-as-context, present moment awareness, values, and committed action. These processes are seen as conceptually overlapping with mindfulness as it is defined by the broader mindfulness literature. Additionally, a recent meta-analysis has provided empirical support for the usefulness of these processes (Levin et al., 2012). It has been argued that acceptance (allowing inner experiences to occur without fight) and defusion (seeing internal experiences as simply thoughts, feelings, or bodily sensations and not what they represent) are central aspects of mindfulness (Fletcher & Hayes, 2005).

As the model pertains to child and adolescent mindfulness assessment, the Avoidance and Fusion Questionnaire for Youth (AFQ-Y) is the first measure of psychological (in)flexibility that has been developed and validated for use with younger populations (Greco et al., 2008). The AFQ-Y taps into the processes of experiential avoidance and cognitive fusion—each conceptualized as the inflexible counterparts of acceptance and defusion processes. The AFQ-Y has been shown to moderately correlate with the CAAM (Greco et al., 2008). There are a growing number of child and adolescent studies which have intervened on psychological flexibility using acceptance and mindfulness-based intervention procedures.

Mindfulness in parents

Assessing mindfulness in parents or caretakers, who often provide shaping and discipline, can also aid in understanding a child's context. It can be a valuable effort to include parent measures, including mindfulness ability. An area that has demonstrated short-term importance in understanding parent symptomatology and ability is within the pediatric surgery preparatory literature. Racine et al. (2016) completed a systematic review of factors predictive of child anticipatory distress prior to invasive surgery and found the parent distress and overall anxious predisposition as two of the top five predictors of child anticipatory distress. This similar relationship is also evidenced between parental distress and maladaptive behaviors for children with autism spectrum disorders (Hall & Graff, 2012; Racine et al., 2016), parental depression and child psychopathology (Pilowsky et al., 2014), and parental attention-deficit hyperactivity-disorder and child internalizing problems (Humphreys et al., 2012). Although parental factors can contribute to childhood problems, they also afford opportunities for improving the lives of children through processes like mindfulness. In the case of parental mindfulness, research shows that parents being more mindful predicts improved childhood outcomes (Parent et al., 2016). Parental trait mindfulness has been shown to predict decreased internalizing and externalizing behaviors in young children (3–7 years), middle childhood (8–12 years), and adolescence (13–17 years).

There are a number of adult measures suitable for state and trait mindfulness assessment. State mindfulness refers to mindfulness related to experience during an intervention or exercise (Shapiro et al., 2008). A state mindfulness measure might assess change in mindfulness before and after completion of a mindfulness exercise. Trait mindfulness is a more commonly measured mindfulness construct that refers to an individual's general disposition (Shapiro & Walsh, 1984). Given the purpose of this chapter and aim of the book, focusing primarily on children and adolescents, only a couple of the most reliable adult mindfulness measures appropriate for assessing individuals with little to no mindfulness experience will be discussed.

The Five Facet Mindfulness Questionnaire (FFMQ; Baer et al., 2006) is a 39-item measure assessing trait mindfulness via the following factors: non-reactivity to inner Experience, Nonjudging of Inner Experience, Observation, Acting with Awareness, and Describing. An example of an item from the Acting with Awareness subscale is "I don't pay attention to what I'm doing because I'm daydreaming, worrying, or otherwise distracted." An example from the Nonjudging of Inner Experience subscale is "I tell myself I shouldn't be feeling the way I'm feeling." All items are scored on a five-point Likert scale (0 = Never or very rarely true to 4 = Very often or always true). Factors range from adequate to excellent internal consistency (α = .75 to α = .91). Recently, the FFMQ was shortened and tested with adolescents with good preliminary support (Cortazar et al., 2019).

The Mindful Attention Awareness Scale (MAAS; Brown & Ryan, 2003) is a 15-item, single-factor questionnaire with good internal consistency (α = 0.82 to 0.87). Items are scored on asix6-point Likert scale (1 = Almost always to 6 = Almost never). An example item of the MAAS is "It seems I am 'running on automatic,' without much awareness of what I'm doing." Both measures evidence strong criterion reliability, as they are sensitive to training or change across time (FFMQ: Bohlmeijer et al., 2011; MAAS; Brown & Ryan, 2003).

While it is not always important or even feasible to obtain parent-specific measures (e.g., measures related to parent ability or functioning), it can be helpful in certain cases. It is important to have a clear rationale for intent in measuring parent mindfulness ability within treatment. Given the importance of considering the context of children and adolescents, it can be of upmost importance to understand parent or caretaker functioning. Additionally, the association between parent mindfulness ability and child functioning (e.g., youth psychological well-being; (Haydicky et al., 2013; Marks et al., 2010) create a strong case for assessing mindfulness in parents, particularly when a mindfulness intervention is present.

One limitation of this measurement approach is that it is fairly global in terms of assessing parent mindfulness. Ultimately, it would be beneficial to have a measure that specifically focuses on mindful parenting interactions. Similar measures have recently been developed with related constructs, such as psychological flexibility (e.g., Burke & Moore, 2015; Cheron et al., 2009; Greene et al., 2015; McCracken & Gauntlett-Gilbert, 2011). For the time being, mindful interactions with children would need to be inferred with validated global mindfulness measures. Consideration might be given to the relationship between child mindfulness ability or functioning and mindful parenting interactions.

Conclusion

Mindfulness has become a central concept in the field of psychology. It is used as an intervention technique in many psychological interventions, as well as a preventative strategy in school, athletics, and other group settings. The benefits of mindfulness are apparent, and in order to support positive changes, recognizing the appropriate uses of mindfulness interventions and measurement (e.g., to whom, when, what setting) are necessary. While the assessments of child and adolescent mindfulness are limited in number, some are strong psychometrically. These measures have been shown to be valid and reliable across a number of studies. Clear guidelines on their use are available including ages as well as populations on which they are normed. When age is a factor, or mindfulness is state dependent, direct observation is a wise decision. Similarly, it is possible that one of the factors in the development and maintenance of low mindfulness is the context in which the child lives. Specifically, sometimes the parents are teaching or modeling actions that are consistent or inconsistent with mindfulness. Measures exist to assess parental or caregiver mindfulness. Finally, there are other psychological constructs similar to mindfulness that may be of interest to those working in this area. Measures of psychological flexibility and values are described. Prudent use of these assessments will help guide service delivery for children and adolescents in a variety of contexts.

We need continued effort in this area as measurement guides research and applied work (Miller et al., 2006; Pallozzi et al., 2017). Future research should focus on clarifying factor structure and content being assessed by these mindfulness measures. This is challenging with children, given single factor solutions often function better, but it seems that the content of these factors vary and are still missing facets relative to other definitions of mindfulness. It is also worth studying if factor structure varies by developmental period. Right now, we are using groupings with large age-ranges. More research on treatment sensitivity is needed. This will increase as treatment outcome research increases in these age ranges. The field needs more state mindfulness measures, as there are times that this is the issue in question. On that note, developing tools to support direct observation of mindfulness is indicated. This could be in the form of a checklist or general direction that teachers could use to guide their work. Assessing mindfulness in child and adolescent populations is imperative to further our understanding of mindfulness differences in non-adult populations (e.g., unique construct definition, clinical utility, change over time).

References

Andronis, P. A. (2004). *The blue books: Goldiamond and Thompson's the functional analysis of behavior*. Cambridge, MA: Cambridge Center for Behavioral Studies.

Baer, R. A., Smith, G. T., & Allen, K. B. (2004). Assessment of mindfulness by self-report the Kentucky inventory of mindfulness skills. *Assessment, 11*(3), 191–206.

Baer, R. A., Smith, G. T., Hopkins, J., Krietemeyer, J., & Toney, L. (2006). Using self-report assessment methods to explore facets of mindfulness. *Assessment, 13*(1), 27–45.

Baer, R. A., Smith, G. T., Lykins, E., Button, D., Krietemeyer, J., Sauer, S., . . Williams, J. M. G. (2008). Construct validity of the five facet mindfulness questionnaire in meditating and nonmeditating samples. *Assessment, 15*(3), 329–342.

Barnert, E. S., Himelstein, S., Herbert, S., Garcia-Romeu, A., & Chamberlain, L. J. (2013). Exploring an intensive meditation intervention for incarcerated youth. *Child and Adolescent Mental Health, 19*(1), 69–73.

Bergomi, C., Tschacher, W., & Kupper, Z. (2015). Meditation practice and self-reported mindfulness: A cross-sectional investigation of meditators and non-meditators using the comprehensive inventory of mindfulness experiences (CHIME). *Mindfulness, 6*(6), 1411–1421.

Black, D. S., Sussman, S., Johnson, C. A., & Milam, J. (2012). Psychometric assessment of the Mindful Attention Awareness Scale (MAAS) among Chinese adolescents. *Assessment, 19*(1), 42–52.

Bögels, S. M., Hellemans, J., van Deursen, S., Römer, M., & van der Meulen, R. (2013). Mindful parenting in mental health care: Effects on parental and child psychopathology, parental stress, parenting, coparenting, and marital functioning. *Mindfulness, 5*(5), 536–551. doi:10.1007/s12671-013-0209-7

Bohlmeijer, E., Klooster, P. M., Fledderus, M., Veehof, M., & Baer, R. (2011). Psychometric properties of the Five Facet Mindfulness Questionnaire in depressed adults and development of a short form. *Assessment, 18*(3), 308–320.

Bond, F. W., Hayes, S. C., Baer, R. A., Carpenter, K. M., Guenole, N., Orcutt, H. K., . . . Zettle, R. D. (2011). Preliminary psychometric properties of the Acceptance and Action Questionnaire—II: A revised measure of psychological inflexibility and experiential avoidance. *Behavior Therapy, 42*(4), 676–688.

Brown, K. W., & Ryan, R. M. (2003). The benefits of being present: Mindfulness and its role in psychological well-being. *Journal of Personality and Social Psychology, 84*(4), 822–848.

Brown, K. W., Ryan, R. M., Loverich, T. M., Biegel, G. M., & West, A. M. (2011). Out of the armchair and into the streets: Measuring mindfulness advances knowledge and improves interventions: Reply to Grossman. *Psychological Assessment, 23*(4).

Brown, K. W., West, A. M., Loverich, T. M., & Biegel, G. M. (2011). Assessing adolescent mindfulness: Validation of an adapted Mindful Attention Awareness Scale in adolescent normative and psychiatric populations. *Psychological Assessessment, 23*(4), 1023–1033.

Burke, K., & Moore, S. (2015). Development of the parental psychological flexibility questionnaire. *Child Psychiatry & Human Development, 46*(4), 548–557.

Cheron, D. M., Ehrenreich, J. T., & Pincus, D. B. (2009). Assessment of parental experiential avoidance in a clinical sample of children with anxiety disorders. *Child Psychiatry and Human Development, 40*(3), 383–403.

Ciarrochi, J., Kashdan, T. B., Leeson, P., Heaven, P., & Jordan, C. (2011). On being aware and accepting: A one-year longitudinal study into adolescent well-being. *Journal of Adolescence, 34*(4), 695–703.

Ciesla, J. A., Reilly, L. C., Dickson, K. S., Emanuel, A. S., & Updegraff, J. A. (2012). Dispositional mindfulness moderates the effects of stress among adolescents: Rumination as a mediator. *Journal of Clinical Child and Adolescent Psychology, 41*(6), 760–770.

Cooper, J. O., Heron, T. E., & Heward, W. L. (2019). *Applied behavior analysis* (3rd ed.). Upper Saddle River, NJ: Pearson.

Cortazar, N., Calvete, E., Fernández-González, L., & Orue, I. (2019). Development of a Short form of the five facet mindfulness questionnaire—adolescents for children and adolescents. *Journal of Personality Assessment*, Online ahead of print.

de Bruin, E. I., Zijlstra, B. J., & Bögels, S. M. (2014). The meaning of mindfulness in children and adolescents: Further validation of the Child and Adolescent Mindfulness Measure (CAMM) in two independent samples from the Netherlands. *Mindfulness, 5*(4), 422–430.

Droutman, V., Golub, I., Oganesyan, A., & Read, S. (2018). Development and initial validation of the Adolescent and Adult Mindfulness Scale (AAMS). *Personality and Individual Differences, 123*, 34–43.

Edwards, M., Adams, E. M., Waldo, M., Hadfield, O. D., & Biegel, G. M. (2014). Effects of a mindfulness group on Latino adolescent students: Examining levels of perceived stress, mindfulness, self-compassion, and psychological symptoms. *The Journal for Specialists in Group Work, 39*(2), 145–163.

Felver, J. C., Celis-de Hoyos, C. E., Tezanos, K., & Singh, N. N. (2016). A systematic review of mindfulness-based interventions for youth in school settings. *Mindfulness*, 7(1), 34–45.

Flesch, R. (1948). A new readability yardstick. *Journal of Applied Psychology, 32*, 221–233.

Fletcher, L., & Hayes, S. C. (2005). Relational frame theory, acceptance and commitment therapy, and a functional analytic definition of mindfulness. *Journal of Rational-Emotive and Cognitive-Behavior Therapy, 23*(4), 315–336.

Goodman, M. S., Madni, L. A., & Semple, R. J. (2017). Measuring mindfulness in youth: review of current assessments, challenges, and future directions. *Mindfulness, 8*(6), 1409–1420.

Greco, L. A., Baer, R., & Smith, G. T. (2011a). Supplemental material for assessing mindfulness in children and adolescents: Development and validation of the Child and Adolescent Mindfulness Measure (CAMM). *Psychological Assessment, 21*(3), 606–614.

Greco, L. A., Baer, R. A., & Smith, G. T. (2011b). Assessing mindfulness in children and adolescents: Development and validation of the Child and Adolescent Mindfulness Measure (CAMM). *Psychological Assessment, 23*(3), 606–614.

Greco, L. A., Lambert, W., & Baer, R. A. (2008). Psychological inflexibility in childhood and adolescence: Development and evaluation of the avoidance and fusion questionnaire for youth. *Psychological Assessment, 20*(2), 93–102.

Greene, R. L., Field, C. E., Fargo, J. D., & Twohig, M. P. (2015). Development and validation of the parental acceptance questionnaire (6-PAQ). *Journal of Contextual Behavioral Science, 4*(3), 170–175.

Hall, H. R., & Graff, J. C. (2012). Maladaptive behaviors of children with autism: Parent support, stress, and coping. *Issues in Comprehensive Pediatric Nursing, 35*(3–4), 194–214.

Haydicky, J., Shecter, C., Wiener, J., & Ducharme, J. M. (2013). Evaluation of MBCT for adolescents with ADHD and their parents: Impact on individual and family functioning. *Journal of Child and Family Studies, 24*(1), 76–94.

Hayes, S. C., Strosahl, K. D., & Wilson, K. G. (2012). *Acceptance and commitment therapy: An experiential approach to behavior change* (2nd ed.). New York, NY: Guilford Press.

Hofmann, S. G., Sawyer, A. T., Witt, A. A., & Oh, D. (2010). The effect of mindfulness-based therapy on anxiety and depression: A meta-analytic review. *Journal of Consulting and Clinical Psychology, 78*(2), 169.

Humphreys, K. L., Mehta, N., & Lee, S. S. (2012). Association of parental ADHD and depression with externalizing and internalizing dimensions of child psychopathology. *Journal of Attention Disorders, 16*(4), 267–275.

Johnson, C., Burke, C., Brinkman, S., & Wade, T. (2017). Development and validation of a multifactor mindfulness scale in youth: The Comprehensive Inventory of Mindfulness Experiences—Adolescents (CHIME-A). *Psychological Assessment, 29*(3), 264–281.

Johnson, W., Logie, R. H., & Brockmole, J. R. (2010). Working memory tasks differ in factor structure across age cohorts: Implications for dedifferentiation. *Intelligence, 38*(5), 513–528.

Keating, D. P. (2004). Cognitive and brain development. In R. M. Lerner & L. Steinberg (Eds.), *Handbook of adolescent psychology* (pp. 45–84). Hoboken, NJ: John Wiley.

Kuby, A. K., McLean, N., & Allen, K. (2015). Validation of the Child and Adolescent Mindfulness Measure (CAMM) with non-clinical adolescents. *Mindfulness, 6*(6), 1448–1455.

Lau, N., & Hue, M. (2011). Preliminary outcomes of a mindfulness-based programme for Hong Kong adolescents in schools: Well-being, stress and depressive symptoms. *International Journal of Children's Spirituality, 16*(4), 315–330.

Lawlor, M. S., Schonert-Reichl, K. A., Gadermann, A. M., & Zumbo, B. D. (2014). A validation study of the mindful attention awareness scale adapted for children. *Mindfulness, 5*(6), 730–741.

Lemberger-Truelove, M. E., Carbonneau, K. J., Zieher, A. K., & Atencio, D. J. (2019). Support for the development and use of the Child Observation of Mindfulness Measure (C-OMM). *Mindfulness, 10*, 1406–1416.

Levin, M. E., Hildebrandt, M. J., Lillis, J., & Hayes, S. C. (2012). The impact of treatment components suggested by the psychological flexibility model: A meta-analysis of laboratory-based component studies. *Behavior Therapy, 43*(4), 741–756.

Marks, A. D. G., Sobanski, D. J., & Hine, D. W. (2010). Do dispositional rumination and/or mindfulness moderate the relationship between life hassles and psychological dysfunction in adolescents? *Australian & New Zealand Journal of Psychiatry, 44*(9), 831–838.

McCracken, L. M., & Gauntlett-Gilbert, J. (2011). Role of psychological flexibility in parents of adolescents with chronic pain: Development of a measure and preliminary correlation analyses. *PAIN, 152*(4), 780–785.

McHugh, R. K., & Behar, E. (2009). Readability of self-report measures of depression and anxiety. *Journal of Consulting and Clinical Psychology*, 77(6), 1100–1112.

Miller, S. D., Duncan, B. L., Brown, J., Sorell, R., & Chalk, M. B. (2006). Using formal client feedback to improve retention and outcome: Making ongoing, real-time assessment feasible. *Journal of Brief Therapy, 5*(1), 5–22.

Oberle, E., Schonert-Reichl, K. A., Lawlor, M. S., & Thomson, K. C. (2011). Mindfulness and inhibitory control in early adolescence. *The Journal of Early Adolescence, 32*(4), 565–588.

Pallozzi, R., Wertheim, E., Paxton, S., & Ong, B. (2017). Trait mindfulness measures for use with adolescents: A systematic review. *Mindfulness, 8*, 110–125.

Parent, J., McKee, L. G., Rough, J. N., & Forehand, R. (2016). The association of parent mindfulness with parenting and youth psychopathology across three developmental stages. *Journal of Abnormal Child Psychology, 44*(1), 191–202.

Petter, M., Chambers, C. T., McGrath, P. J., & Dick, B. D. (2013). The role of trait mindfulness in the pain experience of adolescents. *Journal of Pain, 14*(12), 1709–1718.
Pilowsky, D. J., Wickramaratne, P., Poh, E., Hernandez, M., Batten, L. A., Flament, M. F., . . Weissman, M. M. (2014). Psychopathology and functioning among children of treated depressed fathers and mothers. *Journal of Affective Disorders, 164*, 107–111.
Racine, N. M., Riddell, R. R. P., Khan, M., Calic, M., Taddio, A., & Tablon, P. (2016). Predisposing, precipitating, perpetuating, and present factors predicting anticipatory distress to painful medical procedures in children. *Journal of Pediatric Psychology, 41*(2), 159–181.
Sadoski, M., Goetz, E. T., & Rodriguez, M. (2000). Engaging texts: Effects of concreteness on comprehensibility, interest, and recall in four text types. *Journal of Educational Psychology, 92*(1), 85–95.
Shapiro, D. H., & Walsh, R. N. (1984). *Meditation: Classic and contemporary perspectives*. Chicago, IL: Aldine Transaction.
Shapiro, S. L., Oman, D., Thoresen, C. E., Plante, T. G., & Flinders, T. (2008). Cultivating mindfulness: Effects on well-being. *Journal of Clinical Psychology, 64*(7), 840–862.

Part II

Research

Chapter 4

Mindfulness in education

Mary Katherine A. Schutt and Joshua C. Felver

Introduction

Mindfulness as an applied topic of scientific inquiry has become increasingly popular during the past 30 years (Baer, 2014; Brown et al., 2015; Ivtzan, 2020; Khoury et al., 2015). In parallel with this general interest, clinicians and researchers have also become more interested in exploring the utility of mindfulness-based programs (MBPs) in educational settings. As examples of this surge of research activity, there have been several entire peer-reviewed journal special issues devoted to the topic of MBPs in school settings, including *Research in Human Development* (Frank et al., 2013), *Mindfulness* (Felver & Jennings, 2016), and *Psychology in the Schools* (Renshaw & Cook, 2017), as well as books and manuals devoted to the topic such as the *Handbook of Mindfulness in Education* (Schonert-Reichl & Roeser, 2016) and *Mindfulness in the Classroom* (Felver & Singh, 2020).

Given this surge of applied research into the utility of MBPs with students in school settings, it is useful to periodically take stock of the entirety of the research that has been conducted in order to gain insight into where the field is going and what work still needs to be done. The focus of this chapter is to meet this need by synthesizing the existing research literature on the use of MBP practices with children and adolescents in school settings. In doing so, this chapter intends to provide a snapshot of this quickly evolving research landscape and to provide recommendations for future work on the topic.

This chapter is organized into three sections. The first section summarizes the existing systematic reviews and meta-analyses that have been conducted to date. In order to provide an updated systematic analysis of this research literature, the second section reviews and summarizes research that has been conducted since 2014. The third and final section of the chapter provides recommendations for future research and for those seeking to implement evidence-based MBPs in school settings.

Reviews of MBPs in educational settings: 2005 to 2014

Given the rapid developments that have occurred in this field in the past decade, this section is arranged more or less chronologically, beginning with preliminary reviews and then exploring the more recent systematic reviews and meta-analyses that have been conducted on both MBPs for youth and MBPs in school settings.

Earliest systematic reviews of mindfulness-based practices with youth. The first formal review of MBPs for youth (Jha, 2005; Schoeberlein & Koffler, 2005) was initiated by the Garrison Institute, a nonprofit organization dedicated to contemplative practices, research, and education. The Garrison Report gathered information on the existing contemplative programs for youth, specifically within education contexts. This report detailed a variety of programs that were being utilized at the time across grade levels K–12 and found that these contemplative programs self-reported beneficial outcomes for the youth they served (e.g., increased emotional intelligence and social skills); however, these findings were not collected by objective third-party researchers. The Garrison Report noted that at that time there was "very little published scientific research on the outcomes of school-based contemplative programs" (Schoeberlein & Koffler, 2005, p. 39) and that reports produced by the programs surveyed were either anecdotal or informal evaluations or utilized solely physiological measurements that did not capture cognitive, affective, social, or academic domains of functioning. The report concluded with recommendations including the inclusion of self-report psychological questionnaires and school data (e.g., grades and disciplinary referrals), careful consideration of child development when creating programs, and more rigorous research designs to evaluate programs (e.g., randomized control trials [RCTs]). The report also noted that the field of contemplative practices for students had a "disproportionate ratio of programs-to-research" (Jha, 2005, p. S4), suggesting a need for more replication research relative to the propagation of novel curricula.

The next review came with the influential publication by Thompson and Gauntlett-Gilbert (2008), which is best known in the contemplative literature for detailing specific adaptations, modifications, and practices that are developmentally appropriate for youth. This article reviewed the literature through mid-2006 and found that, similar to the Garrison Report, only a few studies reported formal evaluative data (as opposed to anecdotal or subjective evidence), that sample populations were typically nonclinical, and that studies typically had small sample sizes, which may have created ambiguity in the results obtained.

The first systematic review article of MBPs for youth published in a peer-reviewed scientific journal was conducted by Burke (2010). This paper systematically reviewed the existing scientific literature concerning secular applications of MBPs for youth and included 15 articles. This review found that all studies noted the feasibility and acceptability of MBPs for youth; however, the results reported varied greatly in terms of statistical significance and magnitude of effect sizes obtained (ranging from small to large, according to Cohen's [1977] criteria). Burke also detailed several methodological limitations in the existing literature at the time, including small sample sizes; lack of RCT studies; few objective measurement procedures; sampling biases; overreliance of non-blinded data collection procedures (e.g., self-report or non-blind teacher report); using clinical measures with mostly nonclinical populations; highly variable and poorly defined intervention manuals; and a lack of MBP replication. This review also noted the fidelity of implementation concerns that arise when considering the requisite experience of the MBP instructors, as most programs rely on external MBP facilitators rather than teachers themselves.

Reviewing the totality of contemplative research that had been conducted up to that time, Greenberg and Harris (2012) provided an overview of the state of knowledge of MBPs in education. This review echoed similar findings from previous reviews, namely that contemplative practices (including MBPs) are feasible and effective for supporting youth, although the enthusiasm for the implementation of such programs should be tempered by the overall poor quality of research that had been conducted up to that time. This review focused on critical next steps needed to advance the field's scientific understanding of the feasibility and outcomes of implementing contemplative programs, dividing their findings into MBP/meditative studies and yoga intervention research. In addition to echoing concerns about the overall quality of the research, this review highlighted a few novel considerations for future researchers. For example, it noted the need for active control conditions (as opposed to treatment as usual or wait-list control conditions) in order to help distinguish the key intervention components included in multicomponent MBP curricula. This review also highlighted that researchers need to carefully consider and systematically evaluate logic models for contemplative practice in order to elucidate mechanisms of action. It also noted that there is no existing evidence to inform the dose or amount of contemplative practice needed to create change, a critical next step in mindfulness-based program development and evaluation.

Taken as a whole, the preliminary reviews of MBPs for youth from 2005 to 2011 offered several insights into the development of this nascent field. The earliest reviews conducted between 2005 and 2008 (Jha, 2005; Schoeberlein & Koffler, 2005; Thompson & Gauntlett-Gilbert, 2008) noted that there were very few published research papers on the topic of MBPs for youth and MBPs in educational settings; however, only a few years later, Burke's review (2010) was able to synthesize 15 empirical studies. This highlights the fact that not only was there a dramatic increase in the scientific investigation of the topic but also that virtually all of the research on this topic had taken place just in the past decade or so. To visually represent this, Figure 4.1 presents peer-reviewed publications retrieved from the PsycINFO electronic database with the keyword "mindfulness" and selecting only research involving youth (i.e., age 18 years

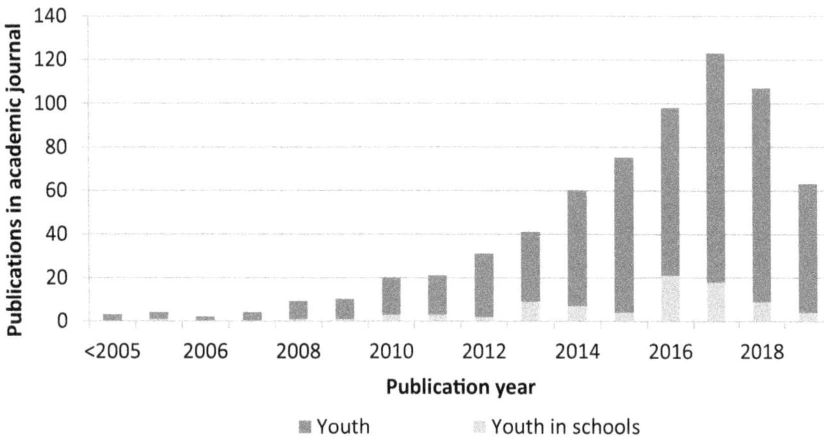

Figure 4.1 Publications retrieved from PsycINFO database search with keyword "mindfulness" and age 18 years or younger

or younger). As can be seen in the figure, virtually all of the research in this emerging field has taken place in the last 10 years (2010–2019). These search terms can be further restricted using the keywords "school" or "classroom" to select studies that took place in educational settings. Inspection of these data clearly indicates the majority of mindfulness research with youth that occurred in educational settings has taken place only in the last few years (e.g., 87% since 2013), highlighting that this is truly an emerging field of scientific inquiry.

All preliminary reviews conducted before 2011 were consistent in noting that youth responded well to MBPs, although the quality of the scientific literature available did not strongly support this claim. Given that the scientific investigation into the use of MBPs for youth was only just beginning, it is not surprising that all of the reviews noted significant limitations in the quality of research conducted, notably a lack of experimental design, heterogeneous interventions with few replications, inadequate outcome measures, and overall poor research quality. By the time the final review of the literature was conducted by Greenberg and Harris (2012), more specific recommendations were provided in order to address these shortcomings.

Reviews and meta-analyses of MBPs for youth from 2011–2019. As more publications and empirical data in support of the use of MBPs for youth accrued, researchers have been able to use more sophisticated methods to summarize and aggregate these results. The first meta-analysis on the benefits of MBPs for youth was conducted on research that was published up until July of 2011 (Zoogman et al., 2015). These researchers aimed to determine the overall magnitude of effects of various MBPs on youth across different outcome dimensions (i.e., psychosocial functioning and attention), as well as explore the various moderating aspects of MBPs that may produce differing results (e.g., length of intervention, variability among different ages of youth). This review included 20 studies, most of which were conducted in school settings. Six of the studies included in this meta-analysis did not use a comparison control condition. Results from this study indicated that overall, MBPs produced a statistically significant but small effect size (Becker's *del* = 0.23). Moderator analyses determined that MBPs were more than twice as effective for clinical samples of youth relative to nonclinical samples (*del* = .50 compared to *del* = 0.20) and that MBPs appeared to be more effective in reducing symptoms of psychopathology relative to other dependent outcomes (i.e., physiological and cognitive outcomes). Interestingly, moderating analyses conducted did not demonstrate significant effects of several variables that were hypothesized by previous researchers, such as instructor experience and training and session length and dosage.

A second meta-analysis (Kallapiran et al., 2015) updated the literature review by including studies published through January 2014 and broadened the inclusion criteria to include multi-component interventions that contained mindfulness practice and theory (i.e., dialectical behavior therapy [Linehan, 1993] and acceptance and commitment therapy [Hayes et al., 2011]) and restricted the inclusion criteria to only RCT study designs. Fifteen studies were included in this meta-analysis. Overall, results obtained found that MBPs were beneficial for youth, specifically in the domains of stress, depression, and anxiety, across both clinical and nonclinical samples. This review noted a few consistent limitations in the literature that precluded more detailed moderator analyses, including lack of blind outcome assessment, lack of statistical treatment of nested data (i.e., statistically accounting for the fact that students were grouped or "nested" within classrooms and schools), small sample sizes, few active control conditions, and little multi-informant (e.g., teachers and students) and multi-method (e.g., physiological outcomes and self-report) outcome measures.

A third meta-analysis (Klingbeil et al., 2017) examined 76 group-design studies of MBPs published through December 2015. Klingbeil et al. reviewed studies that were conducted in both school and nonschool settings with clinical and nonclinical populations. They expanded upon the extant literature by specifically targeting therapeutic processes and outcomes of MBPs. Inclusion criteria was further broadened as Klingbeil et al. analyzed studies that directly targeted youth outcomes; however, there were no inclusion criteria for the types of outcome variables examined, geography or culture of samples, or characteristics of eligible participants. A secondary analysis of the effects of MBPs for both controlled and pre-post designs was completed. Overall, results showed that MBPs had a small positive average treatment effect for both pre-post (Hedges' g = 0.305) and experimental (g = 0.322) study designs, and the effects of MBPs had a slightly larger treatment effect after a follow-up period than post-treatment, which is consistent with previous findings in the literature. Notably, some results differed from previous studies, as Klingbeil et al. found that across all therapeutic outcomes, MBPs produced small positive treatment effects for controlled and pre-post designs, compared to larger effect sizes in previous reviews (Zenner et al., 2014; Zoogman et al., 2015).

Another meta-analysis of RCTs explored the effects of MBPs on cognition and mental health (Dunning et al., 2019). The purpose of this review was to establish efficacy of RCTs for MBPs with children and adolescents under 18 years of age. Dunning et al. included 33 studies published up to October 2017 in their analysis. The outcome measures included mindfulness, cognition (executive functioning and attention), behavior (social and negative behavior), and emotion (depression and stress/anxiety). Results were consistent with previous reviews in that MBPs improved mindfulness and executive functions and decreased depression, anxiety, and stress. Benefits of attention and changing social behavior were not notable; however, MBPs significantly reduced negative behavior. The effect sizes were small (0.10) to small-to-moderate (0.38) for MBPs compared to all control groups. There was a statistically significant level of heterogeneity for mindfulness, executive functions, negative behavior, social behavior, and depression. Seventeen of the studies were analyzed against an active comparison group, with results indicating that only mindfulness, depression, and anxiety/stress were significant.

Reviews and meta-analyses of MBPs for youth in school settings from 2011–2019. In addition to systematic reviews exploring the benefits of MBP for youth generally, the accruing publications have allowed for more narrow reviews focused specifically on the benefits of MBPs in school settings. A meta-analysis was conducted exploring studies that implemented MBPs in school settings (grades 1–12) through the third quarter of 2012 (Zenner et al., 2014). Using a more liberal selection criteria that included unpublished results, this review analyzed 24 studies and aimed to determine domains of effectiveness and to summarize the state of the field at that time. Results indicated that across all outcome domains, on average, MBPs produced a statistically significant but small effect size ($g = 0.40$). Analyses of the various domains of dependent variables yielded statistically significant large effect sizes for cognitive outcomes ($g = 0.80$), small effect sizes for resilience ($g = 0.36$) and stress ($g = 0.39$), and statistically nonsignificant effects for emotional problems ($g = 0.19$) and third-person ratings ($g = 0.25$). This meta-analysis also found that the amount of practice (i.e., combined minutes of mindfulness practice both at school and at home) accounted for a significant amount of the variance across all outcomes for all studies (adjusted $R^2 = 0.21$) and for studies that utilized a RCT design (adjusted $R^2 = 0.52$). Limitations in the studies reviewed were also noted, including poor or absent reporting of student and school demographics, weak control conditions, lack of follow-up measurement, small sample sizes, and overreliance on student self-report as the sole method of data collection.

To better understand the core components of school-based contemplative programming, mindfulness-based, and yoga studies that were published through May 2014 were systematically analyzed (Gould et al., 2016). This review specifically focused on the fidelity of implementation (FOI), or the degree to which the programs adhered to the intervention model (Dane & Schneider, 1998), of 48 different studies utilizing contemplative curricula. Results indicated both strengths and significant limitations. Relative strengths among the reviewed studies were that most studies (63%) assessed at least one aspect of FOI, and some studies (13%) explored whether intervention dosage was related to the results obtained. Significant limitations were also documented in the vast majority of studies (i.e., at least 90%), including not referencing a logic model, not assessing multiple dimensions of FOI, not fully reporting adaptations made to existing MBPs, and not fully articulating the most essential program components.

To understand the current state of school-based MBP research, Felver et al. (2016) conducted a systematic review of the available literature through June 2014. This review analyzed the research methods, participant and program characteristics, and outcomes from 28 school-based MBPs published in peer-reviewed journals. The results identified several strengths in the literature, including generally large and diverse participants, programs implemented in classroom environments to enhance generalizability, and assigned home practice. Several limitations were also reported, including inadequate comparison conditions, quasi-experimental designs, few replication studies, limited reporting of student and school characteristics, and lack of follow-up data. Based on their analysis of the studies, Felver et al. advanced a list of recommendations for future research on contemplative practices in school settings.

Most recently, McKeering and Hwang (2019) conducted a systematic review of 13 quantitative and mixed methods studies of school-based MBPs. Given the criticism qualitative study designs have received in mindfulness research, quality analysis critique was completed for all 13 studies. Results indicated that emotional well-being was a major intervention outcome, as MBPs are shown to more effectively decrease anxiety and negative affect than increase positive affect and prosocial behavior. Both quantitative and qualitative results indicated school-based MBPs were an effective and feasible prevention program for early adolescents. McKeering and Hwang noted several limitations of the quantitative focused studies, including a lack of reporting of FOI, validity measures, and measurement of intervention effects at appropriate times. Limitations of the qualitative studies included a lack of reporting on trustworthiness and credibility, description of the author's biases, and the relationship between the researcher and participant. The authors offered educational and practical considerations for future research and implementation of school-based MBPs.

Current status of research on school-based MBPs: 2014–2019

Given the rapid pace of development of the field and proliferation of studies, we provide a snapshot review of the field in order to best interpret the current state of school-based MBP research. The Felver et al. (2016) search procedures were replicated. In January 2020, keywords "mindfulness" in addition to "school" or "students" were entered into PsycINFO, an electronic online database. This first search yielded 390 articles. Search results were then screened using the following criteria: published in peer-reviewed journal, publication date ranged of 2014–2020, and participants younger than 18 years of age. This initial screening reduced the number of articles to 35. Next, full-text copies of the 35 articles were retrieved and carefully reviewed for appropriateness of inclusion in this review. The eligibility criteria included: not included in Felver et al. (2016) systematic review; school-aged population; the research was a clinical trial; full-text available in English; and included quantitative outcomes. This procedure identified 18 articles eligible for review. Figure 4.2 presents a summary of the full article selection procedures.

To compare the most recent publications involving school-based MBPs, the 18 articles were coded and analyzed using an abbreviated version of the methods detailed in the Felver et al. (2016) review. One aim was to determine if the recommendations advanced by Felver et al. were evident in articles published since 2014. Articles were coded to specifically capture recommendations provided across four categories: research designs, subject characteristics, intervention characteristics, and outcomes. Table 4.1 details these recommendations,

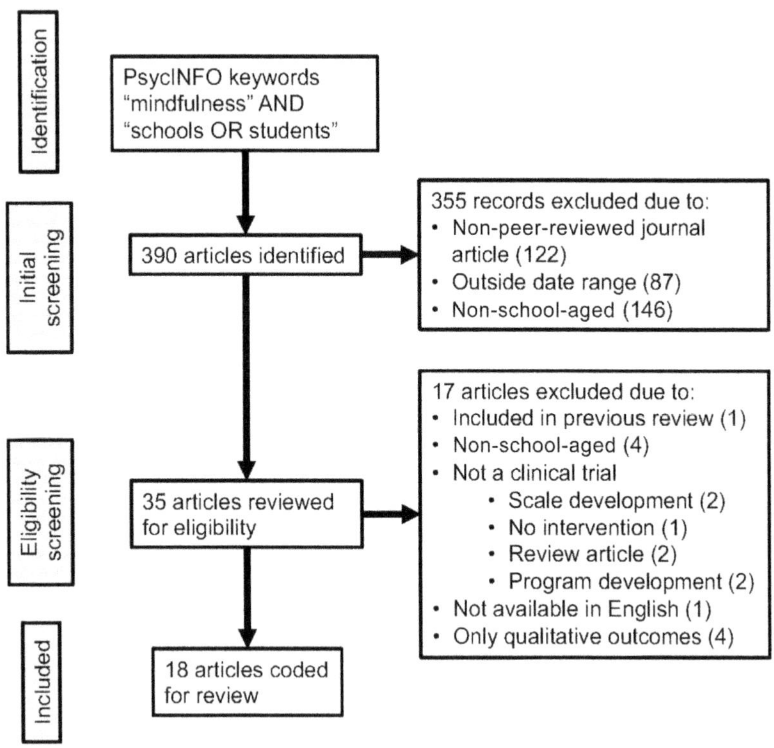

Figure 4.2 Flowchart of article identification

Table 4.1 School-based MBP recommendations with percentage of literature implementation

Category	Recommendations*	Percentage of studies implemented	
		Felver et al. (2016) (n = 28)	*Current review (n = 18)*
Research designs	Use randomized controlled trial design	36%	50%
	Use active control condition that includes both didactic and experiential components	11%	6%
	Account statistically for effect of students being nested within classrooms and schools	n/a	6%
Subject characteristics	Report full subject details: individual characteristics	n/a	22%
	Report full subject details: school characteristics	n/a	22%
	Explore implementation with students with identified disabilities and/or learning disabilities	7%	11%
Intervention characteristics	Replicate existing interventions as opposed to testing new approaches	32%	56%
	MBSR-based	32%	22%
	Need to conduct component analyses including testing for dosage effects	n/a	Not to date
	Scientifically evaluate the amount of preparation needed to effectively deliver MBI	n/a	Not to date
	Meta-analyses of existing intervention outcomes	n/a	Zenner et al., 2014 McKeering and Hwang 2019
Outcomes	Include multi-method outcomes	29%	28%
	Include multi-informant outcomes	14%	22%
	Include data collected by school districts: academic	0	17%

(*Continued*)

Table 4.1 (Continued)

		Percentage of studies implemented	
Category	*Recommendations**	*Felver et al. (2016) (n = 28)*	*Current review (n = 18)*
	Include data collected by school districts: behavioral	0%	11%
	Collect follow-up data	29%	22%

* Recommendations from Felver et al. (2016).

percentages of articles published prior to June 2014 that would have implemented these recommendations (if these data were reported by Felver et al., 2016), and the percentage of articles published since 2014 that implemented these recommendations.

Research designs. The most consistent limitation noted in previous reviews was the inclusion of low-quality research designs. One way to determine the quality of an intervention study is to examine whether it utilized an appropriate experimental research design (e.g., randomized control trial). Half (50%) of the research conducted since June 2014 utilized appropriate experimental designs, an increase from the previously reported 36% of studies.

Another research quality indicator is the utilization of a control condition that includes theoretically non-important intervention elements in order to isolate the hypothesized important components, also known as an active control condition. School-based MBP research has been criticized for its lack of use of active control conditions (e.g., didactic teaching elements and experiential practice components), as control conditions are more commonly wait-list or treatment as usual (i.e., normal educational programming) that do not actually provide the best comparison condition. By way of illustration, it could be that by simply having students meet with an outside facilitator or by engaging in a novel noneducational practice, MBP effects may be produced that have nothing to do with actual mindfulness-based practices. This review found that only 6% of studies utilized active control conditions that attempted to account for didactic and experiential components, which is down slightly from 11% of studies using this approach prior to 2014 as reported by Felver et al. (2016).

A final research design characteristic concerns statistically accounting for the fact that individual students are delivered MBPs in classroom groups, and these groups are also contained within the larger school context, a statistical feature referred to as nesting. This review explored whether studies statistically accounted for nesting, such as by using hierarchical linear modeling statistical techniques, and found that only 6% of studies had accounted for this fact.

Taken as a whole, it would seem that the field is benefitting from employing more rigorous experimental designs, but progress has been slow in this regard.

Subject characteristics. The present review also explored whether research conducted since 2014 has implemented recommendations about the inclusion and reporting of diverse student characteristics. Similar to previous reviews, students ranged in grade level from pre-K through high school, indicating that the study of MBPs in school populations is being considered across the range of school-aged children. More studies that target specific clinical populations of concern were identified, notably the prevention of substance use (Parker et al., 2014) and eating disorders (Johnson et al., 2016). This is a promising finding given the long-term cost of these and other pediatric psychiatric disorders and the potential value of preventing the development of these problems through school-based MBPs.

A surprising finding from this review is that studies continue to not fully report basic characteristics of student populations and school settings. Studies were coded as reporting basic student characteristics if they detailed the age, gender, and ethnicity of their participants. Using these criteria, only 2% of studies reported these characteristics, which is an unfortunate result given the importance of these data for those wishing to understand the results obtained. Studies were coded as reporting basic school characteristics if they reported both the ethnic composition and an objective aspect of the socioeconomic status (SES; often captured using the proxy of percentage of students receiving free and reduced-price lunch) of the total school population. Using these criteria, only 22% of studies detailed this information. This is also a surprising finding given the critical nature that this information supplies about the setting of the study, and also because these data are freely and easily available as public information that can be obtained from the school district's department of education website. Studies were also coded as to whether they specifically explored the utility of MBPs for students with identified disabilities, and only one study (i.e., Singh et al., 2016) focused on this vulnerable subpopulation. Taken as a whole, research published since 2014 continues to largely not report important participant and setting characteristics and to not target students with disabilities. Future research should pay heed to these limitations.

Intervention characteristics. With regard to intervention characteristics, this review found only marginal progress in the field of school-based MBPs relative to the literature reviewed previously (Felver et al., 2016). There has been a notable increase in the relative percentage of publications that replicated an existing protocol (56% of protocol in the current review), which is a promising trend. Although there has yet to be a formal highly controlled study exploring the dose-response relation between mindfulness-based practice and outcomes, there were several studies in this review that did take into account the amount of practice students engaged in, and these studies used this as a proxy for dosage in exploring intervention effects. Although there has not been a formal evaluation of the requisite practice needed to implement MBPs with fidelity, researchers are beginning to consider the relative effectiveness of different modalities of intervention delivery, such as via audio recordings (Bakosh et al., 2016).

Outcomes. School-based studies published since 2014 have made some progress in implementing many of the recommendations with regard to outcome measurement. Slightly fewer articles reviewed included follow-up measurement in addition to simple pre-post outcome assessment, but slightly more articles included multiple informants (e.g., student self-report and teacher report on student) since the Felver et al. (2016) review. Most importantly, researchers are beginning to include data on student academic performance (17% of studies reviewed) and behavioral data (e.g., office-disciplinary referrals, direct observations of classroom behavior; 11% of studies reviewed) as dependent outcomes, as no study in the Felver et al. (2016) review included these data. The inclusion of this "real world" school data is vital to the field's understanding of how school-based MBPs can benefit students and will also be of benefit for those wishing to make a compelling argument to administrators for the adoption of such practices.

Conclusions

School-aged children and youth are faced with many challenges not encountered by previous generations, such as navigating the rapidly evolving landscape of social media and preparing for pressured high-stakes standardized assessments. Given these challenges, twenty-first century schools must be equipped with effective and efficient intervention technologies to reduce stress and support the general health and psychosocial well-being of all students. Accruing scientific evidence indicates that MBPs may offer one solution to meeting the complex needs of children and adolescents in today's school systems, and indeed there is a growing movement among teachers, parents, and students to implement such technology. However, this enthusiasm for implementation and demonstration of exciting new applications must be tempered with the logic and rigor of systematic scientific procedures.

We have covered the existing research evidence to date concerning school-based MBP, and several conclusions can be drawn by taking into account the entirety of the work reviewed. First, evidence strongly suggests that MBPs appear to be feasible to implement in school systems, are acceptable as a practice, and do not appear to cause harm. This is an important step for the field, as MBPs are often associated with Eastern religious practices and caution has been noted about its implementation in secular school environments (Felver et al., 2013), and it would appear that Western culture has embraced the use and utility of these practices without notable reservations. Second, the existing studies do indicate that MBPs, as a whole, would seem to benefit students across multiple domains of functioning, including reducing symptoms of psychopathology, improving their general psychosocial well-being, enhancing certain aspects of cognitive functioning (e.g., attention, self-regulation), and improving academic outcomes. However, these documented benefits should be considered as promising and not definitive, as more research needs to be conducted to confirm and replicate these preliminary results.

It is worth noting that this review is not without limitations. First, the identification and inclusion of articles reviewed was limited in scope and only utilized the PsychINFO electronic search database. Figure 4.1 would indicate that there are certainly additional articles that could have been located by using other search engines (e.g., PubMed, Google Scholar) and by reviewing citation lists. Future systematic reviews should conduct a more thorough and exhaustive review of the published literature in order to give a comprehensive overview of the field. Second, although we replicated the coding procedure proposed by Felver et al. (2016), this method did not code for all of the important characteristics of intervention studies. A more thorough review could have covered quantitative outcomes and drawn conclusions via a meta-analysis.

Taken as a whole, the reviews discussed are consistent in noting both general and specific recommendations for applied scientists seeking to advance the field of school-based MBPs. By far the most important recommendation is to utilize appropriate experimental research designs. The scientific benefits of conducting fewer high-quality RCT studies far outweighs the merit of more nonexperimental pilot studies (Cook, 2002), and it would behoove contemplative scientists who work in school systems to follow this guideline in order to advance the field. In addition, research could be strengthened by utilizing more rigorous experimental designs, such as the inclusion of active control conditions and accounting statistically for the effects of students being nested within classrooms and schools. The quality of outcome measures would be strengthened by including student academic and behavioral data, as well as blinded third-party evaluators of student outcomes. Theoretically, school-based MBP research would be best served by researchers explicitly stating the theoretical model from which they are operating and including mechanistic variables to test these theoretical models of change.

For administrators and clinicians, there are also several recommendations to consider when implementing school-based MBPs. There has been a proliferation of school-based MBPs developed in the past decade, but the majority of these programs have not been researched, and fewer still have been studied multiple times by independent scientists. By way of illustration, if one applies an accepted standard for determining whether an intervention is an empirically validated treatment (Chambless et al., 1998), no school-based MBP intervention meets the criteria for a "well-established treatment," and (arguably) only a few would meet criteria for a "probably efficacious treatment." This is not to say that the available interventions lack any support, but rather, it is meant as a note of caution in that there is currently no "best practice" in how to implement school-based MBPs, and consumers should therefore be wary of claims saying otherwise. It would be wise for those who wish to implement a school-based

MBP to begin with a program that has some research in support of its effectiveness and then refer to the research literature to determine whether the program would be best suited for one's specific student population. In addition to the critical evaluation of the research, it is also recommended that educators consider the sustainability of the program selected. Some school-based MBPs have only been studied in the context of a highly trained external interventionist implementation. Although this approach could be effective, it also may not be feasible or affordable for school districts to hire an external provider year after year or for larger populations of students beyond a few classrooms. There is no consensus on whether teachers can effectively implement school-based MBPs or how much prerequisite training is required to implement such programs with fidelity. These are critical considerations when planning for multiyear sustainable implementation.

The field of contemplative science in general and school-based MBP research in particular is exciting, and new findings are emerging in the scientific literature at an exponential rate. As this field continues to mature, it will be interesting to observe whether appropriate research design characteristics continue to be employed in the scientific evaluation of school-based MBPs. This chapter has highlighted some considerations for those wishing to become involved in this field and what steps are required in order to advance the understanding of this promising technology that may benefit students in today's school settings.

Acknowledgments

A special thank you to Adam Clawson and Melissa Morton for their helpful feedback on drafts of this manuscript.

References

* References marked with an asterisk indicate studies included in the current review.

Baer, R. A. (2014). *Mindfulness-based treatment approaches: Clinician's guide to evidence base and applications*. San Diego, CA: Elsevier.

* Bakosh, L. S., Snow, R. M., Tobias, J. M., Houlihan, J. L., & Barbosa-Leiker, C. (2016). Maximizing mindful learning: Mindful awareness intervention improves elementary school students' quarterly grades. *Mindfulness*, 7, 59–67.

* Bazzano, A. N., Anderson, C. E., Hylton, C., & Gustat, J. (2018). Effect of mindfulness and yoga on quality of life for elementary school students and teachers: Results of a randomized controlled school-based study. *Psychology Research and Behavior Management, 11*, 81–89.

Brown, K. W., Creswell, J. D., & Ryan, R. M. (2015). *Handbook of mindfulness: Theory, research, and practice*. New York, NY: Guilford Press.

Burke, C. A. (2010). Mindfulness-based approaches with children and adolescents: A preliminary review of current research in an emergent field. *Journal of Child and Family Studies, 19*, 133–144.

Chambless, D. L., Baker, M. J., Baucom, D. H., Beutler, L. E., Calhoun, K. S., Crits-Christoph, P., . . Woody, S. R. (1998). Update on empirically validated therapies, II. *The Clinical Psychologist, 51*, 3–16.

Cohen, J. (1977). *Statistical power analysis for the behavioral sciences* (2nd ed.). New York, NY: Academic Press.

Cook, D. T. (2002). Randomized experiments in educational policy research: A critical examination of the reasons the educational evaluation community has offered for not doing them. *Educational Evaluation and Policy Analysis, 24*, 175–199.

Dane, A. V., & Schneider, B. H. (1998). Program integrity in primary and early secondary prevention: Are implementation effects out of control? *Clinical Psychology Review, 18*, 23–45.

* de Carvalho, J. S., Pinto, A. M., & Marôco, J. (2017). Results of a mindfulness-based social-emotional learning program on Portuguese elementary students and teachers: A quasi-experimental study. *Mindfulness, 8*(2), 337–350.

Dunning, D. L., Griffiths, K., Kuyken, W., Crane, C., Foulkes, L., Parker, J., & Dalgleish, T. (2019). The effects of mindfulness-based interventions on cognition and mental health in children and adolescents: A meta-analysis of randomized controlled trials. *Journal of Child Psychology and Psychiatry, 60*, 244–258.

* Edwards, M., Adams, E. M., Waldo, M., Hadfield, O. D., & Biegel, G. M. (2014). Effects of a mindfulness group on Latino adolescent students: Examining levels of perceived stress, mindfulness, self-compassion, and psychological symptoms. *The Journal for Specialists in Group Work, 39*, 145–163.

* Felver, J. C., Butzer, B., Olson, K. J., Smith, I. M., & Khalsa, S. B. S. (2015). Yoga in public school improves adolescent mood and affect. *Contemporary School Psychology, 19*, 184–192.

Felver, J. C., Celis-de Hoyos, C. E., Tezanos, K., & Singh, N. N. (2016). A systematic review of mindfulness-based interventions for youth in school settings. *Mindfulness, 7*, 34–45.

Felver, J. C., Doerner, E., Jones, J., Kaye, N. C., & Merrell, K. W. (2013). Mindfulness in school psychology: Applications for intervention and professional practice. *Psychology in the Schools, 50*, 531–547.

* Felver, J. C., Felver, S. L., Margolis, K. L., Ravitch, N. K., Romer, N., & Horner, R. H. (2017). Effectiveness and social validity of the Soles of the Feet mindfulness-based intervention with special education students. *Contemporary School Psychology, 21*, 358–368.

Felver, J. C., & Jennings, P. A. (2016). Applications of mindfulness-based interventions in school settings: An introduction. *Mindfulness, 7*, 1–4.

Felver, J. C., & Singh, N. N. (2020). *Mindfulness in the classroom: An evidence-based program to reduce disruptive behavior and increase academic engagement.* Oakland, CA: New Harbinger Publications.

* Franco, C., Amutio, A., López-González, L., Oriol, X., & Martínez-Taboada, C. (2016). Effect of a mindfulness training program on the impulsivity and aggression levels of adolescents with behavioral problems in the classroom. *Frontiers in Psychology, 7*, 1385.

Frank, J. L., Jennings, P. A., & Greenberg, M. T. (2013). Mindfulness-based interventions in school settings: An introduction to the special issue. *Research in Human Development, 10*, 205–210.

* Frank, J. L., Kohler, K., Peal, A., & Bose, B. (2017). Effectiveness of a school-based yoga program on adolescent mental health and school performance: Findings from a randomized controlled trial. *Mindfulness, 8*, 544–553.

Gould, L. F., Dariotis, J. K., Greenberg, M. T., & Mendelson, T. (2016). Assessing fidelity of implementation (FOI) for school-based mindfulness and yoga interventions: A systematic review. *Mindfulness*, 7, 5–33.

Greenberg, M. T., & Harris, A. R. (2012). Nurturing mindfulness in children and youth: Current state of research. *Child Development Perspectives*, *6*, 161–166.

Hayes, S. C., Strosahl, K. D., & Wilson, K. G. (2011). *Acceptance and commitment therapy: The process and practice of mindful change*. Guilford Press.

Ivtzan, I. (2020). *Handbook of mindfulness-based programmes: Mindfulness interventions from education to health and therapy*. London, UK: Routledge.

Jha, A. P. (2005). *Garrison institute report: Contemplation and education: Scientific research issues relevant to school-based contemplative programs: A supplement*. New York, NY: Garrison Institute.

* Johnson, C., Burke, C., Brinkman, S., & Wade, T. (2016). Effectiveness of a school-based mindfulness program for transdiagnostic prevention in young adolescents. *Behaviour Research and Therapy*, *81*, 1–11.

* Johnson, C., Burke, C., Brinkman, S., & Wade, T. (2017). A randomized controlled evaluation of a secondary school mindfulness program for early adolescents: Do we have the recipe right yet? *Behaviour Research and Therapy*, *99*, 37–46.

Kabat-Zinn, J. (1990). *Full catastrophe living: Using the wisdom of your body and mind to face stress, pain, and illness*. New York, NY: Dell.

Kallapiran, K., Koo, S., Kirubakaran, R., & Hancock, K. (2015). Effectiveness of mindfulness in improving mental health symptoms of children and adolescents: A meta-analysis. *Child and Adolescent Mental Health*, *20*, 182–194.

Khoury, B., Sharma, M., Rush, S. E., & Fournier, C. (2015). Mindfulness-based stress reduction for healthy individuals: A meta-analysis. *Journal of Psychosomatic Research*, *78*, 519–528.

* Kielty, M., Gilligan, T., Staton, R., & Curtis, N. (2017). Cultivating mindfulness with third grade students via classroom-based interventions. *Contemporary School Psychology*, *21*, 317–322.

Klingbeil, D. A., Renshaw, T. L., Willenbrink, J. B., Copek, R. A., Chan, K. T., Haddock, A., . . Clifton, J. (2017). Mindfulness-based interventions with youth: A comprehensive meta-analysis of group-design studies. *Journal of School Psychology*, *63*, 77–103.

Linehan, M. (1993). *Cognitive-behavioral treatment of borderline personality disorder*. New York, NY: Guilford Press.

* Luiselli, J. K., Worthen, D., Carbonell, L., & Queen, A. H. (2017). Social validity assessment of mindfulness education and practices among high school students. *Journal of Applied School Psychology*, *33*, 124–135.

McKeering, P., & Hwang, Y. S. (2019). A systematic review of mindfulness-based school interventions with early adolescents. *Mindfulness*, *10*, 593–610.

* Mendelson, T., Tandon, S. D., O'Brennan, L., Leaf, P. J., & Ialongo, N. S. (2015). Moving prevention into schools: The impact of a trauma-informed school-based intervention. *Journal of Adolescence*, *43*, 142–147.

* Parker, A. E., Kupersmidt, J. B., Mathis, E. T., Scull, T. M., & Sims, C. (2014). The impact of mindfulness education on elementary school students: Evaluation of the master mind program. *Advances in School Mental Health Promotion*, 7, 184–204.

Renshaw, T. L., & Cook, C. R. (2017). Mindfulness in the schools: Historical roots, current status, and future directions. *Psychology in the Schools*, *54*, 5–12.

* Ricarte, J. J., Ros, L., Latorre, J. M., & Beltrán, M. T. (2015). Mindfulness-based intervention in a rural primary school: Effects on attention, concentration and mood. *International Journal of Cognitive Therapy*, *8*, 258–270.

Schoeberlein, D., & Koffler, T. (2005). *Garrison Institute report: Contemplation and education: A survey of programs using contemplative techniques in K—12 educational settings: A mapping report*. New York, NY: Garrison Institute.

Schonert-Reichl, K. A., & Roeser, R. W. (2016). *Handbook of mindfulness in education: Integrating theory and research into practice*. New York, NY: Springer.

* Singh, N. N., Lancioni, G. E., Karazsia, B. T., Felver, J. C., Myers, R. E., & Nugent, K. (2016). Effects of Samatha meditation on active academic engagement and math performance of students with attention deficit/hyperactivity disorder. *Mindfulness*, 7, 68–75.

Thompson, M., & Gauntlett-Gilbert, J. (2008). Mindfulness with children and adolescents: Effective clinical application. *Clinical Child Psychology and Psychiatry*, *13*, 395–407.

* van de Weijer-Bergsma, E., Langenberg, G., Brandsma, R., Oort, F. J., & Bögels, S. M. (2014). The effectiveness of a school-based mindfulness training as a program to prevent stress in elementary school children. *Mindfulness*, *5*, 238–248.

Zenner, C., Herrnleben-Kurz, S., & Walach, H. (2014). Mindfulness-based interventions in schools—a systematic review and meta-analysis. *Frontiers in Psychology*, *5*, 603.

Zoogman, S., Goldberg, S. B., Hoyt, W. T., & Miller, L. (2015). Mindfulness interventions with youth: A meta-analysis. *Mindfulness*, *6*, 290–302.

Chapter 5

Mindfulness in attention deficit hyperactivity disorder

Esther I. de Bruin, Renée Meppelink, and Susan M. Bögels

Introduction

Although some studies show indications for a slight drop in methylphenidate consumption over the past years (e.g., Piper et al., 2018), overall, dramatic numbers of children still are prescribed ADHD-medication in our Western society (e.g., 4.3% of Dutch children [Association of Pharmaceutical Statistics, 2016] and over 9% of children in parts of the United States, according to the Centers for Disease Control and Prevention [Visser et al., 2014]) which is extremely undesirable. Perhaps, maybe, hopefully, mindfulness may provide an alternative for some of these children and their families. This chapter synthesizes the research literature on the effects of mindfulness practice for children and adolescents with ADHD and their parents.

> I start to feel warmer, my heart beat increases, my palms are sweaty, I feel as if I have had too much caffeine, I'm thirsty and drink lots of water, not hungry, though, so I skip lunch, my mind is jumpy, I constantly switch between tasks, can't stay focused on one thing, my head feels very full, and although I want to, I don't have much space left to attune to others, I talk quicker than usual, my hands want to write faster and faster, and therefore my handwriting becomes messy, like my mind.
>
> (Esther de Bruin and Susan Bögels, after 10 mg of Ritalin)

Is this perhaps how a child with attention deficit hyperactivity disorder (ADHD) feels inside sometimes? Is this the effect of medication? We don't know; whatever it is, this feeling further underlines our sense of urgency in assessing mindfulness as an alternative treatment for children with ADHD and their families.

This combination of inattentive, impulsive, and/or hyperactive behavior that occurs at school, at home, and/or in social situations and that interferes with daily functioning, also known as ADHD, is prevalent in around 5% of children (American Psychiatric Association, 2013). ADHD not only has an impact on all aspects of the child's life but also affects all dimensions of the family system. Adverse effects of ADHD may vary throughout childhood, from excessive motor restlessness in preschoolers, to feeling different or being rejected by peers in primary school, to, for instance, low self-esteem, increased risk of academic failure, or substance abuse in adolescent years (e.g., Harpin, 2005). In addition to the core symptoms of ADHD, 60–100% of the children suffer from comorbid conditions such as oppositional, conduct, depressive, or anxiety disorders (Gillberg et al., 2004). Moreover, parents of children with ADHD suffer from significantly more parenting stress than parents of children with, for example, anxiety disorders (Telman et al. 2017), and the severity of parental stress is positively related to the severity of ADHD symptoms (Theule et al., 2013). Furthermore, parents' own ADHD symptomatology is the strongest predictor of parental stress (Theule et al., 2011). In addition to these very high personal and emotional costs for the families, ADHD is associated with increased economic health care costs. Average annual costs related to childhood ADHD in Europe range from €9,860 to €14,483 per individual, with national annual costs ranging from €1,041 million to €1,529 million (Le et al., 2014). In the United States, the national annual incremental costs of childhood ADHD have been estimated to range from $38 billion to $72 billion, in which the largest cost categories were health care ($21 billion to $44 billion) and education ($15 billion to $25 billion) (Doshi et al., 2012).

Effective treatment for ADHD is available. Methodologically sound randomized controlled trials (RCTs) have repeatedly shown that stimulant medication is effective in reducing symptoms of inattention, hyperactivity, and impulsivity in over 70% of the children with ADHD (e.g., Buitelaar et al., 1995; Gilmore & Milne, 2001; Schachter et al., 2001; Storebø et al., 2016). Therefore, several clinical guidelines advise medication as a first-line treatment for childhood ADHD (National Institute for Health and Care Excellence [NICE], 2018; Taylor et al., 2004). The NICE makes a distinction in their treatment guidelines between moderate and severe ADHD (Clinical Guideline [CG] 72). The first-line treatment for school-age children and young people with severe ADHD is drug treatment. However, for children with ADHD and moderate impairment, group-based parent training is usually considered the first-line treatment for parents, combined with group or individual behavioral treatment for the child. Other guidelines advise parent training combined with behavioral therapy for the child in case of insufficient response to medication (Wolpert et al., 2006). Thus, although psychosocial interventions (e.g., parent training) are part of most comprehensive international guidelines for treatment in addition to medication, and parental preferences are taken into account, it is also notable that, for instance, the guidelines of the American Academy of Child and Adolescent Psychiatry (AACAP; Pliszka, 2007) recommend to administer medication only if sufficient benefits are demonstrated in different areas of functioning. All these international guidelines are based on studies of the highest category of evidence, category 1a: evidence from meta-analyses of multiple RCTs (Shekelle et al., 2000). However, extensive data from methodologically strong studies often show no additional benefit of combined treatment over medication alone (e.g., The Multimodal Treatment of ADHD (MTA) Cooperative Group, 2004; van der Oord et al., 2008).

Methylphenidate is the most widely prescribed drug in the world (Swanson, 2003), steadily increasing over the past decades, with a global consumption of as much as 72 tons in 2013 (International Narcotics Control Board, 2014). However convincing the evidence of the effectiveness of drug treatment for childhood ADHD may seem, there are many reasons for concern about the gigantic numbers of children using stimulant medication. The main concerns are the serious side effects such as insomnia, loss of appetite, headache, anxiety, abdominal pain, and nervousness (e.g., Charach et al., 2004; Graham et al., 2011; Storebø et al., 2015). The MTA study (MTA Cooperative Group, 1999) already showed that nearly two-thirds of children on this drug suffer from at least one of these side effects. Furthermore, currently, only little is known about the long-term side effects. Reduced growth and weight in children that take long-term stimulant medication are documented, and although rare, long-term effects on blood pressure, heart rate, and the occurrence of suicidal, psychotic, and manic symptoms have also been reported (De Loo-Neus et al., 2011; Faraone et al., 2008). A recent study showed that the use of methylphenidates over a period of four months in boys aged 10–12 with ADHD still increased the blood flow in the brain up to one week after quitting the medication, whereas in adult men with ADHD this effect was not found (Schrantee, 2016). Although we do not know exactly what this effect means, it shows that methylphenidate at this young age does have a prolonged impact on the functioning of the brain.

Another disadvantage of drug treatment for ADHD is the low treatment adherence. Adler and Nierenberg (2010) showed that nonadherence to treatment can be as high as 64% in people with ADHD. Particularly for the short-acting stimulant medication methylphenidate, the most commonly prescribed treatment, the adherence is low (Swanson, 2003), which is understandable because these types of medication need to be taken two to three times daily. However, given that these short-acting agents only have a short half-life, effects subside soon after medication is discontinued, and as a consequence symptoms return.

So although medication is used as a first-line treatment for childhood ADHD worldwide and has been shown to effectively reduce symptoms, we feel that with the substantial limitations and disadvantages, it is highly undesirable that in our society, we medicate millions of children from such a young age. As parents, as clinicians, and as researchers, we have the responsibility to at least examine thoroughly what other effective non-pharmacological options are available. This chapter describes how the practice of mindfulness could perhaps be one of those options for children with ADHD and their families.

What bridges mindfulness practice and ADHD?

Both from a behavioral and neuroanatomical perspective, the practice of mindfulness might go straight to the heart of the challenging behaviors encountered by children with ADHD and their families. During mindfulness training one learns to respond (to thoughts, feelings, situations etc.) rather than to instantly react, which can be very useful for children (and parents) who usually are very impulsive and have difficulties inhibiting their responses. In addition, during mindfulness practices one learns to maintain a focused attention and to bring the attention back when it wanders, which might be especially useful for children who suffer from difficulties sustaining and focusing their attention. A variety of studies have indeed shown improvements in attentional monitoring and functioning as a result of the practice of mindfulness (e.g., Chiesa et al., 2011).

From a neuroanatomical viewpoint, the practice of mindfulness also goes straight to the core problems of ADHD. Our monkey mind jumps from one thing to the next, even more so for children with attention, hyperactivity, and impulsivity problems. Monkey mind is a term used by the Buddha to refer to the agitated, easily distracted, and constantly moving human mind, like a monkey jumping from branch to branch. Or perhaps the monkey is sometimes better described as a small lion, like in the book *There Is a Lion inside Me* about a boy with ADHD (Dieltjens & Klompmaker, 2006). In children without ADHD, who also have a lion inside them from time to time, the anterior cingulate (part of the frontal lobe) down-regulates the raw emotions that come up through the limbic system. However, in children with ADHD, activity in the anterior cingulate is reduced (e.g., Liotti et al., 2005), and as a result there seems to be no pause between the raw impulses, reactions, or emotions that shoot up through the limbic system and what is subsequently exerted out in the behavior. The anterior cingulate cortex seems to somehow fail to regulate the limbic system. When stimulants such as methylphenidate are taken, the limbic system is suppressed; therefore, one of the side effects of high doses of stimulant medication is emotional blunting. With mindfulness meditations, however, the inner lion is treated with kindness, compassion, and acceptance, and by practicing mindfulness skills, perhaps children with ADHD can learn to introduce a pause before acting instantly and are able to kindly tame their inner lion. Neuroimaging studies in long-term meditators demonstrate that meditation is indeed associated with activation in the anterior cingulate cortex (e.g., Brefczynski-Lewis et al., 2007).

Offering a combined parent and child mindfulness training, as we have done from the very first time we offered mindfulness to youth with ADHD (Bögels et al., 2008), is a sensible approach for different reasons. First, this way a parent really understands what the child is learning; parents know better how to support their child in practicing mindfulness and help them with the generalization of mindfulness skills in their lives. Second, parents become more aware of certain automatic patterns that they developed toward their child's problem behavior over time ("overreactive parenting") and learn how to cultivate a more accepting and nonjudging attitude toward them. For example, parents may immediately overreact by shouting at their child for throwing a jacket—for the hundredth time—on the couch instead of putting it neatly on the coat rack.

By becoming aware of this automatic reaction to shout, parents now create the opportunity to choose how to respond in a more accepting and nonjudging manner. Third, because of the heritable component of ADHD, parents of children with ADHD often also suffer from ADHD symptoms (Epstein et al., 2000; Thapar et al., 2007). A mindful parent training program, therefore, may also help reducing parents' own ADHD symptoms. Consequently, parents who suffer less from their own ADHD symptoms may become better in structuring the environment of their child and learn to be more consistent, clear, and calm toward their child, which is found to be especially beneficial for children with ADHD (Sonuga-Barke et al., 2002). Lastly, combining a mindful parenting program with a mindfulness training for the children is a more holistic approach in which the implicit message is that we, as a family, experience problems, recognizing that the dynamics and interaction within the family contribute to the behavior of the child and family functioning, so we as a family are going to work on that during the mindfulness training. Such a family systems approach is in contrast to medicating a child, as this may indirectly imply that only the child has a problem, so the child needs to undergo treatment.

Research on mindfulness practices for children with ADHD

Research on mindfulness practices for families with ADHD is rapidly emerging. The first meta-analysis of the effects of mindfulness-based programs (MBPs) on symptoms of ADHD in both children and adults came out in 2016 (Cairncross & Miller, 2016). Of the 10 included studies, six reported on the effectiveness of MBPs on inattention in children with ADHD, with an average effect size of 0.66, and five reported about the effectiveness of MBPs on hyperactivity/impulsivity, with an average effect size of 0.47.

Subsequently, three systematic reviews were published (Evans et al., 2018; Mak et al., 2018; Tercelli & Ferreira, 2019). The majority of the studies included by Evans et al. (2018) showed large effects on symptoms of ADHD; however, some studies did not show any effects or even showed the opposite. In addition, the studies varied largely in methodological quality. Mak et al. (2018) specifically examined the effects on neuropsychological measures of attention and executive functioning. Five of the 13 included studies showed medium to large effects; the other eight studies did not. Tercelli and Ferreira (2019) included 10 studies and found positive effects of MBPs on attention deficits in children with ADHD but showed that in terms of hyperactivity the evidence was less conclusive. MBPs also effectively reduce parental stress and improve family functioning, but overall, published studies still suffered from several methodological limitations, and therefore the current evidence on the impact of MBPs on ADHD is nonconclusive, according to these authors. Finally, a combined systematic review and meta-analysis investigating the effects of yoga and mindfulness interventions for youth with ADHD was published in 2018 (Chimiklis et al., 2018). Eleven studies were included, showing significant effects on hyperactivity and inattention (parent and teacher reports) as well as on parent-child relationship, executive functioning, parental stress, and parental mindfulness. These authors also emphasized the methodological limitations. Thus, although preliminary findings indicate beneficial effects of MBPs for youth with ADHD, positive effects should be interpreted with caution, and MBPs should as yet not be considered first-line interventions for youth with ADHD (Chimiklis et al., 2018).

Two main approaches for assessing the effects of mindfulness practice for children with ADHD and their families can be distinguished in the literature. First is the "individual-based approach," in which individual children (sometimes with their parents) are trained and effects are monitored individually over time, sometimes daily, with a research design consisting of a baseline phase and an intervention phase. These types of studies are also known as single-case experimental designs (SCEDs), of which multiple baseline designs studies are an example. Second is the "group-based approach" which can be divided into three subgroups; the first are studies in which MBPs for (small) groups of children with ADHD are evaluated, usually by using a repeated measures design with wait-list, pretest, posttest, and follow-up assessments. Second are studies in which MBPs are investigated from a family dynamic perspective. Children then follow a mindfulness training, and in conjunction parents take part in a parallel mindful parenting training. And third are the large-scale randomized controlled trials (RCTs), an approach that is rapidly emerging in this field.

A recent review by Cassone (2015) underlines the potential of including the practice of mindfulness as an adjunct to parent training for parents of children with ADHD, or as a mindful parenting training in itself. Interestingly, currently running RCTs (Chan et al., 2018; Lo et al., 2016; Lo et al., 2017; Meppelink et al., 2016a; Siebelink et al., 2018) seem to approach ADHD from this family dynamic perspective. Below an overview is given of the different types of studies and findings so far, and further details of the different studies can be found in Table 5.1.

Individual-based approach

Singh et al. (2010) trained two mother-child with ADHD dyads in mindfulness, in which a 12-session individual mother training was followed by a subsequent 12-session individual child training. Children in this study, in contrast to most of the other studies, were of below average intellectual ability. Mothers recorded their child's behavior on a daily basis. Although core ADHD symptoms were not monitored in this study, compliance of the child improved after the mother-training and improved even further when the child was subsequently trained, as did the parent-child interaction and happiness in parenting. As expected, no changes occurred during the baseline period preceding both training phases. Effects were maintained up to the six-month follow-up.

Table 5.1 Summary of study results assessing the effects of MBPs for children with ADHD and their families

Research group	*Study design*	*Sample size*	*Age in years*	*Type of MBP*	*Primary (borderline) significant outcomes on ADHD measures*	*Secondary (borderline) significant outcomes*
Bögels et al. (2008)[1]	WL; pretest; posttest; FU	*n* = 4	11–18	Previous version of 8-week MYmind program	Reduced: Attention problems (YSR/CBCL) Improved: Sustained attention (D2)	Reduced: Internalizing problems (YSR), externalizing problems (YSR/CBCL) Improved: Happiness (SHS), mindful awareness (MAAS), self-control (SCRS), attunement to others (CSBQ), withdrawal (CSBQ), personal goals (parent and child)
Zylowska et al. (2008)[2]	Pretest; posttest	*n* = 8	15–18	8-week MAP program	Reduced: Inattention and hyperactivity (ADHD Rating Scale IV/SNAP-IV) Improved: Attentional conflict (ANT conflict/SCWT), set-shifting (TMT)	n/a
Grosswald et al. (2008)	Pretest; posttest	*n* = 10	11–14	3-month TM practice	Reduced: ADHD symptoms (YSR) Improved: Expressive attention and accuracy (CAS)	Reduced: Stress (RCMAS), anxiety (RCMAS/YSR/CBCL), total psychopathology (YSR/CBCL) Improved: Executive functioning (BRIEF)

Semple et al. (2010)[3]	RCT (MBCT-C vs. WL) with pretest; posttest; FU	*n* = 5	9–13	12-week MBCT-C Program	Reduced: Attention problems (CBCL)	Reduced: Behavior problems (CBCL)
Singh et al. (2010)	Multiple baseline design	*n* = 2	10; 12	12-week parent training; subsequent 12-week child training	n/a	Improved: Compliance of child, parent-child interaction, happiness parent
van der Oord et al. (2012)	WL; pretest; posttest; FU	*n* = 22	8–12	Previous version of 8-week MYmind program	Reduced: Child and parental Inattention (DBDRS/ASR), child and parental H/I (DBDRS/ASR)	Reduced: Parental stress (PSI), parental overreactivity (PS) Improved: Mindful awareness (MAAS)
Haydicky et al. (2012)[4]	RCT (MMA vs. WL) with pretest; posttest	*n* = 28	12–18	20-week MMA training	n/a	Reduced: Externalizing behavior (CBCL), oppositional defiant problems (CBCL), conduct problems (CBCL)
van de Weijer-Bergsma et al. (2012)	Pretest; posttest; FU1; FU2	*n* = 10	11–15	Previous version of 8-week MYmind program	Reduced: Attention problems (CBCL) Improved: Sustained attention (ANT2.1)	Reduced: Externalizing problems (CBCL/YSR), internalizing problems (CBCL/YSR), paternal parenting stress (PSI), maternal overreactivity (PS) Improved: Executive functioning (BRIEF), paternal overreactivity (PS)

(Continued)

Table 5.1 (Continued)

Research group	*Study design*	*Sample size*	*Age in years*	*Type of MBP*	*Primary (borderline) significant outcomes on ADHD measures*	*Secondary (borderline) significant outcomes*
Haydicky et al. (2015)	WL; pretest; posttest; FU	*n* = 18	13–18	8-week MYmind program	Reduced: Inattention (Conner's 3-P)	Reduced: Depression (Conner's 3-P), CD (Conner's 3-P), ODD (Conner's 3-SR), depression/anxiety (RCADS), learning problems (RCADS), aspects of parenting stress (SIPA) Improved: Executive functioning (Conner's 3-P), peer relations (Conner's 3-P), family relations (Conner's 3-SR), mindful parenting (IM-P), family functioning (FAD)
Zhang et al. (2017)	Pretest; posttest	*n* = 11		8-week MYmind program	Improved: Attention (CPT 3: detectability, omissions), selective/focused attention (TEA-Ch: Skye Search, Map Mission)	n/a

Lo et al. (2017)	RCT	$n = 100$	8-week Mindfulness Matters program	Reduced: Hyperactivity (SWAN) Improved: attention (SWAN)	Reduced: Child internalizing and externalizing problems (CBCL), parental stress (PSI), dysfunctional parent-child interactions (PSI) Improved: Parental quality of life (WHO-5)
Bögels et al. (in preparation)	WL; pretest; posttest; FU1; FU2	$n = 187$	8-week MYmind program	Reduced: Child ADHD symptoms (DBDRS/CBCL/YSR), parental ADHD symptoms (ADHD rating scale/ASR)	Reduced: Child and parental psychopathology (CBCL/ASR), parental over reactivity (PS), parental stress (PSI) Improved: Child executive functioning (BRIEF), mindful parenting (IM-P)

Notes

1 The study by Bögels et al. (2008) included a total sample size of $n = 14$ of adolescents with externalizing problems; $n = 4$ of those met criteria for ADHD. Separate results for this subgroup were not provided.

2 The study by Zylowksa et al. (2008) included a total sample size of $n = 32$ of adults and adolescents; $n = 8$ of those were adolescents. Separate results for adolescents were not provided.

3 The study by Semple et al. (2010) included a total sample size of $n = 25$ children; $n = 5$ of those had clinically elevated attention problems, of which $n = 2$ met criteria for ADHD.

4 The study by Haydicky et al. (2012) included a total sample size of $n = 60$ of adolescents with intellectual disabilities; $n = 28$ of those met criteria for ADHD. ANT = Attention Network Test; ANT2.1 = Amsterdam Neuropsychological Tests version 2.1; ASR = Adult Self Report; BRIEF = Behavior Rating Inventory of Executive Functioning; CAS = Cognitive Assessment System; CBCL = Child Behavior Check List; CD = Conduct Disorder; CPT 3 = Conner's Continuous Performance Test 3rd Edition; CSBQ = Children's Social Behavior Questionnaire; DBDRS = Disruptive Behavior Disorder Rating Scale; FAD = Family Assessment Device; FU = Follow Up; H/I = Hyperactivity/Impulsivity; IM-P = Interpersonal Mindfulness in Parenting Scale; MAAS = Mindful Attention Awareness. Scale; MAP = Mindful Awareness Practices; MBCT-C = Mindfulness Based Cognitive Therapy-Child version; MBPs = Mindfulness-Based Interventions; MMA = Mindfulness Martial Arts; P = Parent; PS = Parenting Styles; ODD = Oppositional Defiant Disorder; PSI = Parenting Stress Index; QoL-C = Quality of Life-Child; QoL-P = Quality of Life-Parent; RCADS = Revised Child Anxiety and Depression Scale; RCMAS = Revised Children's Manifest Anxiety Scale; SCRS = Self Control Rating Scale; SCWT = Stroop Color Word Test; SHS = Subjective Happiness Scale; SIPA = Stress Index for Parents of Adolescents; SNAP = Swanson, Nolan and Pelham; SR = Self Report; SWAN = Strengths and Weaknesses of ADHD Symptoms and Normal Behaviors Rating Scales; TEA-Ch = Test of Everyday Attention for Children; TM = Transcendental Meditation; TMT = Trail Making Test; WHO-5 = World Health Organization Well-Being Index; WL = Wait-List; YSR = Youth Self Report.

Shecter (2013) followed 13 parents and nine adolescents during baseline, eight-week MYmind mindfulness training, parallel for parents and adolescents, with a six-month follow-up period. Both parents and adolescents reported reductions in stress and family conflict, and due to the multiple baseline design, these effects could be contributed to the training. Parents further reported a decrease in the inattention, hyperactivity, and impulsivity of the adolescents; however, adolescents themselves did not report this change. Most effects were maintained up to the six-month follow-up. The author further reported a positive relationship between meditation practice and stress reduction; the more both parents and adolescents meditated, the larger the stress reducing effects they experienced.

Group-based approach

Group studies with mindfulness training focusing only on children with ADHD

In a feasibility study with pretest and posttest assessments of an eight-week mindfulness meditation training (mindful awareness practices [MAPs]) for 24 adults with ADHD, eight adolescents (aged 15–18) with ADHD were included (Zylowska et al., 2008). Although results for adolescents were not presented separately, ADHD symptoms were significantly reduced after training. Furthermore, neurocognitive measures showed improvements in attentional conflict monitoring at posttest and improved set shifting at posttest as compared to pretest.

Another study investigated the effects of 10 minutes of transcendental meditation (TM) twice daily for three months for 10 children with ADHD (aged 11–14) in a school setting (Grosswald et al., 2008). At posttest, as compared to before the training period, they found significant reductions in symptoms of ADHD, stress, and anxiety as well as improved executive functioning.

Semple et al. (2010) adapted mindfulness-based cognitive therapy (MBCT) for children (MBCT-C) and conducted a small RCT in which 25 children (aged 9–13) were randomized to MBCT-C or to a wait-list. MBCT-C is a 12-week group program that aims to enhance self-management of attention and improve affect regulation by learning to decenter from thoughts and emotions and increase social-emotional resiliency. Although this study was not primarily targeting children with ADHD, at the outset, five children met the threshold for clinically elevated attention problems, and two of them met criteria for ADHD. Directly after the intervention, but not after wait-list, the children with ADHD showed significantly fewer attention problems, and these improvements were maintained up to three months after the training.

Haydicky et al. (2012) applied a 20-week mindfulness martial arts (MMA) training to adolescents (aged 12–18) with learning disabilities (n = 60), of which 28 also met criteria for ADHD. Half of the adolescents were randomized to the mindfulness training, and the other half to the wait-list control group. A pretest, posttest design was used. According to parent ratings, the externalizing, oppositional, and conduct behaviors were significantly reduced in the intervention group as compared to the wait-list control group. Further subgroup analyses showed that adolescents with clinically elevated hyperactive/impulsive or attentive symptoms (just below the threshold for a full ADHD classification) showed improved monitoring skills and reduced social problems after the mindfulness training as compared to the wait-list group.

Group studies with combined mindfulness training for children with ADHD and their parents

All group studies described in this section, although carried out by different research groups, have assessed the effects of the (preliminary versions of the) MYmind mindfulness training program, which runs parallel versions for children and parents. This program is described in more detail in the next section. Moreover, all studies have a similar repeated measures study design.

Bögels et al. (2008) carried out the first study, in which the eight-week mindfulness training for children (a preliminary version of the MYmind program) was combined with a parallel eight-week mindful parenting training. The authors included 14 adolescents with externalizing disorders, of which four met criteria for ADHD, and used a wait-list, pretest, posttest, follow-up design. Although results for the adolescents with ADHD were not presented separately, significant improvements on personal goals, happiness, and mindful awareness were found for the whole group. Furthermore, they reported significantly lowered internalizing, externalizing, and attention problems after the training. More objective neuropsychological measures of attention confirmed the improved attentional functioning. Independent of the children, parents confirmed the improvement in their children's personal goals, externalizing, and attention problems, and further reported improved self-control, attunement to others, and a decrease in withdrawal. Parents further reported improvements in their own goals. Most effects were maintained up to two months after the training. Furthermore, mediation analysis showed that increased mindful awareness in the youth-mediated reductions in parent-reported externalizing and attention problems of the youth.

Whereas the study of Bögels et al. (2008) included a heterogeneous group of adolescents, subsequent studies examined groups of children with ADHD as the primary classification. Van der Oord et al. (2012) studied the effects of the combined child and parent MYmind training in 22 children with ADHD (aged 8–12). Parents as well as teachers reported a significant decrease in ADHD symptoms after the training. Moreover, parents showed a decline in their own symptoms of ADHD, stress levels, and reported decreased overreacting in their parenting. Van de Weijer-Bergsma et al. (2012) extended these findings further in a sample of 10 children (aged 11–15) with ADHD and their parents using a pretest, posttest, follow-ups (two follow-up measurements) design. Children themselves as well as their fathers and teachers reported a significant reduction in their symptoms of ADHD. Interestingly, significant improvements in attention were also found on objective computerized tests of attention. In addition, mothers significantly reduced their overreactive parenting style, and fathers reduced their stress levels.

Another research group assessed the effects of the MYmind mindfulness training in 18 adolescents with ADHD (aged 13–18) and their parents (Haydicky et al., 2015). As compared to the wait-list period, in which no changes occurred, after the training, internalizing, inattention, and conduct problems of the adolescents significantly decreased and their peer relationships improved, as rated by the parents. For themselves, parents reported feeling significantly less stressed and more mindful in their parenting role.

A small nonrandomized study on the feasibility, acceptability, and effects of the MYmind program was conducted in a Chinese sample of 11 children with ADHD and their parents (Zhang et al., 2017). Acceptability and feasibility in a different cultural setting was high; attendance rate (≥ 6 out of 8 sessions) was 91%, and only one family withdrew from the training. Results showed a significant improvement in some of the objective attention subtests but not on parent-rated child problems, parent-rated executive functioning of the children, and parents' own stress, mindfulness, and parenting.

A large non-randomized study of the effectiveness of the MYmind program is currently in preparation (Bögels et al. in preparation). Children (n = 187) and their parents (n = 128 fathers and n = 179 mothers) completed measurements at wait-list, pretest, posttest, eight-week, and one-year follow-up. As expected, no changes occurred during the wait-list period. Significant reductions in children's ADHD symptoms were reported at posttest, two months later, and one year later as compared to pretest. Parents' own ADHD symptoms significantly reduced at posttest, two months later, and one year later as compared to pretest. Further improvements were found on children's internalizing and externalizing symptoms, according to parent reports, in some but not all cases, and also according to the children and adolescents themselves. Overreactive parenting significantly decreased after the training and effects were maintained at both follow-ups. At one-year follow-up, mindful parenting and executive functioning of the children significantly improved, and parental stress and parents' own psychopathology significantly decreased.

Recently, critical concerns about a positive reporting bias of mindfulness clinical trials have been raised. Apparently, nearly 90% of the published RCTs, mainly related to depression, reported positive outcomes (Coronado-Montoya et al., 2016). Hardly any mindfulness trials reported negative or null findings. Although the trials that were reviewed did not concern childhood ADHD, it is of great importance to be aware of this pitfall. The studies discussed in this chapter, although there are no large-scale RCTs just yet, show promising results; however, not all findings are as expected. For instance, some studies did not show significant effects for maternal parenting stress, paternal overreactivity, parental and child mindful awareness, teacher-rated ADHD symptoms of the child, and child's self-reported ADHD symptoms (e.g., Shecter, 2013; van de Weijer-Bergsma et al., 2012; van der Oord et al., 2012), as would be expected.

Large scale randomized clinical trials

Findings from uncontrolled trials seem very promising and have now become apparent from a variety of research groups. Moreover, although one small RCT has been carried out (Haydicky et al., 2012), the majority of the currently available studies are of a quasi-experimental nature (category 2b), and only a few include a control group without randomization (category 2a, Shekelle et al., 2000). Therefore, larger-scale RCTs are now a logical next step.

In Hong Kong, two RCTs are being carried out with different age groups and different MBPs. One RCT examines the effects of an eight-week MBP (Snel, 2014) for children aged 5–7 (n = 100) with (symptoms of) ADHD and their parents (Lo et al., 2016). Families are randomized to the mindfulness training or to a wait-list control group, and those assigned to the control group follow the family-based mindfulness training later. Children from families in the MBP showed greater improvements in inattention (effect size 0.60) and hyperactivity (effect size 0.59) than families on the wait-list. In addition, parenting stress and well-being significantly improved for the parents in the MBP, but no changes in parental ADHD symptoms or interpersonal mindfulness were found (Lo et al., 2017).

The second RCT in Hong Kong follows up on the nonrandomized pilot study mentioned earlier (Zhang et al., 2017). The effects of the eight-week MYmind program (Bögels, 2020) are studied in a sample of n = 140 children (aged 8–12) and their parents, randomized over the MBP and an active control group that is offered a CBT program. Primary and secondary outcomes are children's attention, ADHD-related symptoms, executive functioning, and mindfulness levels. Parental stress, parenting styles, ADHD related symptoms, well-being, rumination, and parental mindfulness levels are also measured. Measurements are taken at baseline, immediately after the intervention, and three and six months later (Chan et al., 2018).

Further, two RCTs examining the MYmind program are currently running in the Netherlands. In the "MindChamp" study, children and adolescents (n = 100; aged 8–16) with ADHD are randomized to care-as-usual or care-as-usual plus the MYmind program. Primary outcome is parent-rated self-control of the child, and secondary outcomes are teacher-rated self-control and computerized tasks of self-control of the child. Psychological symptoms, well-being, and level of mindfulness of the child are also measured. Similar measures of self-control, psychological symptoms, well-being, and mindfulness are included for the parents (Siebelink et al., 2018).

The RCT "ADHD: Medication or Meditation?" is being carried out by the authors of this chapter (Meppelink et al., 2016a, 2016b). In this RCT, the (cost) effectiveness of medication versus mindfulness training for children with ADHD (n = 91, aged 8–18) and their parents (n = 172) is examined. Primary outcomes of this trial are symptoms of ADHD; rated by parents and children but also by teachers (n = 81) and independent observers (n = 85). In addition, the two treatments are compared on other measures of child functioning (i.e., psychopathology, stress, sleep), and measures of parent functioning (i.e., own symptoms of ADHD, stress, quality of life, sleep). Furthermore, underlying mechanisms of change are assessed. For instance, it is hypothesized that the effects of MYmind mindfulness training on a reduction in ADHD symptoms of the child will be mediated by improved mindful awareness and self-compassion in the parents, elements that are specifically targeted in the mindful parenting training but that are obviously not necessarily part of medication treatment. After randomization into the trial, eight-week mindfulness or methylphenidate treatment is administered. Pretest is completed before the start of the treatment, followed by posttest immediately after eight weeks of treatment. Subsequently, for children in the MYmind mindfulness group, a period of eight weeks of own mindfulness practice follows, whereas children in the medication group keep taking daily methylphenidate. After eight weeks, a booster session follows in the mindfulness training, and subsequent measurements in both groups are taken. A second follow-up measurement is taken after six months to determine long-term effects. Between the first and the second follow-up measurement, however, children and their families are free to choose other treatment, stop treatment, or change to the other intervention group (for ethical reasons). Since it is expected that not all families want to be randomized and/or have a strong preference for either medication or mindfulness training, a nonrandomized preference trial (n = 29 children and n = 52 parents) is also being carried out, in which families are assessed that take part in the treatment of their choice.

MYmind program for children and adolescents with ADHD and their parents

The MYmind program consists of eight weekly 1.5-hour sessions for the children and separately for their parents in group format, followed by a booster session eight weeks after the last session. Children follow the MYmind program: Mindfulness training for Youngsters with ADHD (Bögels, 2020), and the parents of children with ADHD follow an adapted version of the Mindful Parenting program, as described by Bögels and Restifo (2014), is used. Both children and parents are asked to practice daily meditations at home; for the children, the home practice is around 15 minutes a day, whereas for the parents this is around 30–45 minutes a day. Children practice focusing and sustaining their attention, becoming aware of being distracted and bringing back their attention to the original focus, and enhanced bodily awareness, by practicing (short) meditations, yoga, and playful exercises and games to make it fun. For instance, in one exercise the children take turns in being the "meditators" versus the "distractors." The meditators sit in a small circle with the trainer leading a meditation with focus on the breath, while the distractors walk around the room and make all sorts of distracting noises. The meditators experience how hard it is to keep meditating with all these distractors around them, and at the same time, the trainers experience how amazingly well these children can actually keep their attention focused on the breath already after a few weeks of practice. In the session where "Home in our Body" is the theme, the children are asked where they feel the ADHD in their bodies. They draw their bodies life-size on a large piece of paper and color in where the ADHD inhabits their bodies. Sometimes children color in their arms and legs, and when asked, they explain the feeling of hyperactive motor movements in their limbs that we recognize as part of ADHD. But very often they color in their heads and their brains and explain that their head is so full, so chaotic, so messy, so unorganized, and how they would like to be able to feel calmer, less jumpy, think more before they act, pause more, and pay more attention to daily chores.

Parents, in turn, practice awareness of their own physical responses to the challenging behavior of their child and how to calmly respond instead of overreacting to such challenging behavior from their child. They cultivate an attitude of nonjudgmental acceptance of the ADHD of their child. They also practice being fully present with their child, as well as with themselves, in the parent-child interaction. They further practice self-compassion and learn how to (better) take care of themselves. For instance, in one exercise the parents are asked to visualize the morning stress they encounter taking their unwilling child to school in a rush. During the meditation they are invited to observe their bodily signals, thoughts, emotions, and action tendencies and learn to see what happens when under stress, and how hard one can sometimes be on oneself as a parent. A more detailed description of themes and exercises in the children's and parents' sessions is outlined in Table 5.2.

Conclusion

Overall, the evidence base of promising effects of the practice of mindfulness for children and families with ADHD seems to be building gradually, with overall medium-sized effects in the reduction of core symptoms of ADHD and similar effects on parental stress and parental functioning. However, at this moment, a cautious attitude is warranted, since most currently published studies are small, nonrandomized and noncontrolled, and measures are often self-reports. However, with several currently running RCTs with active comparison groups in different countries and different cultures, the level and quality of evidence is expected to improve in the near future so firmer conclusions can be drawn about the effectiveness of mindfulness for children with ADHD and their families.

Table 5.2 Overview of sessions of the MYmind training for children with ADHD and their parents

Session	Session's theme	Core practices children	Core practices parents
Session 1	Beginner's Mind	Man from Mars; sitting meditation	Exercise Morning Stress; sitting meditation
Session 2	Home in our Body	Body scan with stretches; Exercise Ragdoll Robot, yoga	Body scan; Exercise Morning Stress with Compassion
Session 3	The Breath	Breathing Space: Exercise Rubber Duck; yoga	Body scan; Breathing Space
Session 4	Distractors!	Distractor Meditation; sound meditation; yoga	Sitting meditation with sounds and thoughts; exercise attention for yourself
Session 5	Stress	Halfway evaluation; body scan relax only; exercise stress	Halfway evaluation; sitting meditation choice less awareness; exercise parenting stress
Session 6	Highway, Walkway	Role-play exercise: conflict breathing space; walking meditation	Imagination practice and role-play exercise: rupture and repair; walking meditation
Session 7	Autonomy	Repetition of the past session in the form of a quiz; children as meditation and yoga teachers	Imagination practice: acceptance and autonomy; role-play exercise: limits
Session 8	The Future	Children as meditation and yoga teachers; making a meditation plan for the next eight weeks	Meditation and yoga practices guided by the children; making a meditation plan for the next eight weeks
Session 9	Each time beginning anew	Body scan; sharing experiences of the past eight weeks; making a meditation plan for the next year; individual evaluation per family	Body scan; sharing experiences of the past eight weeks; making a meditation plan for the next year; individual evaluation per family

Note: Session 9 is a booster session, at about two months follow-up after the MYmind training.

If the practice of mindfulness turns out to be a good alternative for the current standard treatment of medication for childhood ADHD, that is, if the effects are similar on some primary outcomes such as attention problems, hyperactivity, and impulsivity, this will be of substantial clinical, economical, ethical, and scientific relevance for our society. Perhaps the next generation of child psychiatrists, psychologists, and pediatricians will prescribe these families "five minutes of meditation twice a day" to learn to tame their inner lion. However, the practice of mindfulness is not a quick fix, or as a father in one of our groups put it nicely, "Mindfulness is great, but in a way similar to taking medication for ADHD; in order to maintain the effects, you have to continue taking the pills, I have realized that I (and my son) need to keep meditating."

> Working as a mindfulness teacher with children with ADHD, and trying to cultivate an open mind, an attitude of not-knowing, non-judging, and not-expecting, leads to surprising outcomes every time. Imagine for instance a very impulsive, overly active boy with ADHD who faced big behavioral challenges, also during the MYmind training, who was leading the Man from Mars exercise for all the children and parents in the last session: "So now, all look at your decorated cake . . . what do you see? . . . . . and what can you smell when you put it by your nose? . . . . . and now put the cake by your ears . . . can you hear anything? . . . . . and now try and taste just one small piece with only your lips and tongue . . . what do you notice? . . . and now, you can slowly swallow and eat the rest of your cake with full attention to all your senses. . . ." The next moment this boy started laughing and put the cake with the fruit and lots of cream all over his face. Everybody laughed with him and genuinely applauded him. What a brilliant eating meditation, and an amazing sense of control over his feelings, impulses, and action tendencies he had just displayed; he managed to tame his inner lion! He only forgot that being mindful also includes to not judge yourself and others. When his father could not inhibit his action tendency to take a lick of the cream during the meditation, the boy looked at him in irritation and said: "That's not allowed yet dad!"

References

Adler, L. D., & Nierenberg, A. A. (2010). Review of medication adherence in children and adults with ADHD. *Postgraduate Medicinal Journal, 122*, 184–191.

American Psychiatric Association. (2013). *Diagnostic and statistical manual of mental disorders* (DSM-5). Arlington: American Psychiatric Pub.

Bögels, S. M. (2020). MYmind mindfulness voor kinderen en adolescenten met ADHD en hun ouders: Trainershandleiding [*MYmind mindfulness for children and adolescents with ADHD and their parents: Manual for professionals*]. Houten, the Netherlands: Lannoo Campus.

Bögels, S. M., Hoogstad, B., van Dun, L., de Schutter, S., & Restifo, K. (2008). Mindfulness training for adolescents with externalizing disorders and their parents. *Behavioral Cognitive Psychotherapy, 36*, 193–209.

Bögels, S. M., Potharst, E., Formsma, A. R., Oort, F. J., van Roosmalen, R., Williams, J. M. G., et al. (in preparation). Mindfulness for children and adolescents with ADHD and parallel mindful parenting for their parents ("MYmind") reduces child, paternal and maternal attention- and hyperactivity/impulsivity problems up to 1 year after training.

Bögels, S. M., & Restifo, K. (2014). *Mindful parenting: A guide for mental health practitioners*. New York, NY: Springer.

Brefczynski-Lewis, J. A., Lutz, A., Schaefer, H. S., Levinson, D. B., & Davidson, R. J. (2007). Neural correlates of attentional expertise in long-term meditation practitioners. *Proceedings of the National Academy of Sciences (USA), 104*, 11483–11488.

Buitelaar, J. K., van der Gaag, R. J., Swaab-Barneveld, H., & Kuiper, M. (1995). Prediction of clinical response to methylphenidate in children with attention deficit hyperactivity disorders. *Journal of American Child and Adolescent Psychiatry, 34*, 1025–1032.

Cairncross, M., & Miller, C. J. (2016). The effectiveness of mindfulness-based therapies for ADHD: A meta-analytic review. *Journal of Attention Disorders, 20*, 1–17.

Cassone, A. R. (2015). Mindfulness training as an adjunct to evidence-based treatment for ADHD within families. *Journal of Attention Disorders, 19*, 147–157.

Chan, S. K. C., Zhang, D., Bögels, S. M., Chan, C. S., Lai, K. Y. C., Lo, H. H. M., . . Wong, S. Y. S. (2018). Effects of a mindfulness-based intervention (MYmind) for children with ADHD and their parents: Protocol for a randomized controlled trial. *BMJ Open, 8*, e022514.

Charach, A., Ickowicz, A., & Schachar, R. (2004). Stimulant treatment over five years: Adherence, effectiveness, and adverse effects. *Journal of American Academy of Child and Adolescent Psychiatry, 43*, 559–567.

Chiesa, A., Calati, R., & Serretti, A. (2011). Does mindfulness training improve cognitive abilities? A systematic review of neuropsychological findings. *Clinical Psychology Review, 31*, 449–464.

Chimiklis, A. L., Dahl, V., Spears, A. P., Goss, K., Fogarty, K., & Chacko, A. (2018). Yoga, mindfulness, and meditation interventions for youth with ADHD: Systematic review and meta-analysis. *Journal of Child and Family Studies, 19*(2), 133–144.

Coronado-Montoya, S., Levis, A. W., Kwakkenbos, L., Steele, R., Turner, E. H., & Thombs, B. D. (2016). Reporting of positive results in randomized controlled trials of mindfulness-based mental health interventions. *PloS ONE, 11*, 1–18.

De Loo-Neus, V., Gigi, H. H., Rommelse, N., & Buitelaar, J. K. (2011). To stop or not to stop? How long should medication treatment of attention deficit hyperactivity disorder be extended? *European Neuropsychopharmacology, 21*, 584–599.

Dieltjens, K., & Klompmaker, M. (2006). Er zit een leeuw in mij. [*There is a lion inside me*]. Hasselt/Amsterdam, The Netherlands: Clavis Publisher.

Doshi, J. A., Hodgkins, P., Kahle, J., Sikirica, V., Cangelosi, M. J., Setyawan, J., . . Neumann, P. J. (2012). Economic impact of childhood and adult attention deficit hyperactivity disorder in the United States. *Journal of the American Academy of Child & Adolescent Psychiatry, 51*, 990–1002.

Epstein, J. N., Conners, C. K., Erhardt, D., Arnold, L. E., Hechtman, L., Hinshaw, S. P., . . Vitiello, B. (2000). Familial aggregation of ADHD characteristics. *Journal of Abnormal Child Psychology, 28*, 585–594.

Evans, S., Ling, M., Hill, B., Rinehart, N., Austin, D., & Sciberras, A. (2018). Systematic review of meditation-based interventions for children with ADHD. *European Child and Adolescent Psychiatry, 27*, 9–27.

Faraone, S. V., Biederman, J., Morley, C. P., & Spencer, T. J. (2008). Effect of stimulants on height and weight: A review of the literature. *Journal of American Academy of Child and Adolescent Psychiatry*, *47*, 994–1009.

Gillberg, C., Gillberg, I. C., Rasmussen, P., Kadesjö, B., Söderström, H., Råstam, M., . . Niklasson, L. (2004). Co-existing disorders in ADHD: Implications for diagnosis and intervention. *European Child and Adolescent Psychiatry*, *13*, 80–92.

Gilmore, A., & Milne, R. (2001). Methylphenidate in children with hyperactivity: Review and cost-utility analysis. *Pharmacoepidemiology and Drug Safety*, *10*, 85–94.

Graham, J., Banaschewski, T. Buitelaar, J., Coghill, D., Danckaerts, M., Dittmann, R., . . Taylor, E. (2011). European guidelines on managing adverse effects of medication for ADHD. *European Child and Adolescent Psychiatry*, *20*, 17–37.

Grosswald, S. J., Stixrud, W. R., Travis, F., & Bateh, M. A. (2008). Use of the transcendental meditation technique to reduce symptoms of Attention Deficit Hyperactivity Disorder (ADHD) by reducing stress and anxiety: An exploratory study. *Current Issues in Education*, *10*(2).

Harpin, V. A. (2005). The effect of ADHD on the life of an individual, their family, and community from preschool to adult life. *Archives of Diseases in Childhood*, *90*(Suppl), 2–7.

Haydicky, J., Shecter, C., Wiener, J., & Ducharme, J. M. (2015). Evaluation of MBCT for adolescents with ADHD and their parents: Impact on individual and family functioning. *Journal of Child and Family Studies*, *24*, 76–94.

Haydicky, J., Wiener, J., Badali, P., Milligan, K., & Ducharme, J. M. (2012). Evaluation of a mindfulness-based intervention for adolescents with learning disabilities and co-occurring ADHD and anxiety. *Mindfulness*, *3*, 151–164.

International Narcotics Control Board. (2015). *Annual report 2014*. New York, NY: United Nations.

Le, H. H., Hodgkins, P., Postma, M. J., Kahle, J., Sikirica, V., Setyawan, J., Doshi, J. A. (2014). Economic impact of childhood/adolescent ADHD in a European setting: The Netherlands as a reference case. *European Child and Adolescent Psychiatry*, *23*, 587–598.

Liotti, M., Pliszka, S. R., Perez, R., Kothmann, D., & Woldorff, M. G. (2005). Abnormal brain activity related to performance monitoring and error detection in children with ADHD. *Cortex*, *41*, 377–388.

Lo, H. H. M., Wong, S. Y. S., Wong, J. Y. H., Wong, S. W. L., & Yeung, J. W. K. (2016). The effect of a family-based mindfulness intervention on children with attention deficit and hyperactivity symptoms and their parents: Design and rationale for a randomized, controlled clinical trial (Study protocol). *BMC Psychiatry*, *16*, 65–74.

Lo, H. H. M., Wong, S. W. L., Wong, J. Y. H., Yeung, J. W. K., Snel, E., & Wong, S. Y. S. (2017). The effects of a family-based mindfulness intervention on ADHD symptomology in young children and their parents: A randomized control trial. *Journal of Attention Disorders*, *21*, 1–14.

Mak, C., Whittingham, K., Cunnington, R., & Boyd, R. N. (2018). Efficacy of mindfulness-based interventions for attention and executive function in children and adolescents: A systematic review. *Mindfulness*, *9*, 59–78.

Meppelink, R., de Bruin, E. I., & Bögels, S. M. (2016a). Meditation or medication? Mindfulness training versus medication in the treatment of childhood ADHD: A randomized controlled trial. *BMC Psychiatry*, *16*, 267–283.

Meppelink, R., de Bruin, E. I., & Bögels, S. M. (2016b). Mindfulness training for childhood ADHD: A promising and innovative treatment. *ADHD in Practice*, *8*, 33–36.

MTA Cooperative Group. (1999). A 14-month randomized clinical trial of treatment strategies for attention deficit hyperactivity disorder. *Archives of General Psychiatry*, *56*, 1073–1086.

MTA Cooperative Group. (2004). National Institute of Mental Health Multimodal Treatment Study of ADHD follow-up: 24-month outcomes of treatment strategies for attention deficit hyperactivity disorder. *Pediatrics, 113*, 754–761.

National Institute for Health and Clinical Excellence (NICE). (2018). *Attention deficit hyperactivity disorder—diagnosis and management*. NICE Guideline 87. Available from: www.nice.org.uk/ng87

Piper, B. J., Ogden, C. L., Simoyan, O. M., Chung, D. Y., Caggiano, J. F., Nichols, S. D., & McCall, K. (2018). Trends in use of prescription stimulants in the United States and Territories, 2006 to 2016. *PLoS ONE, 13*, Article e0206100.

Pliszka, S. (2007). AACAP Work group on quality issues: Practice parameter for the assessment and treatment of children and adolescents with attention deficit hyperactivity disorder. *Journal of the American Academy of Child and Adolescent Psychiatry, 46*, 894–921.

Schachter, H. M., Pham, B., King, J., Langford, S., & Moher, D. (2001). How efficacious and safe is short-acting methylphenidate for the treatment of attention deficit hyperactivity disorders in children and adolescents? A meta-analysis. *Canadian Medical Association Journal, 165*, 475–488.

Schrantee, A., Tamminga, H. G., Bouziane, C., Bottelier, M. A., Bron, E. E., Mutsaerts, H. J. M., . . Reneman, L.(2016). Age-dependent effects of methylphenidate on the human dopaminergic system in young vs adult patients with attention deficit hyperactivity disorder: A randomized clinical trial. *JAMA Psychiatry, 73*, 955–962.

Semple, R. J., Lee, J., Rosa, D., & Miller, L. F. (2010). A randomized trial of mindfulness-based cognitive therapy for children: Promoting mindful attention to enhance social-emotional resiliency in children. *Journal of Child and Family Studies, 19*, 218–229.

Shecter, C. (2013). *Mindfulness training for adolescents with ADHD and their families: A time-series evaluation*. Toronto: University of Toronto.

Shekelle, P., Woolf, S., Eccles, M., & Grimshaw, J. (2000). Developing guidelines. In M. Eccles & J. M. Grimshaw (Eds.), *Clinical guidelines: From conception to use*. Abingdon: Radcliffe Medical.

Siebelink, N. M., Bögels, S. M., Boerboom, L. M., de Waal, N., Buitelaar, J. K., Speckens, A. E., & Greven, U. C. (2018). Mindfulness for children with ADHD and Mindful Parenting (MindChamp): Protocol of a randomised controlled trial comparing a family mindfulness-based intervention as add-on to care-as-usual with care-as-usual only. *BMC Psychiatry, 18*, 237–256.

Singh, N. N., Singh, A. N., Lancioni, G. E., Singh, J., Winton, A. S., & Adkins, A. D. (2010). Mindfulness training for parents and their children with ADHD increases the children's compliance. *Journal of Child and Family Studies, 19*, 157–166.

Snel, E. (2014). Mindfulness matters: Mindfulness for children, ages 5–8. In *Trainer's handbook 1*. Amsterdam, The Netherlands: Author.

Sonuga-Barke, E. J. S., Daley, D., & Thompson, M. (2002). Does maternal ADHD reduce the effectiveness of parent training for preschool children's ADHD? *Journal of the American Academy of Child & Adolescent Psychiatry, 41*, 696–702.

Stichting Farmaceutische Kengetallen [Association of Pharmaceutical Statistics]. (2016). Gebruik methylphenidaat groeit steeds minder sterk [*Use of methylphenidate increases less strongly*]. Retrieved from https://www.sfk.nl/publicaties/PW/2016/gebruik-methylfenidaat-groeit-steeds-minder-sterk

Storebø, O. J., Krogh, H. B., Ramstad, E., Moreira-Maia, C. R., Holmskov, M., Skoog, M., . . Gluud, C. (2015). Methylphenidate for attention deficit hyperactivity disorder in children and adolescents: Cochrane systematic review with meta-analyses and trial sequential analyses of randomized clinical trials. *British Medical Journal, 351*, 1–14.

Storebø, O. J., Simonsen, E., & Gluud, C. (2016). Methylphenidate for attention deficit hyperactivity disorder in children and adolescents. *JAMA, 315*, 2009–2010.

Swanson, J. (2003). Compliance with stimulants for attention deficit hyperactivity disorder. *CNS Drugs, 17*, 117–131.

Taylor, E., Döpfner, M., Sergeant, J., Asherson, P., Banaschewski, T. Buitelaar, J. K., . . Zuddas, A. (2004). European clinical guidelines for hyperkinetic disorder-first upgrade. *European Child and Adolescent Psychiatry, 13*, 7–30.

Telman, L. G. E., van Steensel, F. J. A., Maric, M., & Bögels, S. M. (2017). Are anxiety disorders in children and adolescents less impairing than ADHD and Autism Spectrum Disorders? Associations with child quality of life and parental stress and psychopathology. *Child Psychiatry and Human Development, 48*, 891–902.

Tercelli, I., & Ferreira, N. (2019). A systematic review of mindfulness-based interventions for children and young people with ADHD and their parents. *Global Psychiatry, 2*, 1–17.

Thapar, A., Langley, K., Asherson, P., & Gill, M. (2007). Gene—environment interplay in Attention Deficit Hyperactivity Disorder and the importance of a developmental perspective. *British Journal of Psychiatry, 190*, 1–3.

Theule, J., Wiener, J., Rogers, M. A., & Marton, I. (2011). Predicting parenting stress in families of children with ADHD: Parent and contextual factors. *Journal of Child and Family Studies, 20*, 640–647.

Theule, J., Wiener, J., Tannock, R., & Jenkins, J. M. (2013). Parenting stress in families of children with ADHD: A meta-analysis. *Journal of Emotional and Behavioral Disorders, 21*, 3–17.

van de Weijer-Bergsma, E., Formsma, A. R., De Bruin, E. I., & Bögels, S. M. (2012). The effectiveness of mindfulness training on behavioral problems and attentional functioning in adolescents with ADHD. *Journal of Child and Family Studies, 21*, 775–787.

van der Oord, S., Bögels, S. M., & Peijnenburg, D. (2012). The effectiveness of mindfulness training for children with ADHD and mindful parenting for their parents. *Journal of Child and Family Studies, 21*, 139–147.

van der Oord, S., Prins, P. J., Oosterlaan, J., & Emmelkamp, P. M. (2008). Efficacy of methylphenidate, psychosocial treatments and their combination in school-aged children with ADHD: A meta-analysis. *Clinical Psychological Review, 28*, 783–800.

Visser, S. N., Danielson, M. L., Bitsko, R. H., Holbrook, J. R., Kogan, M. D., Ghandour, R. M., . . Blumberg, S. J. (2014). Trends in the parent-report of health care provider diagnosed and medicated attention deficit hyperactivity disorder: United States, 2003–2011. *Journal of the American Academy of Child & Adolescent Psychiatry, 53*, 34–46.

Wolpert, M., Fuggle, P., Cottrell, P., Fonagy, P., Phillips, J., Pilling, S., & Target, M. (2006). *Drawing on the evidence: Advice for mental health professionals working with children and adolescents*. London, UK: CAMHS Publications.

Zhang, D., Chan, S. K. C., Lo, H. H. M., Chan, C. Y. H., Chan, J. C. Y., Ting, K. T., . . Wong, S. Y. S. (2017). Mindfulness-based intervention for Chinese children with ADHD and their parents: A pilot mixed method study. *Mindfulness, 8*, 859–872.

Zylowska, L., Ackerman, D. L., Yang, M. H., Futrell, J. L., Horton, N. L., Hale, T. S., . . Smalley, L. S. (2008). Mindfulness meditation training in adults and adolescents with ADHD: A feasibility study. *Journal of Attention Disorders, 11*, 737–746.

Chapter 6

Mindfulness in intellectual and developmental disabilities

Nirbhay N. Singh and Yoon-Suk Hwang

Introduction

The history of services for people with intellectual and developmental disabilities (IDD) is fraught with lapses in good judgment and well-intentioned but harmful interventions. At the height of the institutionalization movement, it was thought that the quality of life of people with IDD could be enhanced through the use of the first-generation antipsychotic drugs from the phenothiazine drug group, especially thioridazine and chlorpromazine, but their long-term adverse effects outweighed their benefits. Over the years, mainstream and fringe treatment providers have advocated numerous non-evidence-based and often bogus treatments, especially for those with autism spectrum disorder (ASD), including antifungal interventions, auditory integration training, bleach-based therapies, chelation therapy, CocoKefir probiotics, craniosacral therapy, detoxifying clay baths, dolphin-assisted therapy, essential oils, facilitated communication training, gentle teaching, gluten- and casein-free diets, holding therapy, hyperbaric oxygen therapy, intravenous secretin, Lupron therapy, magnetic shoe inserts, miracle mineral solution, rapid prompting method, raw camel milk, sensory integration therapy, sheep stem-cell injections, vision therapy, weighted vests, and many more. While these interventions initially gave hope to parents, they failed miserably to produce much of a change in the condition of their children.

When a mindfulness-based program first appeared in the field of developmental disabilities, it was justifiably treated with much skepticism. How could meditation on the breath and shifting the focus of one's attention from an emotionally arousing situation to a neutral point on the body inhibit anger and aggression, especially in people with compromised cognitive abilities? After a slow start, there is evidence of growing interest, acceptance, and research studies evaluating the effectiveness of established and customized mindfulness-based programs in the field of developmental disabilities.

In this chapter, we present a chronological but not exhaustive narrative of this research. The research can be broadly divided into three groups: (a) research on mindfulness-based programs that are taught directly to individuals with IDD by an experienced meditation teacher or by parents, caregivers, or teachers who have been taught by a meditation teacher to teach the individuals using a train-the-trainer model; (b) the meditation teacher has taught only the parents, caregivers, or teachers a mindfulness-based program, with the expectation that the effects of their meditation practice will cascade and spill over when engaged in mindful caregiving to people with IDD; and (c) when the mindfulness-based programs are taught to parents and their children in parallel, such that effects of the teaching on people with IDD is enhanced not only by the cascading and spill over effects from parental mindfulness but also from their own meditation practice. In addition, there is research on teaching mindfulness to parents so that they can then teach mindfulness activities to their children. The summarized research includes participants with IDD from children to adults. The reason for including adults is that in the field of developmental disabilities it is the level of functioning, not age, that is correlated to learning. While acknowledging that with age comes experiential knowledge, the level of functioning generally establishes the floor effects for conceptual learning. Due to space considerations, only intervention studies based on mindfulness meditation have been included.

Mindfulness-based programs for individuals with IDD

A number of mindfulness-based programs and practices have been researched with individuals with IDD, especially those with ASD. These include Soles of the Feet (SoF), SOBER Breathing Space, Surfing the Urge, mindfulness-based smoking cessation program, mindfulness-based health wellness program (MBHW), and mindfulness-based stress reduction (MBSR) and mindfulness-based cognitive therapy (MBCT) or their adaptations.

Soles of the Feet for aggressive behaviors

The first mindfulness-based practice was developed and informally evaluated with adolescents diagnosed with ASD. Following several developmental iterations of the practice based on intensive observations of its use by several adolescents with ASD, it was labeled as *meditation on the Soles of the Feet* (SoF). It was described as a meditation because it included two key elements of meditation (i.e., attention and awareness). In essence, the practice involves paying attention to the triggers of one's anger, awareness of negative emotional arousal state, a pause to discern whether the emotional arousal is wholesome or unwholesome, and skillfully using an antidote for the rising negative emotion. The antidote is a simple shift of one's attention from a negative emotional arousal to a neutral point on the body, the soles of the feet. Proposed theoretical mechanisms of action of the SoF practice include top-down and bottom-up neurocognitive control models (Hölzel et al.,

2011; Chiesa & Serretti, 2013; Tang et al., 2015) and behavioral models based on operant conditioning (Felver & Singh, 2020).

In the initial case study that provided a glimpse of the potential of a mindfulness-based program to help individuals with intellectual disability (ID) to self-manage their physical and verbal aggression, Singh et al. (2003) described the case of a young man who was diagnosed with mild ID and mental illness. He was repeatedly in and out of hospital placements because he was aggressive toward others in community group homes. He was taught the SoF practice until he was able to use it with arising triggers for his verbal and physical aggression. When discharged from a psychiatric hospital following training in SoF and six months of being aggression free, he was successful in controlling his anger and aggression and successfully maintained his community placement over several years. Given the study was based on a weak pre- and posttest design, it did not actually demonstrate that learning SoF was responsible for his success, even though positive changes were noted on 12 variables (e.g., number of episodes of physical and verbal aggression, injuries to staff and peers, need for medication). On the other hand, several years after learning to use SoF, he demonstrated his mastery of the practice by successfully teaching it to his peers for controlling their anger and aggression (Singh et al., 2011e).

This case study was followed by two multiple baseline design studies that evaluated the effects of SoF on aggressive behavior by individuals with mental illness (Singh et al., 2007c) and adolescents with conduct disorder (Singh et al., 2007a). In a third study using the same research design, three individuals who functioned at the moderate level of intellectual disability were taught SoF to manage their aggressive behavior so that they could maintain their community placement (Singh et al., 2007b). Their cognitive impairment hindered learning the SoF practice because they could not visualize a past instance of aggressive behavior, but adding *recreating-the-scene* (van Houten & Rolider, 1988) as a mediational procedure enabled staff to successfully teach the SoF practice to them. Results indicated the individuals were able to manage their aggressive behavior and maintain their post-training community placement during the two-year follow-up period. This study was important not only for pointing to the possible lower limits of cognitive functioning required to master the SoF practice but also for indicating that, with some ingenuity, it may be possible to overcome this problem with some individuals through the use of adjunctive behavioral procedures.

Adult offenders with IDD who are incarcerated for long periods in secure facilities sometimes engage in aggressive behavior toward staff and peers because of frustration with the monotony of their placement. However, when taught to use SoF, they can substantially decrease and eventually eliminate their aggressive behaviors, require no emergency medication or physical restraints for their aggressive behavior, and refrain from injuring staff and peers (Singh et al., 2008b). In addition, benefit-cost analysis of the use of SoF in this study showed a 95.7% reduction in agency costs when assessed in terms of the number of days injured staff members were absent from work, the cost of medical care related to their injuries, and salary or workers compensation costs. This study provided the first indication that mindfulness-based programs may not only be clinically effective but also cost-effective.

The SoF practice works well when the training is provided by an experienced meditation teacher. Adkins et al. (2010) reported a study in which a community-based therapist taught individuals with mental illness who functioned at a mild level of ID. They engaged in maladaptive behaviors (i.e., verbal and physical aggression, disruptive behavior) severe enough to threaten their group home placement. They were referred to their local community-based therapist for training in the use of the SoF practice. The individuals were able to gradually reduce their maladaptive behaviors to near-zero levels and maintain their group home placement. In addition, self-ratings by the individuals indicated clinically significant reductions in obsessive-compulsive behaviors, depression, state anxiety, property destruction, rectal digging, and urinary incontinence. This study indicated that it might be feasible for community-based therapists to learn how to utilize SoF in their clinical practice and that the effects of SoF may generalize to conditions beyond the targeted maladaptive behaviors.

A pair of studies showed that adolescents with Asperger syndrome (Singh et al., 2011b) and autism (Singh et al., 2011a)—using DSM IV diagnostic terminology for ASD—could learn to use SoF to manage their anger and aggression. One interesting aspect of these two studies was the fact that experienced meditation teachers had taught the mothers of the adolescents to use SoF in their own lives before teaching their adolescents. They used verbal instructions and modeling to teach the task-analyzed steps of the SoF practice and then prompted them to use SoF when they anticipated angry or aggressive behavior from the adolescents. The mothers also recorded the SoF instructions on the adolescents' iPods for use during self-practice. The other aspect of these two studies that is worth noting is that follow-up data were collected for four and three years, respectively. The results showed maintenance of zero rates of physical aggression by the adolescents with Asperger syndrome and a near-zero rate by those with autism.

In another study, both parents (instead of just mothers) were taught to use SoF and then teach it to their adolescent children with Prader-Willi syndrome (PWS) who engaged in verbal and physical aggression (Singh et al., 2017b). Results showed that three sets of parents successfully taught their adolescent children with PWS to reduce their verbal aggression to very low levels and to eliminate their physical aggression. During the 12-month follow-up period, the adolescents were able to maintain their verbal aggression at very low levels and not reengage in physical aggression. In a related study, telehealth technology was used to teach teachers to learn and practice SoF in their own lives, and then to demonstrate their competency by teaching the SoF practice to another teacher (Singh et al., 2017a). Once competency was achieved, the teachers taught SoF to their students. Results showed that the teachers were able to learn and then teach their students with IDD to use SoF with precursors of their verbal and physical aggression, reducing both behaviors to near-zero levels. In addition, the data showed that the students were able to maintain these behaviors at near-zero levels for 12 months during the follow-up period.

In a systematic replication and extension of SoF studies, Chinese mothers of adolescents with ASD were taught basic meditation on the breath, followed by instructions on using SoF in their own lives (Ahemaitijiang et al., 2020). When they developed a disciplined practice of mindfulness of the breath meditation and achieved fluency in using SoF, they taught their adolescents to use SoF for precursors of aggressive and destructive behaviors. Results showed that the adolescents were able to reduce their verbal aggression to very low levels, eliminate their physical aggression, and reduce their destructive behavior to low levels following training. In addition, they were able to maintain these behavioral gains during a 12-month follow-up period. This study provided an independent replication of the effectiveness of SoF in reducing aggression and destructive behaviors in a non-US culture.

The evidence for the effectiveness of SoF for self-management of anger and aggression by individuals with IDD was based almost exclusively on well-controlled, internally valid single-subject experimental design studies (Barlow et al., 2009). To demonstrate external validity of SoF, a small randomized controlled trial (RCT) was undertaken in a two-arm study (Singh et al., 2013a). Individuals who functioned at the mild level of ID were randomly assigned to either SoF or to a wait-list control group. Results showed that their verbal and physical aggression was significantly reduced only in the SoF condition and that the wait-list group showed similar reductions when they were provided training in SoF. While the data clearly favored the experimental group (i.e., SoF condition), the drawback was the use of a wait-list instead of an active control condition. By its very nature, the wait-list group participants know that they are in the control group, thus breaking the blinding to group assignment. This produces differential demand characteristics in the two groups, thus weakening the conclusions that can be drawn from the RCT.

In sum, there is substantial evidence that supports the effectiveness of SoF in reducing verbal aggression and destructive behaviors, as well as substantially reducing or eliminating physical aggression in individuals with IDD. Also, recent research suggests that individuals with IDD find SoF to be highly acceptable, with some participants reporting not only reduced aggression but also increased sociability and higher quality of life (Griffith et al., 2019).

SOBER Breathing Space for aggressive behaviors

SOBER Breathing Space is an acronym for *S*top and be aware of what is happening in the moment, *O*bserve the physical sensations and emotional regulation changes in the body, *B*reathe by deliberately and quietly bringing attention to the breath, *E*xpand awareness of the situation, response options, and the consequences of those response options, and then *R*espond mindfully by taking skillful action. This informal mindfulness-based practice has been used in the context of addiction treatment and forms a part of the Mindfulness-Based Relapse Prevention (MBRP) program. However, it can be used in a variety of other contexts as a skillful means of regulating emotions, thoughts, feelings, perceptions, and desires.

SOBER Breathing Space was recently used as an informal mindfulness-based practice for responding to precursors of verbal and physical aggression (Singh et al., 2018). Four children with ASD aged between 10 and 12 years of age were included in a multiple baseline across participants study because of the high frequency of their verbal and physical aggression. An experienced mindfulness teacher individually taught the children the SOBER Breathing Space practice at home until they reached competency in using it with fluency when needed. Given that they were aggressive both at home and at school, data were collected at home (by their parents) and at school (by their teachers). While the training was based at home, the school data provided a measure of unprogrammed generalization across settings. Results showed a statistically significant change in the children's frequency of verbal and physical aggression to near-zero in both home and school settings. A 12-month follow-up showed maintenance of behavioral gains in both settings. This study demonstrated that young children could use SOBER Breathing Space to manage their verbal and physical aggression, generalize their use of the practice across settings, and maintain behavioral gains for at least 12 months during the follow-up period. A collateral effect of the informal mindfulness-based practice was that the parents discontinued their use of physical restraints for their children's physical aggression, which they had often resorted to for their own safety as well as that of their children.

Surfing the Urge for aggressive behaviors

Surfing the Urge is another informal mindfulness-based practice that has been used to achieve behavioral control in situations that may result in relapse of addictive behavior. This practice was first used in the context of substance use when an urge arises to ingest, for example, alcohol or use illicit drugs. These urges arise like waves in the ocean, increase in size and intensity, peak, and then dissolve or dissipate. Giving in to these urges reinforces them and leads to strengthening of the addiction. However, refocusing on one's breath provides a skillful means of riding out the waves of urges by simply observing each urge with an open, nonjudgmental, equanimous attitude, and nonattachment to the urge. By not reinforcing the urges, thereby essentially putting them on extinction, eventually frees the individual from the urges. This practice involves recognizing the impermanence of the urge and resting in a state of equanimity in its presence. It enables the individual to face the urges head-on without engaging in escape or avoidance behavior and thus being able to live with it but without giving in to it.

Given the probable mechanism of action of Surfing the Urge as an informal mindfulness-based practice, it is likely applicable not only in the context of substance abuse but also in any context in which unwanted or maladaptive urges arise. Thus, it could be applicable in situations which give rise to anger and aggression. This was tested with three adolescents with ASD in a multiple baseline design across participants study (Singh et al., 2019b). The adolescents were taught Surfing the Urge practice customized for precursors of anger and aggression for each adolescent by an experienced meditation teacher. Results showed a statistically significant reduction in both verbal and physical aggression, as well as discontinuation of the adolescents' psychotropic medication that had originally been prescribed for their aggressive behavior. Obviously, a single study using SOBER Breathing Space and another with Surfing the Urge do not prove anything about their utility for self-management of maladaptive behavior, but they do provide the basis for testing their utility with other participants for proof-of-concept.

Mindfulness-based smoking cessation program

As in the general population, smoking has similar outcomes for people with IDD, even though it is a preventable cause of disease, disability, and death (e.g., 87% of lung cancer deaths are caused by smoking). In the short term, smoking results in shortness of breath and nagging coughs, reduced ability to smell and taste, premature aging of the skin, bad breath, and stained teeth. In the long term, it may cause heart disease, aneurysms, bronchitis, emphysema and stroke, worsen pneumonia and asthma, and negatively impact the immune system. The prevalence of smoking in people with IDD varies depending on the parameters of the sample surveyed. For example, in terms of those who function at the mild level of disabilities, about 26% of adolescents (Kalyva, 2007) and 36% of those who live in independent community settings (Tracy & Hosken, 1997) are occasional or regular smokers. Although smoking is clearly a health hazard, there has been a dearth of research on smoking cessation in this population.

In the first application of a mindfulness-based program for smoking cessation in this population, Singh et al. (2011d) developed a protocol that included the following components: concentration meditation; daily intention; mindful observation of thoughts; and the SoF practice. They tested its feasibility with one individual who functioned at the mild level of ID and had been a long-term smoker. When he began the mindfulness-based program he was restricted by his group home staff to 12 cigarettes a day, even though he had previously averaged up to 30 cigarettes a day. The study used a changing criterion design (Barlow et al., 2009) to enable the individual to determine the pace at which he would decrease the number of cigarettes smoked per day. Results showed that he was able to reduce and eliminate smoking in 82 days on the program and not smoke for four years during the maintenance and follow-up periods.

In a proof-of-concept study that followed, using the same research design and mindfulness-based program, the results were replicated with a further three individuals (Singh et al., 2013b).

In a small RCT, individuals who functioned at the mild level of ID were randomized into the mindfulness-based smoking cessation program or a no-treatment control group (Singh et al., 2014a). The same program components—concentration meditation, daily intention, mindful observation of thoughts, and SoF as a default control strategy for times when the urge to smoke was overwhelming—were used by the active treatment participants. The no-treatment control group participants did not engage in any formal or informal smoking cessation activities. Both intention-to-treat and per-protocol analyses indicated significantly greater reduction in smoking in participants in the mindfulness-based smoking cessation program when compared to the control group. In addition, participants in the active treatment program were significantly more successful in abstaining from smoking during the one-year follow-up period than those in the control group. A weakness of this RCT was that it did not include a third arm—an alternative active treatment group—to control for nonspecific factors that are usually embedded in each type of active treatment. Of course, this would require that the participants be blinded as to whether they are assigned to the experimental group or the alternative active treatment control group. Blinding is not necessary for the no-treatment control group participants because they will know that they are not receiving instructions on how to stop smoking. Such a trial awaits future research.

Mindfulness-based health wellness program

Prader-Willi syndrome (PWS), which has a point prevalence of 1 in 8,000 individuals, is a phenotypically expressed genetic disorder that has major neurologic, cognitive, endocrine, and behavioral characteristics. Most individuals with PWS have ID, often at the mild, borderline, or low normal level of functioning, with only about 20% functioning at the moderate level of ID (Dykens et al., 1992). A majority of them (over 70%) evince maladaptive behavior, such as temper tantrums, aggression, stubbornness, and controlling and manipulative behavior (Dykens, 2004). However, the most debilitating behavioral effects of PWS arise from their hyperphagia and obesity. The hyperphagia appears to delay their satiation response to food, thus leading them to eat much longer and consume three times more calories than people without PWS (Hinton et al., 2006; Holland et al., 1993). They develop life-threatening obesity if given unlimited access to food because of overeating and low metabolic rate. If access to food is restricted, they may engage in relentless food-seeking and maladaptive behavior (e.g., stealing food or money to buy food). There has been no viable treatment for their food-seeking behavior and obesity, given that it arises from a biological dysfunction. The typical management that parents and other caregivers use is to keep all food and drinks locked, thus denying access except at mealtimes.

A customized mindfulness-based health wellness (MBHW) program was developed to assist an adolescent with PWS to self-manage his eating and obesity issues (Singh et al., 2008a). The MBHW program includes five components: physical exercise, food awareness, mindful eating, visualizing and labeling hunger, and SOF as a default self-control strategy when the urge to eat becomes almost irresistible. Using a changing criterion design (Barlow et al., 2009) that enabled the adolescent to determine the pace of weight reduction, he used the MBHW program and was able to reach his target weight and maintain it for three years during the follow-up period. In a follow-up replication study, three adolescents used the MBHW program with their mothers acting as their primary therapists (Singh et al., 2011c). With the assistance of their mothers, all three adolescents were able to successfully use the MBHW program to reach their desired body weight, reduce their body mass index (MBI) to within normal range, enhance their lifestyles, and maintain these gains during the three-year follow-up period. Recently, in a proof-of-concept study, 30 adolescents and young adults with IDD but without PWS completed the MBHW program and reported similar findings (Myers et al., 2018). On average they reduced their weight by 38 lbs., BMI from 29.54 to 22.80, and maintained their average body weight at 127 lbs. and BMI at 23.03 during the four-year follow-up period.

Mindfulness-based programs: standard and customized

There has been an effort to evaluate the effects of standard mindfulness-based programs, such as mindfulness-based stress reduction (MBSR; Kabat-Zinn, 1990) and mindfulness-based cognitive therapy (MBCT; Segal et al., 2002), or various adaptations of such programs. For example, Spek et al. (2013) tested the effectiveness of MBT-AS, an adaptation of the MBCT program sans the cognitive elements of the program because of the information-processing deficits of individuals with ASD. The small randomized controlled trial evaluated MBT-AS vs. a treatment-as-usual (TAU) control group. Results showed significant reductions in depression, anxiety, and rumination, as well as increased positive affect, in participants with ASD in the MBT-AS group when compared to the control group. This study is suggestive of the effectiveness of the MBT-AS program, but the lack of an active control condition precludes a more definitive conclusion. In a repeated measures design study of MBT-AS, 50 adults with ASD were assessed three times: before the first training session; following the final training session; and nine weeks later (Kiep et al., 2015). Results showed mixed findings. For example, symptoms of anxiety, depression, agoraphobia, somatization, inadequacy in thinking and acting, distrust and interpersonal sensitivity, and sleeping problems significantly declined during the treatment and were maintained post-treatment. However, general psychological and physical well-being also declined during treatment. This finding is counterintuitive if the participants' mental health generally improved at the same time. Given the lack of an active control group, and common method bias inherent in the study due to the use of multiple self-report measures, no firm conclusions can be drawn from this study.

The feasibility of using the standard MBSR program with adults with ASD was recently reported in a small pilot study (Beck et al., 2020). Twelve individuals volunteered for the training. Following an orientation session and individual interview, the individuals attended eight weekly 2.5 hour sessions and a full-day (7.5 hours) silent meditation retreat following week 6. They were required to engage in meditation practice for 45 minutes a day and 5 to 15 minutes of informal mindfulness practice for six days a week. In all, the MBSR course consisted of 29 hours of class time and 42 to 48 hours of homework. Results indicated feasibility and acceptability of the training and effectiveness on a number of variables, including positive outlook, satisfaction with life, mindfulness, and quality of life. Although no generalizable conclusions can be drawn from this pilot study, the utility of the standard MBSR training in this population deserves further research.

The effects of a 12-week MBSR course adapted for people with ID was evaluated in a small uncontrolled pilot study with 10 participants (Anderson et al., 2019). Although there were no differences before and after the course on well-being and understanding of the concepts of mindfulness, additional practice resulted in self-reported reduced stress, increased self-control, and confidence. These results are encouraging but not definitive due to the small sample size, lack of active comparison treatment and a no-treatment control condition, and common method bias. Conner and White (2018) reported a feasibility and preliminary efficacy study of the effects of mindfulness- and acceptance-based interventions (MABI). Of the nine participants with ASD, seven reported improvement in at least one of the following variables: impulse control, access to emotion regulation strategies, and emotional acceptance. These findings are suggestive, but the small sample size and lack of control conditions makes it difficult to draw any substantive conclusions. In another small pilot study, the effects of a customized mindfulness-based program (Calming Thoughts and Calming Minds Program) were assessed in a group of eight teenagers with IDD (Heifetz & Dyson, 2017). The data from this study were too preliminary from which conclusions can be drawn about the effects of the program.

In a rather elegant study, Ridderinkhof et al. (2020) examined the performance of children with ASD and matched typically developing children on the Attention Network Test prior to and two months following engagement in the MYmind program, a customized mindfulness-based program adapted from MBCT. Baseline results showed that both groups of children performed equally well in the speed of the attention systems, but the children with ASD were less accurate than the matched controls in their orienting and executive attention. Furthermore, two months following their engagement in the

MYmind program, there was no significant change in the attention of the children with ASD, but there was a hint of improvement in their orienting and executive attention. This study provides an example of research needed to study the underlying processes that affect cognitive functioning in children with ASD and whether these processes can be influenced through training in mindfulness-based programs.

There have been a number of qualitative studies that have investigated the experiences of individuals with IDD when participating in mindfulness-based programs (e.g., Chapman & Mitchell, 2013; Currie et al., 2019; Dillon et al., 2018; Idusohan-Moizer et al., 2015; Yildiran & Holt, 2014). Given that mindfulness is experiential and mindfulness-based training targets a person's interoceptive experiences, qualitative methodologies provide a way of sampling the person's lived experiences during and following such training. Such data could be particularly helpful in beginning to understand the psychological mechanisms that may underlie such experiences. However, we need to be particularly careful in moving from descriptive-level qualitative analysis to developing theories of mechanisms of action. One of the pitfalls of such an endeavor is that different qualitative methods of analysis of the same data set may lead to somewhat different findings (Frank et al., 2019), thus questioning the validity and reliability of the findings obtained through a single method of analysis. Furthermore, there are issues that are specific to people with IDD that need to be taken into account, such as their understanding of mindfulness practice, understanding of the nature, meaning, and nuances of the questions being asked, the effects of the mindfulness-based programs, nonspecific factors associated with the program, and so on. This is not to say that qualitative investigation is a poor substitute for quantitative investigation but that researchers should know and acknowledge its pitfalls, should not go beyond the soft data it offers, and (as with quantitative studies) should refrain from offering clinical, practice, or policy implications based on a single study.

In sum, the research literature on teaching mindfulness-based practices to people with IDD is increasing, with commensurate growth in the quality of the investigations. Overall, the findings are fairly positive, maybe a little overstated, and applicable only to those who are at the higher end of intellectual functioning. Objective behavioral measures provide the most reliable and valid indicators of outcomes of training in mindfulness-based programs. Collecting data based on self-reported rating scales of mindfulness is highly questionable because there is no way of knowing what the items actually mean to each individual with IDD, how important the concepts being measured are to them, and the reliability of their ratings.

Effects of parent, caregiver, and teacher mindfulness on individuals with IDD

There are many studies of mindful parenting in developmental disabilities, but most of these focus on its effects on the parents and not on their children (for reviews, see Myers et al., 2014; Singh & Hwang, 2020). The literature on mindfulness for caregivers and teachers is not as extensive as that for parents. We review only those studies in these areas of research in which the effects of mindfulness training cascades on the children without the mindfulness training directed at the children themselves.

Parent mindfulness

In the earliest study, mothers of three 4- to 6-year-old children with ASD were enrolled in a customized 12-week mindful parenting program (Singh et al., 2006b). This was essentially a behavioral study that used a mindful parenting program as the intervention in a multiple-baseline design across participants. The aim of the study was to assess if teaching mindful parenting to the mothers would translate into changes in their children's behavior. Target child behaviors included physical aggression directed at the mother (e.g., hitting, biting, kicking, slapping, pushing, and shoving), noncompliance with mother's instructions, and self-injury (i.e., biting self on the arm, banging head against hard surfaces, and slapping own face). Results showed that, in comparison to the baseline (control) condition, the children's frequency of aggression began decreasing soon after the mothers started their training in mindful parenting and continued to decrease to zero levels following the completion of training. Compliance with mother's requests was an issue with two of the children, and self-injury with the remaining child. Both noncompliance and self-injury decreased substantially following mothers' training in mindful parenting and remained at near-zero levels toward the end of the study. Unlike behavioral interventions in which sharp decreases in challenging behaviors are evident with the introduction of the treatment, there was a slower arrival of effects with mindful parenting. This was expected because training effects in mindful parenting takes time to mature and then to cascade to other family members. However, when the reductions in the children's behaviors occur, they tend to be maintained for long periods.

In a systematic replication of the Singh et al. (2006b) study with four mothers of children with developmental disabilities, mindful parenting resulted in aggressive behavior being reduced to near-zero levels, substantial decreases in child negative social interaction with siblings, and significant increases in positive interactions (Singh et al., 2007d). In addition, the mothers reported increased practice of mindfulness in daily life, increased satisfaction with their parenting, more positive interactions with their children, and lowered parenting stress.

The effects of teaching mindfulness-based positive behavior support (MBPBS) to mothers of adolescents with ASD were assessed on the behavior of the adolescents (Singh et al., 2014b). MBPBS is the braiding of two evidence-based programs—mindfulness and positive behavior support—with mindfulness being responsible for emotional regulation of the parents and the positive behavior support providing the basis for positive behavioral management of the child (Singh et al., 2020a). This proof-of-concept study showed that the adolescents' aggressive and disruptive behaviors decreased to near-zero levels, accompanied by a substantial increase in their compliance to parental requests. Significant changes in the adolescents' behavior was achieved simply by teaching MBPBS to their mothers. Furthermore, the MBPBS training produced a significant reduction in the mothers' perceived stress. A large comparison group study investigated the differential effects of MBPBS on the stress levels of mothers of adolescents with ASD and mothers of adolescents with IDD (Singh et al., 2019a). The results indicated no differential effects, with both groups of mothers showing statistically significant reductions in their perceived stress. Furthermore, statistically significant reductions in aggression and disruptive behavior and increases in compliance were evident in both groups of adolescents. The findings of this study suggest that customized mindfulness-based programs may not be needed for specific etiological groups of children with developmental disabilities.

In a wait-list control study, Neece (2014) investigated the effectiveness of the standard MBSR program on parental stress and, secondarily, whether reduced parental stress would lead to reductions in the challenging behaviors of their children with developmental delays. Results showed that parents who completed the MBSR program reported significantly reduced stress and depression and greater life satisfaction than the wait-list group of parents. Furthermore, the children of parents in the MBSR group were reported to have fewer attention problems and ADHD symptomology when compared to the children of parents in the wait-list control group. Further analysis of data from 24 families included in the Neece (2014) sample of parents showed increased child self-control which resulted from two parent-child relational factors, namely, attachment and discipline practices (Lewallen & Neece, 2015). In two further studies that also included samples from the Neece (2014) study, Chan and Neece (2018a) replicated the findings from the Neece (2014) study with a larger sample and reported that the gains in the parents' mental health and reduced child behaviors were maintained at a six-month follow-up. In the other study, Chan and Neece (2018b) found that reductions in parenting stress predicted reductions in child emotion dysregulation. The final study in this series using the same cohort of parents showed that MBSR is equally effective in improving parent and child outcomes in Latino and non-Latino families (Neece et al., 2019). This series of studies provide interesting data on the use of MBSR in families with a child with developmental delays, but the interpretation of the findings is somewhat complicated given the overlapping sample across studies.

Caregiver mindfulness

In the first study on the cascading effects of mindfulness in caregivers, three pairs of caregivers were selected based on their observed interactions with individuals who functioned at profound levels of intellectual and physical disability, with one of each pair provided training in mindfulness and the other as a yoked control (Singh et al., 2004). Levels of happiness displayed by the individuals with ID were recorded during baseline (no training), eight-week training in mindfulness, and 16 weeks following training. Results showed that the individuals' levels of happiness increased substantially only in the presence of the three caregivers trained in mindfulness, while their happiness remained at baseline levels in the presence of the other three caregivers who were not trained in mindfulness. This study suggested that the personal transformation that occurred in the caregivers due to training in mindfulness cascaded to the individuals in their care, without direct training being provided to the individuals.

In a larger study, caregivers from three community group homes were provided training in behavior management, followed by training in mindfulness (Singh et al., 2006a). The three key variables among the large number monitored included staff interventions needed for the aggressive behavior of the individuals with IDD, use of physical restraints by the caregivers for the individuals' aggressive behavior, and the number of objectives the individuals mastered. Results showed that caregiver training in behavior management produced a small reduction in the frequency of aggression, minimal increase in the number of learning objectives mastered, and small reduction in caregiver use of physical restraints for their aggressive behavior. With the introduction of caregiver training in mindfulness, there were significant reductions in the individuals' aggressive behavior, increases in learning objectives, and elimination of caregiver use of physical restraints. The results were encouraging, but the experimental design was flawed in that sequence effects successive trainings could not be ruled out. However, a further study replicated the finding that caregivers can substantially reduce their use of physical restraints following training in a 12-week mindfulness-based program (Singh et al., 2009). That caregivers can reduce their use of restrictive interventions was further demonstrated in a study with disability support workers trained in a customized occupational mindfulness program (Brooker et al., 2014).

The effects of caregiver training in MBPBS were explored in four studies across several variables in community group homes and a congregate care facility. In the first study, caregivers from community group homes participated in a seven-day intensive MBPBS program (Singh et al., 2015). Results showed that the individuals with IDD decreased and then eliminated their aggressive behavior toward staff and peers, and that the staff eliminated their use of physical restraints in line with the findings from previous studies. In addition, caregivers reported significant reductions in their perceived psychological stress. The second study replicated and extended these findings with a larger sample size and additional outcome variables (Singh et al., 2016b). In the third study, caregivers from a congregate care facility participated in a two-arm RCT, with training in MBPBS in one arm and training-as usual (in-service training) in the other (Singh et al., 2016a). Results showed that MBPBS was significantly more effective than the training-as-usual for both the caregivers and the individuals with IDD in their care. For caregivers, their perceived psychological stress was significantly reduced. Caregivers significantly reduced their use of physical restraints and stat medication for aggressive behavior by the individuals in their care, but only following training in MBPBS. The individuals significantly reduced their use of aggressive behavior, defined as hitting, biting, scratching, punching, kicking, slapping, and destroying property. In the final study, the comparative effectiveness of caregiver training in MBPBS and PBS alone was examined in a two-arm 40-week RCT (Singh et al., 2020b). Results showed that both MBPBS and PBS were effective, but caregiver, individuals with IDD, and agency outcomes were significantly superior for MBPBS than PBS alone. That is, the outcomes for the individuals were significantly better when the caregivers were trained in MBPBS than in PBS alone.

Teacher mindfulness

There has been increasing emphasis on teacher mindfulness training, but virtually all of it has been directed at teachers of typically developing children or those with mental health conditions. In perhaps the only study which focused on teachers of students with ID, Singh et al. (2013) taught three teachers a series of meditations in an eight-week course (two hours per week) within a multiple baseline design across participants. The mindfulness training program included sitting and walking meditations, observation of thoughts, beginner's mind, present moment awareness, lovingkindness, compassion, equanimity, and *shenpa*. The teachers practiced sitting meditation for about 20 to 30 minutes at least five days a week. Results showed that the preschool children who functioned at the mild level of ID showed significant reductions in their maladaptive behavior (defined as screaming, kicking, biting, pushing and shoving, hitting, slapping, throwing or destroying property, and grabbing food) commensurate with the mindfulness training of the teachers. The preschool children also substantially increased their compliance with teacher requests. Finally, although there was virtually no change in the children's positive interactions with peers, their negative interactions decreased significantly, and their isolate or self-initiated play increased significantly. This study hinted at the interdependence of teacher and student behavior (Dalai Lama, 2002) and suggested that the teacher-student transactions moved from a negative to a positive trajectory (Sameroff, 1995; Singh & Singh, 2001). Although the findings are interesting, the data are preliminary and await further research.

In sum, there is an emerging research literature attesting to the cascading or spill over effects of parent, caregiver, and teacher mindfulness on individuals with IDD. The initial findings from single-subject experimental design studies on parent and caregiver mindfulness appear to be confirmed by recent proof-of-concept and RCTs. Research on teacher mindfulness cascading to their students is still meager and ripe for future research.

Mindfulness training for parents and their children with ASD

There are a small number of studies that have investigated the effectiveness of teaching mindfulness practices to individuals with ID or ASD and teaching mindful parenting to their parents in parallel or teaching mindfulness practices to the parents to fluency and then having the parents teach the practices to their children. This emerging area of training mindfulness practices to children and adolescents takes advantage of the bidirectional effects of training inherently embedded in such a format.

In the earliest study, parents and their adolescent children were provided training in mindfulness in parallel; that is, the parents and their children were trained at the same time but separately (Bögels et al., 2008). This enabled the mindfulness program to be customized for the parents and for their children. This pilot study included children with externalizing disorders, including ASD, but the data were not examined separately for those with ASD. The parents and their children attended an eight-week mindfulness-based program modeled on MBCT (Segal et al., 2002), with data being collected at baseline, following the training, and at eight-week follow-up. Results showed substantial benefits for both parents and their children. For the children, the mindfulness training produced substantial gains in self-reported personal goals, internalizing and externalizing complaints, attention problems, happiness, and mindful awareness. In addition, they performed better on a sustained attention test when compared to pre-mindfulness training. This study opened the field of mindful parenting, showing the beneficial effects of teaching mindfulness to both the parents and their children in parallel.

In another study, mothers of children with ASD participated in an eight-week mindfulness program, and when they attained fluency in the theory and practice of mindfulness meditation, they taught mindfulness activities to their children (Hwang et al., 2015). Mindfulness training of the mothers resulted in increased self-reported mindfulness, decreased stress, and reductions in anxiety and thought problems. Mindfulness training for the children resulted in reductions in anxiety, thought problems, and aggressive behavior, with the reductions being at different levels across the children. One of the strengths of this study was the intensive study of each mother-child dyad that provided valuable information on what happens during mindfulness training of parents and their children. The limitations of the study include the small sample size, the lack of a comparison or control group, and that the self-ratings by the parents may have resulted in common method bias.

MYmind, which is based on MBCT and MBSR programs, is a mindfulness training program for adolescents with ASD and other disorders (e.g., ADHD).

Using a repeated measures design, de Bruin et al. (2015) evaluated the effects of MYmind with adolescents with ASD and parallel mindful parenting for their parents. Assessments were undertaken a week pre-training, a week post-training, and nine weeks post-training. Self-ratings by the adolescents indicated an increase in quality of life and a decrease in rumination. The adolescents reported no changes in their levels of worry, ASD core symptoms, or mindful awareness. Their parents also indicated no changes core symptoms of ASD but rated improvements in their children's social responsiveness, social communication, social cognition, preoccupations, and social motivation. Parental self-ratings indicated improvements in their parenting competence, overall parenting styles, and increased quality of life. The initial data on the use of MYmind with children with ASD provided cautious optimism about its effectiveness balanced by the fact that the study did not include a control or comparison group.

In a subsequent study of MYmind, also using a repeated measures design with a one-year follow-up, Ridderinkhof et al. (2018) systematically replicated and extended the de Bruin et al. (2015) study. Self-reported ratings by the children with ASD indicated decreased social communications problems and improvements in emotional and behavioral functioning, but virtually no change in their mindful awareness. The children indicated most improvements at the two-month post-training, but these improvements decreased by the one-year follow-up. In contrast, parental ratings of the children's behaviors suggested that the changes in the children were evident during both follow-up assessments. Parents rated improvements in their own emotional and behavioral functioning, parenting, and mindful awareness at both follow-up assessments. These ratings were bolstered by qualitative data based on open-ended questions. This study provided supportive evidence of positive outcomes for teaching mindfulness to parents and their children with ASD in parallel sessions.

In another study of MYmind, 14 children with ASD and 31 parents who had been participants in earlier studies (de Bruin et al., 2015; Ridderinkhof et al., 2018, 2020) took part in a qualitative investigation of their perceptions of the change processes involved in the MYmind mindfulness training (Ridderinkhof et al., 2019). The children and their parents were interviewed two to five months after the nine-week MYmind training. Their responses were analyzed using constructivist grounded theory to develop an understanding of the relations among the key change processes. Ridderinkhof et al. developed a model that reflected the interdependency and direction of the change processes identified by the participants. The eight main change processes identified were connecting with peers; pausing, being aware; being in the here and now; letting be; determining a strategy; being and responding calm; and attuning to others. These change processes were explored in terms of current conceptions of the mechanisms of action of mindfulness and Buddhist foundations of mindfulness. This study provides a plethora of testable hypotheses for future research.

In the final study on MYmind, a 10-week pre-training assessment was added as a control condition in a within-subject repeated measures design study

(Salem-Guirgis et al., 2019). Procedurally, this study was essentially similar to the earlier investigations but with the addition of a pre-intervention control condition. Results indicated improvements in autism symptoms, emotion regulation, and adaptive skills. The addition of the pre-training control condition strengthened the study design, but it is still not ideal because the efficacy or effectiveness of a training program can only be established in an RCT that includes random assignment of participants to the target program, an alternative active control of comparison program, and a no-training control condition.

In sum, studies that have investigated the effects of mindfulness-based training for parents and their children with ID or ASD, either in parallel or successively, indicate positive changes for both the parents and their children. The data indicate the need for further studies that are methodologically robust to reach more definitive conclusions.

Conclusions

A diverse range of mindfulness-based programs and practices have been developed and/or researched in the field of IDD. A majority of the research has focused on developing or adapting mindfulness-based practices for teaching individuals with ID or ASD how to regulate their emotions. Finding ways of helping individuals to inhibit their anger and aggression has been a priority because such behavior is not only harmful to self and others but also threatens the welfare of the individuals themselves. For example, uncontrolled anger and aggression always threaten community placement of these individuals and preclude their social acceptance by typically developing peers. The studies reviewed suggest that such individuals may include specific mindfulness-based practices in their toolbox of effective approaches for self-managing anger and aggression. There is a growing research base on the positive effects of parent, caregiver, and teacher mindfulness that cascade to people in their care. This is also a small but growing research literature attesting to the benefits of teaching mindfulness-based programs to both parents and their children in parallel or teaching mindfulness practices to the parents, who then teach the practices to their children. Overall, the research is in its early stages and mainly positive in terms of outcomes, but much remains to be accomplished.

References

Adkins, A. D., Singh, A. N., Winton, A. S. W., McKeegan, G. F., & Singh, J. (2010). Using a mindfulness-based procedure in the community: Translating research to practice. *Journal of Child and Family Studies*, *19*, 175–183.

Ahemaitijiang, N., Hu, X., Yang, X., & Han, Z. H. (2020). Effects of Meditation on the Soles of the Feet on aggressive and destructive behaviors of Chinese adolescents with autism spectrum disorders. *Mindfulness*, *11*, 230–240.

Anderson, R., McKenzie, K., & Noone, S. (2019). Effects of a mindfulness-based stress reduction course on the psychological well-being of individuals with an intellectual disability. *Learning Disability Practice, 22*(2), 20–25.

Barlow, D. H., Nock, M. K., & Hersen, M. (2009). *Single case experimental designs: Strategies for studying behavior change* (3rd ed.). Boston, MA: Allyn and Bacon.

Beck, K. B., Greco, C. M., Terhorst, L. A., Skidmore, E. R., Kulzer, J. L., & McCue, M. P. (2020). Mindfulness-based stress reduction for adults with autism spectrum disorder: Feasibility and estimated effects. *Mindfulness, 11*, 1286–1297.

Bögels, S. M., Hoogstad, B., van Dun, L., de Schutter, S., & Restifo, K. (2008). Mindfulness training for adolescents with externalizing disorders and their parents. *Behavioural and Cognitive Psychotherapy, 36*, 193–209.

Brooker, J. E., Webber, L., Julian, J., Shawyer, F., Graham, A. L., Chan, J., & Meadows, G. (2014). Mindfulness-based training shows promise in assisting staff to reduce their use of restrictive interventions in residential services. *Mindfulness, 5*, 598–603.

Chan, N., & Neece, C. L. (2018a). Mindfulness-based stress reduction for parents of children with developmental delays: A follow-up study. *Evidence-Based Practice in Child and Adolescent Mental Health, 3*(1), 16–29.

Chan, N., & Neece, C. L. (2018b). Parenting stress and emotional dysregulation among children with developmental delays: The role of parenting behaviors. *Journal of Child and Family Studies, 27*, 4071–4082.

Chapman, M. J., & Mitchell, D. (2013). Mindfully valuing people now: An evaluation of introduction to mindfulness workshops for people with intellectual disabilities. *Mindfulness, 4*(2), 168–178.

Chiesa, A., & Serretti, A. (2013). Are mindfulness-based interventions effective for substance use disorders? A systematic review of the evidence. *Substance Use & Misuse, 49*(5), 492–512.

Conner, C. M., & White, S. W. (2018). Feasibility and preliminary efficacy of individual mindfulness therapy for adults with autism spectrum disorder. *Journal of Autism and Developmental Disorders, 48*, 290–300.

Currie, T. L., McKenzie, K., & Noone, S. (2019). The experiences of people with an intellectual disability of a mindfulness-based program. *Mindfulness, 10*, 1304–1314.

Dalai Lama. (2002). *How to practice: The way to a meaningful life*. New York, NY: Atria Books.

De Bruin, E. I., Blom, R., Smit, F. M., van Steensel, F. J., & Bögels, S. M. (2015). MYmind: Mindfulness training for youngsters with autism spectrum disorders and their parents. *Autism, 19*, 906–914.

Dillon, A., Wilson, C., & Jackman, C. (2018). Be here now: Service users' experiences of a mindfulness group intervention. *Advances in Mental Health and Intellectual Disabilities, 12*(2), 77–87.

Dykens, E. M. (2004). Maladaptive and compulsive behavior in Prader-Willi syndrome: New insights from older adults. *American Journal on Mental Retardation, 109*, 142–153.

Dykens, E. M., Hodapp, R. M., Walsh, K., & Nash, L. J. (1992). Profiles, correlates, and trajectories of intelligence in Prader-Willi syndrome. *Journal of the American Academy of Child and Adolescent Psychiatry, 31*, 1125–1130.

Felver, J. C., & Singh, N. N. (2020). *Mindfulness in the classroom: An evidence-based program to reduce disruptive behavior and increase academic achievement*. Oakland, CA: New Harbinger Publications.

Frank, P., Stanszus, L., Fischer, D., Kehnel, K., & Grossman, P. (2019). Cross-fertilizing qualitative perspectives on effects of a mindfulness-based intervention: An empirical comparison of four methodical approaches. *Mindfulness, 10*, 2452–2467.

Griffith, G. M., Hastings, R. P., Williams, J., Jones, R. S. P., Roberts, J., Crane, R. S., . . Edwards, R. T. (2019). Mixed experiences of a mindfulness-informed intervention: Voices from people with intellectual disabilities, their supporters, and therapists. *Mindfulness, 10*, 1828–1841.

Heifetz, M., & Dyson, A. (2017). Mindfulness-based group for teens with developmental disabilities and their parents: A pilot study. *Mindfulness, 8*(2), 444–453.

Hinton, E. C., Holland, A. J., Gellatly, M. S. N., Soni, S., Patterson, M., Ghatei, M. A., & Owen, A. M. (2006). Neural representations of hunger and satiety in Prader-Willi syndrome. *International Journal of Obesity, 30*, 313–321.

Holland, A. J., Treasure, J., Coskeran, P., Dallow, J., Milton, N., & Hillhouse, E. (1993). Measurement of excessive appetite and metabolic changes in Prader-Willi syndrome. *International Journal of Obesity and Related Metabolic Disorders, 17*, 527–532.

Hölzel, B. K., Lazar, S. W., Gard, T., Schuman-Olivier, Z., Vago, D. R., & Ott, U. (2011). How does mindfulness meditation work? Proposing mechanisms of action from a conceptual and neural perspective. *Perspectives on Psychological Science, 6*, 537–559.

Hwang, Y. S., Kearney, P., Klieve, H., Lang, W., & Roberts, J. (2015). Cultivating mind: Mindfulness interventions for children with autism spectrum disorder and problem behaviors, and their mothers. *Journal of Child and Family Studies, 24*, 3093–3106.

Idusohan-Moizer, H., Sawicka, A., Dendle, J., & Albany, M. (2015). Mindfulness-based cognitive therapy for adults with intellectual disabilities: An evaluation of the effectiveness of mindfulness in reducing symptoms of depression and anxiety. *Journal of Intellectual Disability Research, 59*(2), 93–104.

Kabat-Zinn, J. (1990). *Full catastrophe living: Using the wisdom of your body and mind to face stress, pain, and illness*. New York, NY: Delta.

Kalyva, E. (2007). Prevalence and influences on self-reported smoking among adolescents with mild learning disabilities, attention deficit hyperactivity disorder, and their typically developing peers. *Journal of Intellectual Disabilities, 11*, 267–279.

Kiep, M., Spek, A. A., & Hoeben, L. (2015). Mindfulness-based therapy in adults with an autism spectrum disorder: Do treatment effects last? *Mindfulness, 5*, 637–644.

Lewallen, A. C., & Neece, C. L. (2015). Improved social skills in children with developmental delays after parent participation in MBSR: The role of parent-child relational factors. *Journal of Child and Family Studies, 24*, 3117–3129.

Myers, R. E., Karazsia, B. T., Kim, E., Jackman, M. M., McPherson, C. L., & Singh, N. N. (2018). A telehealth parent-mediated mindfulness-based health wellness intervention for adolescents and young adults with intellectual and developmental disabilities. *Advances in Neurodevelopmental Disorders, 2*, 241–252.

Myers, R. E., Winton, A. S. W., Lancioni, G. E., & Singh, N. N. (2014). Mindfulness in developmental disabilities (pp. 209–240). In N. N. Singh (Ed.), *Psychology of meditation*. New York, NY: Nova Science.

Neece, C. L. (2014). Mindfulness-based stress reduction for parents of young children with developmental delays: Implications for parental mental health and child behavior problems. *Journal of Applied Research in Intellectual Disabilities, 27*, 174–186.

Neece, C. L., Chan, N., Klein, K., Roberts, L., & Fenning, R. M. (2019). Mindfulness-based stress reduction for parents of children with developmental delays: Understanding the experiences of Latino families. *Mindfulness, 10*, 1017–1030.

Ridderinkhof, A., de Bruin, E. I., Blom, R., & Bögels, S. M. (2018). Mindfulness-based program for children with autism spectrum disorder and their parents: Direct and long-term improvements. *Mindfulness, 9*(3), 773–791.

Ridderinkhof, A., de Bruin, E. I., Blom, R., Singh, N. N., & Bögels, S. M. (2019). Mindfulness-based program for autism spectrum disorder: A qualitative study of the experiences of children and parents. *Mindfulness, 10,* 1936–1951.

Ridderinkhof, A., de Bruin, E. I., van den Driesschen, S., & Bögels, S. M. (2020). Attention in children with autism spectrum disorder and the effects of a mindfulness-based program. *Journal of Attention Disorders, 24*(5), 681–692.

Salem-Guirgis, S., Albaum, C., Tablon, P., Riosa, P. B., Nicholas, D. B., Drmic, I. E., & Weiss, J. A. (2019). MYmind: A concurrent group-based mindfulness intervention for youth with autism and their parents. *Mindfulness, 10,* 1730–1743.

Sameroff, A. J. (1995). General systems theories and developmental psychopathology. In D. Cicchetti & D. J. Cohen (Eds.), *Developmental psychopathology. Vol. 1: Theory and methods* (pp. 659–695). New York, NY: John Wiley.

Segal, Z. V., Williams, J. M. G., & Teasdale, J. D. (2002). *Mindfulness-based cognitive therapy for depression: A new approach to preventing relapse.* New York, NY: Guilford Press.

Singh, N. N., Chan, J., Karazsia, B. T., McPherson, C. L., & Jackman, M. M. (2017a). Telehealth training of teachers to teach a mindfulness-based procedure for self-management of aggressive behavior to students with intellectual and developmental disabilities. *International Journal of Developmental Disabilities, 63*(4), 195–203.

Singh, N. N., & Hwang, Y.-S. (2020). Mindfulness-based programs and practices for people with intellectual and developmental disability. *Current Opinion in Psychiatry, 33*(2), 88–91.

Singh, N. N., Lancioni, G. E., Chan, J., Jackman, M. M., & McPherson, C. L. (2020a). Mindfulness-based positive behavior support. In I. Ivtzan (Ed.), *Handbook of mindfulness-based programmes: Mindfulness interventions from education to health and therapy* (pp. 42–52). London, UK: Routledge.

Singh, N. N., Lancioni, G. E., Joy, S. D. S., Winton, A. S. W., Sabaawi, M., Wahler, R. G., & Singh, J. (2007a). Adolescents with conduct disorder can be mindful of their aggressive behavior. *Journal of Emotional and Behavioral Disorders, 15,* 56–63.

Singh, N. N., Lancioni, G. E., Karazsia, B. T., Chan, J., & Winton, A. S. W. (2016a). Effectiveness of caregiver training in mindfulness-based positive behavior support (MBPBS): A randomized controlled trial. *Frontiers in Psychology, 7,* 1549.

Singh, N. N., Lancioni, G. E., Karazsia, B. T., & Myers, R. E. (2016b). Caregiver training in mindfulness-based positive behavior support (MBPBS): Effects on caregivers and adults with intellectual and developmental disabilities. *Frontiers in Psychology, 7,* 98.

Singh, N. N., Lancioni, G. E., Karazsia, B. T., Myers, R. E., Hwang, Y.-S., & Bhikkhu Anālayo. (2019a). Effects of Mindfulness-Based Positive Behavior Support (MBPBS) training are equally beneficial for mothers and their children with autism spectrum disorder or with intellectual disabilities. *Frontiers in Psychology, 10,* 385.

Singh, N. N., Lancioni, G. E., Karazsia, B. T., Myers, R. E., Kim, E., Chan, J., . . Janson, M. (2019b). Surfing the urge: An informal mindfulness practice for the self-management of aggression by adolescents with autism spectrum disorder. *Journal of Contextual Behavioral Science, 12,* 170–177.

Singh, N. N., Lancioni, G. E., Karazsia, B. T., Myers, R. E., Winton, A. A. W., Latham, L. L., & Nugent, K. (2015). Effects of training staff in MBPBS on the use of physical restraints, staff stress and turnover, staff and peer injuries, and cost effectiveness in developmental disabilities. *Mindfulness, 6,* 926–937.

Singh, N. N., Lancioni, G. E., Karazsia, B. T., Winton, A. S. W., Myers, R. E., Singh, A. N. A., . . Singh, J. (2013a). Mindfulness-based treatment of aggression in individuals with intellectual disabilities: A waiting list control study. *Mindfulness, 4,* 158–167.

Singh, N. N., Lancioni, G. E., Manikam, R. Winton, A. S. W., Singh, A. N. A., Singh, J., & Singh, A. D. A. (2011a). A mindfulness-based strategy for self-management of aggressive behavior in adolescents with autism. *Research in Autism Spectrum Disorders, 5*, 1153–1158.

Singh, N. N., Lancioni, G. E., Medvedev, O. N., Myers, R. E., Chan, J., McPherson, C. L., . . Kim, E. (2020b). Comparative effectiveness of caregiver training in mindfulness-based positive behavior support (MBPBS) and positive behavior support (PBS) in a randomized controlled trial. *Mindfulness, 11*, 99–111.

Singh, N. N., Lancioni, G. E., Myers, R. M., Karazsia, B. T., Courtney, T. M., & Nugent, K. (2017b). A mindfulness-based intervention for self-management of verbal and physical aggression by adolescents with Prader-Willi syndrome. *Developmental Neurorehabilitation, 20*(5), 253–260.

Singh, N. N., Lancioni, G. E., Myers, R. M., Karazsia, B. T., McPherson, C. L., Jackman, M. M., . . Thompson, T. (2018). Effects of SOBER Breathing Space on aggression in children with autism spectrum disorder and collateral effects on parental use of physical restraints. *Advances in Neurodevelopmental Disorders, 2*, 362–374.

Singh, N. N., Lancioni, G. E., Myers, R. M., Karazsia, B. T., Winton, A. S. W., & Singh, J. (2014a). A randomized controlled trial of a mindfulness-based smoking cessation program for individuals with mild intellectual disability. *International Journal of Mental Health and Addictions, 12*, 153–168.

Singh, N. N., Lancioni, G. E., Singh, A. D. A., Winton, A. S. W., Singh, A. N. A., & Singh, J. (2011b). Adolescents with Asperger Syndrome can use a mindfulness-based strategy to control their aggressive behavior. *Research in Autism Spectrum Disorders, 5*, 1103–1109.

Singh, N. N., Lancioni, G. E., Singh, A. N. A., Winton, A. S. W., Singh, A. D. A., & Singh, J. (2011c). A mindfulness-based health wellness program for individuals with Prader-Willi Syndrome. *Journal of Mental Health Research in Intellectual Disabilities, 4*, 90–106.

Singh, N. N., Lancioni, G. E., Singh, A. N. A., Winton, A. S. W., Singh, J., McAleavey, K. M., & Adkins, A. D. (2008a). A mindfulness-based health wellness program for an adolescent with Prader-Willi Syndrome. *Behavior Modification, 32*(2), 176–181.

Singh, N. N., Lancioni, G. E., Winton, A. S. W., Adkins, A. D., Singh, J., & Singh, A. N (2007b). Mindfulness training assists individuals with moderate mental retardation to maintain their community placements. *Behavior Modification, 31*, 800–814.

Singh, N. N., Lancioni, G. E., Winton, A. S. W., Adkins, A. D., Wahler, R. G., Sabaawi, M., & Singh, J. (2007c). Individuals with mental illness can control their aggressive behavior through mindfulness training. *Behavior Modification, 31*, 313–328.

Singh, N. N., Lancioni, G. E., Winton, A. S. W., Curtis, W. J., Wahler, R. G., Sabaawi, M., . . McAleavey, K. (2006a). Mindful staff increase learning and reduce aggression in adults with developmental disabilities. *Research in Developmental Disabilities, 27*, 545–558.

Singh, N. N., Lancioni, G. E., Winton, A. S. W., Fisher, B. C., Wahler, R. G., McAleavey, K., Singh, J., & Sabaawi, M. (2006b). Mindful parenting decreases aggression, noncompliance, and self-injury in children with autism. *Journal of Emotional and Behavioral Disorder, 14*(3), 169–177.

Singh, N. N., Lancioni, G. E., Winton, A. S. W., Karazsia, B. T., Myers, R. E., Latham, L. L., & Singh, J. S. (2014b). Mindfulness-based positive behavior support (MBPBS) for mothers of adolescents with autism spectrum disorder: Effects on adolescents' behavior and parental stress. *Mindfulness, 5*, 646–657.

Singh, N. N., Lancioni, G. E., Winton, A. S. W., Karazsia, B. T., Singh, A. D. A., Singh, A. N. A., & Singh, J. (2013b). A mindfulness-based smoking cessation program for individuals with mild intellectual disability. *Mindfulness, 4*, 148–157.

Singh, N. N., Lancioni, G. E., Winton, A. S. W., Karazsia, B. T., & Singh, J. (2013). Mindfulness training for teachers changes the behavior of their preschool students. *Research in Human Development, 10*(3), 211–233.

Singh, N. N., Lancioni, G. E., Winton, A. S. W., Singh, A. N., Adkins, A. D., & Singh, J. (2008b). Clinical and benefit-cost outcomes of teaching a mindfulness-based procedure to adult offenders with intellectual disabilities. *Behavior Modification, 32*, 622–637.

Singh, N. N., Lancioni, G. E., Winton, A. S. W., Singh, A. N., Adkins, A. D., & Singh, J. (2009). Mindful staff can reduce the use of physical restraints when providing care to individuals with intellectual disabilities. *Journal of Applied Research in Intellectual Disabilities, 22*, 194–202.

Singh, N. N., Lancioni, G. E., Winton, A. S. W., Singh, A. N., Singh, J., & Singh, A. D. A. (2011d). Effects of a mindfulness-based smoking cessation program for an adult with mild intellectual disability. *Research in Developmental Disabilities, 32*, 1180–1185.

Singh, N. N., Lancioni, G. E., Winton, A. S. W., Singh, J., Curtis, W. J., Wahler, R. G., & McAleavey, K. M. (2007d). Mindful parenting decreases aggression and increases social behavior in children with developmental disabilities. *Behavior Modification, 31*(6), 749–771.

Singh, N. N., Lancioni, G. E., Winton, A. S. W., Singh, J., Singh, A. N. A., & Singh, A. D. A. (2011e). Peer with intellectual disabilities as a mindfulness-based anger and aggression management therapist. *Research in Developmental Disabilities, 32*, 2690–2696.

Singh, N. N., Lancioni, G. E., Winton, A. S. W., Wahler, R. G., Singh, J., & Sage, M. (2004). Mindful caregiving increases happiness among individuals with profound multiple disabilities. *Research in Developmental Disabilities, 25*, 207–218.

Singh, N. N., & Singh, S. D. (2001). Developmental considerations in treatment. In H. Orvaschel, J. Faust, & M. Hersen (Eds.), *Handbook of conceptualization and treatment of child psychopathology* (pp. 9–38). Amsterdam, The Netherlands: Pergamon.

Singh, N. N., Wahler, R. G., Adkins, A. D., & Myers, R. E. (2003). Soles of the feet: A mindfulness-based self-control intervention for aggression by an individual with mild mental retardation and mental illness. *Research in Developmental Disabilities, 24*, 158–169.

Spek, A. A., van Ham, N., & Nyklíček, I. (2013). Mindfulness-based therapy in adults with an autism disorder: A randomized controlled trial. *Research in Developmental Disabilities, 34*, 246–253.

Tang, Y. Y., Hölzel, B. K., & Posner, M. I. (2015). The neuroscience of mindfulness meditation. *Nature Reviews Neuroscience, 16*(4), 213–215.

Tracy, J., & Hosken, R. (1997). The importance of smoking education and preventive health strategies for people with intellectual disability. *Journal of Intellectual Disability Research, 41*, 416–421.

van Houten, R., & Rolider, A. (1988). Recreating the scene: An effective way to provide delayed punishment for inappropriate motor behavior. *Journal of Applied Behavior Analysis, 21*, 187–192.

Yildiran, H., & Holt, R. R. (2014). Thematic analysis of the effectiveness of an inpatient mindfulness group for adults with intellectual disabilities. *British Journal of Learning Disabilities, 43*, 49–54.

Chapter 7

Mindfulness in mental health

Nirbhay N. Singh and Subhashni D. Singh Joy

Introduction

Like adults, many children and adolescents occasionally experience anxiety, worries, and fears. Some of these are linked to their changing developmental status, but when these problems become severe and persistent and interfere with daily activities either at home or school, or in the community, then they might be diagnosed as mental health problems or disorders. The prevalence of mental health problems in children and adolescents varies depending on the nature of the study and the population studied. In terms of frequency, the more commonly diagnosed mental disorders include attention deficit hyperactivity disorder (ADHD; 9.4%), general behavior problems or externalizing behaviors (7.4%), anxiety (7.1%), and depression (3.2%) (Centers for Disease Control and Prevention [CDC], 2013; Danielson et al., 2018). Comorbidity, or the co-occurrence of these disorders, is fairly common in children and adolescents, making life much more difficult for them. For example, of those with a primary diagnosis of depression, almost 74% also have anxiety and 48% have behavior problems; of those with anxiety, almost 38% have behavior problems and 33% have depression; and of those with behavior problems, almost 37% have anxiety and 21% also have depression (Danielson et al., 2018). Furthermore, rates of these disorders increase as children grow older. Most of the data on the prevalence of mental health disorders of children and adolescents are based on parent reports. While there is good concordance between parent-reported diagnoses and those based on medical records, it is likely that parent reports do not capture the full range of mental disorders in their children (Visser et al., 2013).

Given the prevalence of mental health problems in children and adolescents, there are many treatment options for specific disorders, with various degrees of evidence backing each one. In terms of psycho-pharmacological treatments for ADHD, stimulants (e.g., methylphenidate) have the best research evidence base for reducing the core symptoms of ADHD, followed by atomoxetine, extended-release guanfacine, and extended-release clonidine (Wolraich et al., 2019). Parent training in behavior management alone is the usual recommendation for the treatment of preschool children with ADHD (i.e., 6 years and younger) and when combined with medication for children older than 6 years. Additional interventions for school-age children may include specific behavioral interventions at home and at school.

Children and adolescents sometimes argue, get angry and aggressive, and engage in disruptive or destructive behaviors. When these behaviors become severe and cause serious problems at home, school, or in the community, they might be diagnosed as a mental disorder and fall within the general group of behaviors known as externalizing behaviors. Typically, the treatment of choice is behavioral interventions, with adjunctive medication as a default treatment when other interventions alone fail to produce adequate control of specific behavior problems, for example, physical aggression.

Anxiety disorders in children and adolescents include separation anxiety, specific phobia, social anxiety disorder, generalized anxiety disorder, panic disorder, and agoraphobia. Psychological interventions provide the first-line treatment for anxiety disorders in this population, with cognitive behavior therapy (CBT) having the best evidence base. Other interventions used alone or adjunctively with CBT include social skills training, relaxation, and problem solving. The short-term effects of psychopharmacological interventions on child and adolescent anxiety are on par with psychological treatment. Antidepressant medication (especially the selective serotonin reuptake inhibitors [SSRIs] and the serotonin norepinephrine reuptake inhibitors [SNRIs]) are somewhat effective in reducing anxiety symptoms, but the tricyclics and benzodiazepines have limited effects on anxiety symptoms in this population (Creswell et al., 2020). The long-term maintenance of treatment gains is unproven for either psychological or psychopharmacological treatments.

Pharmacotherapy is the first-line treatment for pediatric major depressive disorder (MDD), with SSRIs being the recommended treatment. The Food and Drug Administration (FDA) has approved only two antidepressants, fluoxetine and escitalopram, for pediatric MDD, and the National Institute for Health and Care Excellence guidelines (NICE, 2019) recommend fluoxetine as the drug of choice, but only in conjunction with psychotherapy. However, there does not appear to be strong evidence supportive of any particular drug over other SSRIs (Dwyer & Bloch, 2019). Psychotherapy is the treatment of choice for mild pediatric depression, typically without concurrent pharmacotherapy (National Institute for Health and Care Excellence, 2019), but its effects may be limited for pediatric MDD. A number of different modes of psychotherapy have proven effective for mild pediatric depression, including CBT, interpersonal psychotherapy for adolescents (IPT-A), short-term psychoanalytic psychotherapy (STPP), and brief psychosocial intervention (Eckshtain et al., 2019; Goodyer et al., 2017; Weersing et al., 2017). Although initial studies indicated superiority of combined psychotherapy and pharmacotherapy of pediatric MDD, recent studies have suggested that a complex set of interactive variables are involved, including doses of both treatments, as well as the nature of the components of psychotherapy that may contribute the most to positive outcomes (Davey et al., 2019; Goodyer et al., 2017; Scott et al., 2019). The evidence base for treating pediatric treatment-resistant depression is pretty slim for adolescents who have failed with first- and second-line treatments (Dwyer et al., 2020).

Children and adolescents present with a wide variety of mental health problems, although ADHD, externalizing behaviors, anxiety, and depression are the most common. The traditional interventions are pharmacotherapy and a range of psychotherapies, all with variable outcomes when provided alone and in combination. Recently, mindfulness-based programs have been developed specifically for this population or adapted from programs used with adults with mental health problems. In this chapter, we present a narrative review of this research. We will not review mindfulness-based programs used with children and adolescents specifically for ADHD because they have been presented by de Bruin et al. (2021) in Chapter 5 of this book. Specifically, we will present a review of mindfulness-based interventions for externalizing behaviors, anxiety, depression, multiple internalizing and externalizing conditions, substance use, and stress.

Mindfulness-based programs for externalizing behaviors

A small number of mindfulness-based programs and practices have been developed and evaluated for their effectiveness in managing externalizing behaviors (e.g., physical aggression, disruption, property destruction, conduct problems) in children and adolescents. In an early study, Bögels et al. (2008) provided an eight-week group mindfulness training to 14 clinically referred adolescents with a range of externalizing disorders that included ADHD, oppositional-defiant and/or conduct disorder, and autism spectrum disorder. In parallel, their parents received training in mindful parenting. Post-training assessments by both the adolescents and their parents showed statistically significant improvements on personal goals, attention, and awareness (i.e., indicators of enhanced mindfulness), impulsivity (suggesting increased inhibitory control), being attuned, social problems, and happiness. Furthermore, there were statistically significant reductions in internalizing and especially externalizing symptoms. These outcomes were maintained at eight-week follow-up. Given that this was an early study, there were several study limitations (e.g., use of a quasi-experimental design, no control condition, common method bias), but nonetheless it demonstrated that training in mindfulness could be a viable alternative to pharmacotherapy and psychotherapy for adolescents with externalizing behaviors.

Similar results were obtained in a follow-up study with adolescents with ADHD, but the effects decreased at 16-week follow-up (van de Weijer-Bergsma et al., 2012). In a third study in this series, van der Oord et al. (2012) provided an eight-week mindfulness training to children with ADHD, and parallel mindful parenting training to their parents. Parent ratings showed decreased ADHD behavior in the children following mindfulness training, with maintenance effects at the eight-week follow-up. However, independent teacher ratings indicated no generalization of the children's behavioral gains from home to school. Finally, a similar study by Haydicky et al. (2015) reported that parent ratings but not adolescents' self-ratings showed reductions in conduct problems and negative peer relations with training in mindfulness.

In a randomized wait-list trial, Semple et al. (2010) evaluated the effects of mindfulness-based cognitive therapy for children (MBCT-C) on social resiliency of elementary school-aged children. Twenty-five children were provided training in MBCT-C, which is a 12-week manualized program delivered in 90-min sessions, in a group format with up to eight children and one or two therapists. Furthermore, there was substantial involvement of the children's parents in all phases of the mindfulness training. Assessments were undertaken at pre- and post-training and at three-month follow-up. The results were mixed, with the clearest finding being reduction in attention-related problems. There was a strong hint of reduction in anxiety symptoms and behavior problems in those children who had clinically elevated levels of anxiety. The study had a few limitations, most notably the use of a wait-list control design that may conflate mindfulness training effects with a general treatment effect. Without an active control group comparison, purported intervention effects could have resulted from nonspecific factors such as quality of therapeutic alliance and relationship, empathy, being nonjudgmental, time spent with a reflective person, and so on. The strength of this study was that it demonstrated the promise of a manualized mindfulness-based training program for increasing social-emotional resilience in children.

In another wait-list control group study, Haydicky et al. (2012) evaluated the effects of a mindfulness-based program on adolescents with learning disabilities and co-occurring ADHD and anxiety. The multicomponent program included elements of mindfulness meditation, cognitive behavior therapy, behavior modification, and mixed martial arts. This 20-week program, delivered in 90-minute sessions, was designed to manage general problem behavior and increase self-awareness, self-control, adaptability, social skills, and self-defense skills in adolescents. Results were analyzed for subgroups of adolescents. For example, when compared to wait-list participants, those with co-occurring ADHD showed improvements in externalizing behavior, oppositional defiant problems, and conduct problems. In addition to the usual wait-list limitations, without a component analysis, there is no way of determining the effects of the mindfulness meditation component on treatment outcomes.

In a school-based study, Parker et al. (2014) assessed the effects of student participation in a customized mindfulness-based substance abuse prevention program (Master Mind) when compared to a wait-list control condition. Although there was no difference between the mindfulness and wait-list control participants on their intention to use alcohol or tobacco, the results indicated statistically significant reductions in aggression and social problems in both boys and girls, and anxiety only in the girls. Britton et al. (2014) evaluated the effects of a classroom-based meditation and an active control condition with sixth-grade children. The children were taught three meditation techniques (i.e., breath awareness; awareness of thoughts, feelings, and sensations; and body scan), and they could choose to use one of these during the final two weeks of a six-week mindfulness program. The active control condition was a six-week curriculum on ancient African history that included the construction of a three-dimensional life-sized model of a pharaoh's tomb to control for nonspecific effects in the mindfulness condition. Among several measures, externalizing behaviors as measured on the Youth Self-Report (YSR) rating scale significantly decreased under both conditions; however, there was no difference between the mindfulness and active control condition, suggesting the effects were probably due to nonspecific treatment factors. A strength of this study was that it used an experimental design that was a cut above the wait-list controls used in previous studies.

In a small series of studies, single mindfulness-based practices have been used to teach inhibitory control to children and adolescents for self-management of their anger and aggression. Anger and aggression are included in the constellation of externalizing behaviors that may lead to other mental health conditions. *Soles of the Feet* (SoF) is a mindfulness-based practice that enables a person to notice arising negative emotional arousal, pause, and then shift their attention from the emotionally arousing situation that may lead to anger to a neutral part of the body, the soles of their feet. Essentially, mastering the SoF practice enables the person to shift from an automatic reaction to an internal event (e.g., when a negative thought arises) or an external event (e.g., when someone says something that is hurtful) to a skillful mindful response. The time it takes the individual to shift their attention from the arising emotional thoughts or an event to a neutral place provides a pause, which enables the arising of a mindful response from a state of calmness (see the Felver & Singh, 2020 manual for using SoF in individual or group training).

Adolescents with conduct disorder evince aggressive behaviors that threaten or cause physical harm to others or engage in nonaggressive conduct that may result in disruptive or destructive behavior. In a multiple baseline design study, three adolescents were taught to use the SoF practice to manage their aggressive behavior at school (Singh et al., 2007). Training on SoF was provided for 15 minutes three times a week for four weeks. Following the training, their aggressive and collateral behaviors continued to be monitored for 25 weeks until the end of the school year. Results showed that the adolescents were able to inhibit their anger and physical aggression at school. In two related studies, adolescents with autism (Singh et al., 2011a) and Asperger syndrome (Singh et al., 2011b)—using DSM-IV-TR terminology (American Psychiatric Association, 2000)—were taught to engage in inhibitory control of their physical aggression using the SoF practice. The adolescents with autism successfully controlled their physical aggression and maintained it at near-zero levels during the three-year follow-up. Those with Asperger syndrome were able to eliminate their aggression and maintain the behavioral gains during the four-year follow-up.

In the initial SoF studies, experienced mindfulness teachers provided the training to the children and adolescents. In more recent studies, parents and teachers were taught to provide the training. For example, parents of adolescents with Prader-Willi syndrome were taught to use the SoF practice, to use it in their own lives, and when fluent in its use to teach it to their children (Singh et al., 2017b). The parents successfully taught their adolescents to use SoF to reduce verbal aggression to minimal levels and to eliminate physical aggression. The adolescents were able to maintain low rates of verbal aggression and zero rates of physical aggression during the 12-month follow-up. In a similar study, telehealth training was used to teach teachers to use the SoF practice and then to teach it to students with IDD in their classrooms (Singh et al., 2017a). The students learned and used the SoF practice to reduce verbal and physical aggression to very low levels and to maintain the behavioral gains during the 12-month follow-up. Ahemaitijiang et al. (2020) systematically replicated and extended the use of SoF practice with Chinese adolescents for aggressive and destructive behaviors. First, the mothers of these adolescents were taught the SoF practice, and once they achieved fluency in its use, they taught it to their own adolescents. Results, which were analyzed using weighted average Tau-U scores across the adolescents, showed significantly reduced verbal and physical aggression and destructive behaviors to near-zero levels. The adolescents were able to maintain their behavioral gains during the 12-month follow-up.

Two informal mindfulness-based practices have been used to teach inhibitory control to children and adolescents for self-management of verbal and physical aggression. In one study, Singh et al. (2018) taught children with autism spectrum disorder (ASD) to use SOBER Breathing Space to control their verbal and physical aggression in the family home and to assess whether it would generalize to the children's school environment in the absence of training being provided there. SOBER is an acronym: S = Stop, O = Observe, B = Breathe, E = Expand, and R = Respond. Thus, using SOBER Breathing Space requires a person to stop and be aware of what is happening in that moment, observe the physical sensations and emotional regulation changes in the body, breathe by deliberately bringing attention to the breath, expand awareness of the situation and potential skillful and unskillful response options, and then respond mindfully to the arising negative emotional arousal. Results indicated the children were able to reduce their verbal and physical aggression to near-zero levels and maintain them at these levels during the 12-month follow-up. In addition, there was generalization of their inhibitory control from home to school, without training in the school setting.

In the other study, Singh et al. (2019) taught adolescents with ASD to use Surfing the Urge, an informal mindfulness-based practice to overcome the urge to respond to a negative internal or external event with anger and aggression. This practice requires the person to move the focus of their attention from the urge to the breath and to use the breath like a surfboard to ride out the waves of urges by simply observing each urge with an open, equanimous, and curious attitude, without self-judgment, and with nonattachment to the urge. Mindful attention to the urge, without engaging in escape or avoidance, provides an alternative context for experiencing the negative event, thereby putting it on extinction. Results indicated that the adolescents were able to master this informal mindfulness-based practice and to reduce their verbal and physical aggression to very low levels. In addition, their psychiatrist was able to eliminate the use of psychotropic medications that had been prescribed for their uncontrolled physical aggression.

In sum, a range of formal and informal mindfulness-based interventions have been investigated for externalizing behavior, mainly for adolescents, and there is suggestive evidence that they may be effective. However, many studies were not methodologically robust enough from which generalizable conclusions can be drawn about their efficacy or effectiveness. Given that no single intervention has proven effective in the self-management of responses to negative emotional states, it is important to offer children and adolescents a number of equally effective options.

Mindfulness-based programs for anxiety

In an open clinical trial focused on feasibility and acceptability of a mindfulness-based training program for anxious children, Semple et al. (2005) provided group training for five elementary school children. Training was provided in 45-minute sessions, one session a week, for six weeks. The program was adapted from the standard mindfulness-based stress reduction (MBSR; Kabat-Zinn, 1990) and mindfulness-based cognitive therapy (MBCT; Segal et al., 2002) and structured to be developmentally appropriate for children 7 to 8 years of age. The results indicated that it was feasible to use a mindfulness-based program with anxious elementary-aged children. Each of the children improved in at least one area, which included academic functioning, internalizing problems, and externalizing problems. This study had the usual limitations of case studies, including small sample, pre- and posttest design, and no controls, but it was suggestive of the utility of mindfulness-based training in young children. In another early study, Beauchemin et al. (2008) tested the feasibility of a five-week mindfulness meditation program that was provided to 34 adolescents with learning disabilities. Results indicated feasibility and acceptability of the program, with decreased state and trait anxiety and enhanced social skills. However, the limitations inherent in the pre-post, no-control quasi-experimental design preclude any definitive conclusions about effectiveness.

In a pilot study, Cotton et al. (2016) reported the feasibility, acceptability, and preliminary findings of a trial of MBCT-C (Semple & Lee, 2011). The training was provided to only 10 adolescents in 12 weekly sessions, with the mindfulness exercises focusing on attention regulation and nonjudgmental acceptance of present moment thoughts, emotions, and experiences. Ratings by clinicians showed significant reductions in anxiety, the participants self-ratings indicated reduced trait anxiety, and parental ratings showed increased emotional regulation. The results indicated feasibility of the training program, and the parents and their children indicated high levels of acceptability and utility of the MBCT-C program.

Lam (2016) reported a pilot study using a wait-list control design to assess the effectiveness of a customized school-based cognitive mindfulness intervention for internalizing problems of young children (9- to 13-year-olds). The mindfulness program was adapted from at least four other programs to meet the developmental, cognitive, and cultural needs of the participants. Results indicated reduction in internalizing problems, including worry and generalized anxiety disorder. The majority of the participants rated the program as being helpful in handling emotions and interpersonal relationships.

In another pilot study, the effects of the standard MBSR course (Kabat-Zinn, 1990) were evaluated with eleventh-grade students and their teachers (Gouda et al., 2016). Three assessments were undertaken within a wait-list control design. Medium effect sizes were reported for mindfulness, anxiety, and creativity for the children, and similar effect sizes were reported for the teachers on anxiety and emotion regulation. While the results of these pilot studies are encouraging, the wait-list design limitations and absence of active control or comparison group require us to be cautious about drawing any general conclusions.

In a small open trial, Crowley et al. (2018) reported the feasibility, acceptability, and preliminary effectiveness of an after-school group mindfulness therapy (GMT) program for adolescents with anxiety problems. The GMT program included present moment awareness, mindfulness in everyday life (breathing, eating, walking), body scan, lovingkindness, and self-acceptance. The 10-week after school program was delivered to 12 sixth- and seventh-grade adolescents in 60-minute weekly sessions in a regular classroom. Results indicated large effect sizes for anxiety, internalizing problems, stress, and attention. While demonstrating feasibility and acceptability, little can be said about effectiveness from a pre-post quasi-experimental design study that did not include a control or comparison condition.

In a wait-list control group study, Lu et al. (2019) evaluated the effectiveness of a customized eight-week mindfulness program based on MBCT and MBSR protocols that was delivered weekly in one-hour sessions. The group sessions included mindful eating, body scan, mindfully working with Silly Putty, and group discussions. In addition, the program required the adolescents to complete 30- to 45-minute homework exercises. When compared to the wait-list control group, participants in the mindfulness group showed significant increment in their level of mindfulness as measured on the 15-item Chinese version of the Mindful Attention Awareness Scale (MAAS) and decreased social anxiety and suicidal ideation. Even though this study endeavored to provide better controls, it still suffered from shortcomings of the wait-list design, common method bias (use of only self-rating scales), and the use of MAAS as a measure of mindfulness.

In sum, there is reason for optimism that anxiety in children and adolescents may be responsive to training in mindfulness, but the data are minimal and derived mainly from pilot and feasibility studies. Robust randomized controlled trials (RCTs) would be the next step in this area of research.

Mindfulness-based programs for depression

In a school-based study, Joyce et al. (2010) assessed the effects of a 10-week, 45-minute per session, customized mindfulness program on children aged 10 to 12 years. This was a pre-post study with no control or comparison group, with the teachers taught to deliver the course materials in the best way they could within the existing classroom conditions. Results indicated a decrease in the children's self-rated depression score on the Children's Depression Inventory (CDI; Kovacs, 2003). Although the data are suggestive of positive effects of the mindfulness program, the study suffered from design limitations that preclude any conclusions about effectiveness.

In a pilot study, Lau and Hue (2011) assessed the effects of a six-week mindfulness program that was modified and culturally adapted from the standard MBSR program on well-being, stress, and depressive symptoms of 14- to 16-year-old students in Hong Kong. The six-week mindfulness program was delivered in two-hour weekly sessions. Outcomes were based on self-ratings by the students. When compared to the students in the control condition, those receiving mindfulness training showed significant reduction in depressive symptoms. There was no significant difference between the two groups on perceived stress, but there were comparable changes on one dimension of well-being. The authors noted the need for implementing the mindfulness program in school settings in a more tightly controlled study that includes appropriate outcome measures and avoids common method bias.

In a nonrandomized feasibility study, Kuyken et al. (2013) assessed the acceptability and effectiveness of the Mindfulness in Schools Programme (MiSP) with 12- to 16-year-old students against a matched control group of students. The MiSP, a nine-week program, is designed to be taught as a universal intervention by integrating it within a school's standard curriculum. Six schools participated in the MiSP training, and these schools were matched to a control school. Results indicated high acceptability of MiSP. When compared to the control participants, those in the MiSP training reported fewer depressive symptoms and lower stress at post-treatment and two-month follow-up. The results are supportive of MiSP in decreasing internalizing problems of students, although the possibility of common method bias and reference bias problems may be limiting factors that should be addressed in future studies.

In another acceptability study, Ames et al. (2014) assessed the effects of MBCT adapted for adolescents on their depressive symptoms. This was a very small study in which only 7 of 11 adolescents recruited for the study completed the mindfulness training. Qualitative data indicated that the program was acceptable to the participants, and quantitative data indicated reductions in depressive symptoms in this clinical sample of adolescents. The findings are limited because of the shortcomings of a quasi-experimental design, which did not include a control or comparison condition.

In a recent pilot study, Bluth et al. (2016) reported the feasibility and acceptability of the Learning to BREATHE school-based mindfulness program (Broderick, 2013) in an ethnically diverse student population. The mindfulness program was delivered over 11 sessions to 14 students, and outcomes were compared to those of 13 control group students who did not receive such training. Results indicated reductions in self-reported depression only in those students who received mindfulness training. The results are encouraging and bear replication with a larger sample size.

In a cluster-randomized controlled trial, Raes et al. (2014) assessed the efficacy of a group mindfulness program for reducing and preventing depression in an adolescent school-based population. The mindfulness program included elements of the standard MBCT and MBSR programs and was delivered weekly in eight 100-minute sessions with homework assignments. The students in both the active and control conditions provided self-ratings of depression at baseline, post-mindfulness training, and at a six-month follow-up. Results showed statistically significant reductions in depressive symptoms at post-training and six-month follow-up only in the group of adolescents who received training in mindfulness. This was a well-controlled trial of mindfulness-based training for adolescents with depression.

In sum, the research on mindfulness-based programs for depression in children and adolescents is very much at the feasibility and acceptability stage. However, the emerging data are positive for the effects of mindfulness training on depressive symptoms, and further well-controlled studies are needed, especially with clinical populations of children and adolescents.

Mindfulness-based programs for multiple conditions

A number of research studies assessed the effectiveness of MBSR for multiple adolescent conditions. For example, Biegel et al. (2009) reported an RCT in which the effects of a modified MBSR program were evaluated against a wait-list control that received treatment as usual. The participants were 14- to 18-year-olds from an outpatient child and adolescent psychiatry clinic. Given that all participants were under psychiatric care at the time of study entry, the

MBSR training was provided as an adjunct to standard care only for those in the active condition. The eight-week MBSR course was provided for two hours each week, with 20- to 35-minute at-home mindfulness practice and no daylong retreat. A broad range of self-reported assessments were taken at pretest, posttest, and three-month follow-up. When compared to the control condition, adolescents in the MBSR group reported reduced symptoms of anxiety, depression, and somatic distress and increased self-esteem and sleep quality. To counter common method bias, condition-naive clinicians also rated the adolescents' conditions. Their ratings showed MBSR participants had a higher percentage of diagnostic improvement during the study period and significant increases in global functioning when compared to the control participants. This study provided evidence of the beneficial effects of MBSR on a broad range of adolescent mental health variables. However, these findings should be interpreted cautiously because of the limitations of a wait-list design and the possible interactive effects of psychiatric treatment and MBSR training.

In a small RCT, with an active control condition, Sibinga et al. (2013) tested the effects of a modified MBSR program with 42 seventh- and eighth-grade boys, with 95% being African American. When compared to the boys in the active control condition, those in the MBSR group had less anxiety and rumination following mindfulness training. A comparison of pretest and post-program salivary cortisol levels showed that stress remained stable for those in the MBSR condition but increased for those in the active control condition. These results were essentially confirmed in a large-scale replication of this study with 300 fifth- to eighth-grade urban public school students (Sibinga et al., 2016). When compared to the control group of students, those receiving MBSR had significantly lower levels of somatization, depression, negative affect, rumination, self-hostility, and severity of post-traumatic symptoms. Given self-ratings on multiple mental health rating scales, there may have been common method bias in the reported data.

In a small feasibility study, Bennett and Dorjee (2016) evaluated the effects of MBSR on depression, anxiety, and academic attainment of 16- to 18-year-old students in a longitudinal nonequivalent group design study. Reported attendance at MBSR training was high (94%), attrition was low (1 of the 11 participants dropped out), and most of the participants (90%) would recommend the course to others. When compared to the control group, those in the MBSR group had lower depression scores at posttest and at three-month follow-up and lower anxiety at follow-up. Only the MBSR group had a medium-sized effect on academic attainment. The preliminary outcome data are positive, but the sample size and design limitations preclude any general conclusions. Finally, the beneficial effects of MBSR were reported in a qualitative study with adolescents with serious mental health concerns (van Vliet et al., 2017). The themes that emerged from semi-structured interviews included improved mood, enhanced relationship with self, increased self-control, improved problem-solving, awareness of the present, and enhanced interpersonal relationships.

In addition to MBSR, other mindfulness-based programs have been used with children and adolescents with multiple conditions. In a feasibility study, Vickery and Dorjee (2016) investigated the acceptability and emotional well-being outcomes of the eight-week *Paws b* mindfulness program for children 7 to 9 years old. The teachers were trained to deliver the program within the regular school curriculum. Three schools were involved, with the first two being assigned to the mindfulness training and the third to the control group. The children in both groups completed a brief demographic questionnaire, four outcome rating scales, and an acceptability questionnaire. Both parents and teachers completed a rating scale for executive function, taking into account the child's executive functioning during the previous six months. A majority of the participating children gave the program high acceptability score and indicated that they wished to continue with the mindfulness program at school. When compared to the control participants, those in the mindfulness training condition showed significant decreases in negative affect at follow-up and improved their metacognition. The results are encouraging, but the study suffered from nonrandomization of the children, reference bias due to schools being assigned to either the active or control condition, and common method bias due to only the students rating the mindfulness and mental health rating scales.

In an RCT, Johnson et al. (2016) assessed the effectiveness of *Dot b*, a school-based mindfulness program, on anxiety, depression, and eating disorder risk factors in young adolescents. Classes within each school were randomized into active and control conditions, with the mindfulness training conducted in the classroom and practice at home. Assessments were scheduled at pretest, posttest, and follow-up at 11 weeks post-training. Training was provided in eight lessons of 35- to 60-minute sessions. While the mindfulness program was acceptable, there were no differential effects between the two conditions on any of the outcome variables at posttest and 11-week follow-up.

In another evaluation of the *Dot b* program, Santa Maria et al. (2020) provided mindfulness training to sheltered youth experiencing homelessness in a pretest-posttest quasi-experimental design. Given the short length of stay of the adolescents in the shelter environment, the training was delivered in five sessions within a 2.5-week period. The adolescents rated the acceptability of the mindfulness program and delivery format highly, and their self-ratings showed significant pre-post training differences in frustration, restlessness, stress, depression, boredom, and mindfulness. The study was limited due to small sample size and use of quasi-experimental design.

In sum, several but not all group design studies have reported positive findings on the purported effects of mindfulness-based programs on multiple adolescent mental health and other conditions. The studies were concerned mainly with feasibility and acceptability, and future research would do well to assess the effects of the mindfulness-based programs against active control or comparison groups in RCTs.

Mindfulness-based programs for substance use

In a systematic review of intervention studies, Chiesa and Serretti (2014) concluded that mindfulness-based interventions are effective in reducing the use of a number of substances including alcohol, cocaine, amphetamines, marijuana, cigarettes, and opiates when compared to wait-list controls, nonspecific educational support groups, and some specific control groups. In addition, there was a hint in some studies that mindfulness-based interventions may be effective in reducing craving for these substances as well. However, the findings were based on studies that left much to be desired in terms of methodological robustness of the studies. Furthermore, with respect to the present context, of note is that of the 24 studies reviewed, all included adult participants. Mindfulness-based interventions for adolescents still remain a rarity, and we review what little is currently available.

In an early study, Himelstein (2011) reported on open trial of a customized eight-week mindfulness-based substance use program with 48 incarcerated youth. The mindfulness training was provided once a week in 90-minute sessions in a group format of 8 to 12 participants. Results indicated that it was feasible to run mindfulness groups with incarcerated youths in terms of attendance (80%) and receptivity of the course by the participants. Impulsivity decreased and perceived risk of drug use *increased* from pretest to posttest. Given the limitations of the research design and common method bias (given self-ratings by the participants), the best that can be said is that it is feasible to use mindfulness-based programs in juvenile justice settings, which by itself is a promising finding. Although variations of this kind of research have been reported (e.g., Himelstein et al., 2012, 2015), with the mindfulness training being adjunct to psychotherapy, none have included data on whether the mindfulness training actually makes a difference to the participants' substance use following training or discharge from the juvenile facility.

The additive effects of mindfulness meditation (MM) were assessed in a three-arm RCT across classes in six schools, with 404 of 468 adolescents 13 to 17 years of age completing the study (Patton et al., 2019). The three interventions included universal cognitive-behavioral therapy (CBT) plus progressive muscle relaxation (PMR), CBT plus MM, and assessment only control condition. The interventions ranged from 110 mins to 210 minutes (mean = 173 mins) across the schools, with training provided in groups of 8 to 23 students. The outcomes were self-rated by the students and took 80 minutes to complete. Assessments were scheduled at four times: pretraining, post-training, three-month follow-up, and six-month follow-up, and included alcohol use, alcohol-related cognitions, impulsivity, family affluence, and mindfulness. Results indicated that while both active interventions were equally effective for reducing the rate of alcohol consumption and for increasing negative alcohol expectancies, neither had any effect on mindfulness, drinking refusal self-efficacy, or impulsivity. Essentially, there were no additive effects of mindfulness meditation on any of the measured variables. Although this was a well-controlled study, it had its limitations as well, such as that psychology graduate students delivered the interventions, the mindfulness intervention was not fully described and thus cannot be replicated, the training time was too short, and all outcomes were self-rated (with the possibility of common method bias being a confounding factor). Furthermore, there is strong suggestion in the literature that the mindfulness rating scale used in this study may actually measure acting with awareness rather than mindfulness per se.

In sum, research on mindfulness-based programs for substance use or addictions in child and adolescent populations has barely begun, and thus not much can be said about its present status. There is a scattering of intervention studies in such areas as adolescent smoking (Pbert et al., 2020) and eating disorders (e.g., Atkinson & Wade, 2015), but not enough to provide a meaningful review at present.

Mindfulness-based programs for stress

Stress occurs in the rhythm of our life across the lifespan. Up to a certain level, stress can energize us to respond in a meaningful way to the ups and downs of life, but when it becomes chronic it can lead to mental health problems. For children and adolescents, family issues such as discord or divorce and the demands of school, bullying, and anxiety about academic performance may lead to chronic stress. In addition, developmental and social changes during adolescence may result in chronic stress among adolescents. In a nationwide study, teens reported experiencing emotional and physical symptoms of stress, including feeling irritable or angry, nervous, or anxious (American Psychological Association, 2014). Given that chronic stress can be a precursor to mental health problems, stress has been the target of some mindfulness-based programs in children and adolescents. We briefly touch on this research for the sake of completeness.

In a feasibility study, Mendelson et al. (2010) instituted a 12-week school-based mindfulness and yoga program for 97 fourth- and fifth-grade students in urban public schools. Results showed that the program was feasible and acceptable to the students, teachers, and school administrators. In addition, outcome data from the study indicated that the students were able to reduce their rumination, intrusive thoughts, and emotional arousal due to stress. In a similar study, White (2012) provided mindfulness training through yoga to 155 fourth- and fifth-grade public school girls. The eight-week program was run weekly, for an hour, in a group format with 10 minutes of daily homework. When compared to a control group, the girls in the mindfulness group reported greater appraisal of stress and frequency of coping. In an exploratory study, Costello and Lawler (2014) assessed the effects of a customized five-week school-based mindfulness intervention with 63 primary school children (11–12 years old). Although there was a significant decrease in the children's stress scores on the Perceived Stress Scale (Cohen et al., 1983), the absolute level of stress still remained high. In a stress prevention study, van de Weijer-Bergsma et al. (2014) assessed the effects of a school-based mindfulness training program with 208 elementary school children aged 8 to 12 years. The six-week mindfulness program was delivered in 12 30-minute sessions. Results indicated preventive effects of the mindfulness program on stress, well-being, and behavior of the children based on self- and parent-reports. If this study can be replicated in a robust RCT, with adequate controls for nonspecific factors, it certainly has public health implications for school-based mindfulness programs for children and adolescents.

Conclusions

We know from the current research literature that mindfulness-based programs can be effective in ameliorating a number of mental health disorders in adults. Similar research with children and adolescents is just emerging. Extant research is relatively meager in this population and appears to be still at the feasibility and acceptability stage, with most studies being pilot studies. Unfortunately, even the feasibility studies are rather weak and are not well designed to truly assess many of its essential components. Future studies should be grounded within a model of feasibility research, such as that proposed by Bowen et al. (2009), so that the findings can better inform the development of RCTs. What research is available is strongly suggestive of positive effects of mindfulness-based programs on the mental health of children and adolescents. However, methodology has been a major weakness even in the few RCTs that have been conducted in this population. This is to be expected in an emerging field, and especially one in which the participants experience developmental issues as confounding factors. But on balance, the field is ripe for the next generation of research with children and adolescents who have mental health concerns.

References

Ahemaitijiang, N., Hu, X., Yang, X., & Han, Z. H. (2020). Effects of meditation on the soles of the feet on aggressive and destructive behaviors of Chinese adolescents with autism spectrum disorders. *Mindfulness, 11*, 230–240.

American Psychiatric Association. (2000). *Diagnostic and statistical manual of mental disorders* (4th ed., text rev.). Washington, DC: Author.

American Psychological Association. (2014). *Stress in America: Are teens adopting adults' stress habits?* Washington, DC: Author.

Ames, C. S., Richardson, J., Payne, S., Smith, P., & Leigh, E. (2014). Innovations in practice: Mindfulness-based cognitive therapy for depression in adolescents. *Child and Adolescent Mental Health, 19*(1), 74–78.

Atkinson, M. J., & Wade, T. D. (2015). Mindfulness-based prevention for eating disorders: A school-based cluster randomized controlled study. *International Journal of Eating Disorders, 48*(7), 1024–1037.

Beauchemin, J., Hutchins, T. L., & Patterson, F. (2008). Mindfulness meditation may lessen anxiety, promote social skills, and improve academic performance among adolescents with learning disabilities. *Complementary Health Practice Review, 13*(1), 34–45.

Bennett, K., & Dorjee, D. (2016). The impact of a mindfulness-based stress reduction course (MBSR) on well-being and academic attainment of sixth-form students. *Mindfulness, 7*, 105–114.

Biegel, G. M., Brown, K. W., Shapiro, S. L., & Schubert, C. M. (2009). Mindfulness-based stress reduction for the treatment of adolescent psychiatric outpatients: A randomized clinical trial. *Journal of Consulting and Clinical Psychology*, 77(5), 855–866.

Bluth, K., Campo, R. A., Pruteanu-Malinici, S., Reams, A., Mullarkey, M., & Broderick, P. C. (2016). A school-based mindfulness pilot study for ethnically diverse at-risk adolescents. *Mindfulness*, 7, 90–104.

Bögels, S. M., Hoogstad, B., van Dun, L., de Schutter, S., & Restifo, K. (2008). Mindfulness training for adolescents with externalizing disorders and their parents. *Behavioural and Cognitive Psychotherapy, 36*(2), 193–209.

Bowen, D. J., Kreuter, M., Spring, B., Cofta-Woerpel, L., Linnan, L., Weiner, D., . . Fernandez, M. (2009). How we design feasibility studies. *American Journal of Preventive Medicine, 36*(5), 452–457.

Britton, W. B., Lepp, N. E., Niles, H. F., Rocha, T., Fisher, N. E., & Gold, J. S. (2014). A randomized controlled pilot trial of classroom-based mindfulness meditation compared to an active control condition in sixth-grade children. *Journal of School Psychology, 52*, 263–278.

Broderick, P. (2013). *Learning to BREATHE: A mindfulness curriculum for adolescents to cultivate emotion regulation, attention, and performance.* Oakland, CA: New Harbinger Publications.

Centers for Disease Control and Prevention. (2013). Mental health surveillance among children—United States, 2005–2011. *Morbidity and Mortality Weekly Report, 62*(Suppl; May 16), 1–35.

Chiesa, A., & Serretti, A. (2014). Are mindfulness-based interventions effective for substance abuse disorders? A systematic review of the evidence. *Substance Use & Misuse, 49*, 492–512.

Cohen, S., Kamarck, T., & Mermelstein, R. (1983). A global measure of perceived stress. *Journal of Health and Social Behavior, 24*(4), 385–396.

Costello, E., & Lawler, M. (2014). An exploratory study of the effects of mindfulness on perceived levels of stress among school children from lower socioeconomic backgrounds. *International Journal of Emotional Education, 6*(2), 21–39.

Cotton, S., Luberto, C. M., Sears, R. W., Strawn, J. R., Stahl, L., Wasson, R. S., & Delbello, M. P. (2016). Mindfulness-based cognitive therapy for youth with anxiety disorders at risk for bipolar disorder: A pilot trial. *Early Intervention in Psychiatry, 10*(5), 426–434.

Creswell, C., Waite, P., & Hudson, J. (2020). Anxiety disorders in children and young people—assessment and treatment. *Journal of Child Psychology and Psychiatry, 61*(6), 628–643.

Crowley, M. J., Nicholls, S. S., McCarthy, D., Greatorex, K., Wu, J., & Mayes, L. C. (2018). Group mindfulness for adolescent anxiety: Results of an open trial. *Child and Adolescent Mental Health, 23*(2), 130–133.

Danielson, M. L., Bitsko, R. H., Ghandour, R. M., Holbrook, J. R., & Blumberg, S. J. (2018). Prevalence of parent-reported ADHD diagnosis and associated treatment among U.S. children and adolescents, 2016. *Journal of Clinical Child and Adolescent Psychology, 47*, 199–212.

Davey, C. G., Chanen, A. M., Hetrick, S. E., Cotton, S. M., Ratheesh, A., Amminger, G. P., . . Berk, M. (2019). The addition of fluoxetine to cognitive behavioural therapy for youth depression (YoDA-C): A randomised, double-blind, placebo-controlled, multicentre clinical trial. *Lancet Psychiatry, 6*, 735–744.

de Bruin, E. I., Meppelink, R., & Bögels, S. (2021). Mindfulness in attention-deficit hyperactivity disorder. In N. N. Singh & S. D. Singh Joy (Eds.), *Mindfulness-based interventions with children and adolescents: Research and practice* (pp. 74–95). London, UK: Routledge.

Dwyer, J. B., & Bloch, M. H. (2019). Antidepressants for pediatric patients. *Current Psychiatry, 18*, 26–42.

Dwyer, J. B., Stringaris, A., Brent, D. A., & Bloch, M. H. (2020). Defining and treating pediatric treatment-resistant depression. *Journal of Child Psychology and Psychiatry, 61*(3), 312–332.

Eckshtain, D., Kuppens, S., Ugueto, A., Ng, M. Y., Vaughn-Coaxum, R., Corteselli, K., & Weisz, J. R. (2019). Meta-analysis: 13-Year follow-up of psychotherapy effects on youth depression. *Journal of the American Academy of Child and Adolescent Psychiatry, 59*, 45–63.

Felver, J. C., & Singh, N. N. (2020). *Mindfulness in the classroom: An evidenced-based program to reduce disruptive behavior and increase academic engagement*. Oakland, CA: New Harbinger Publications.

Goodyer, I. M., Reynolds, S., Barrett, B., Byford, S., Dubicka, B., Hill, J., . . Fonagy, P. (2017). Cognitive behavioural therapy and short-term psychoanalytical psychotherapy versus a brief psychosocial intervention in adolescents with unipolar major depressive disorder (IMPACT): A multicentre, pragmatic, observer-blind, randomised controlled superiority trial. *Lancet Psychiatry, 4*, 109–119.

Gouda, S., Luong, M. T., Schmidt, S., & Bauer, J. (2016). Students and teachers benefit from mindfulness-based stress reduction in a school-embedded pilot study. *Frontiers in Psychology*, 7(590), 1–18.

Haydicky, J., Shecter, C., Wiener, J., & Ducharme, J. M. (2015). Evaluation of MBCT for adolescents with ADHD and their parents: Impact on individual and family functioning. *Journal of Child and Family Studies, 24*(1), 76–94.

Haydicky, J., Wiener, J., Badali, P., Milligan, K., & Ducharme, J. M. (2012). Evaluation of a mindfulness-based intervention for adolescents with learning disabilities and co-occurring ADHD and anxiety. *Mindfulness, 3*, 151–164.

Himelstein, S. (2011). Mindfulness-based substance abuse treatment for incarcerated youth: A mixed method pilot study. *International Journal of Transpersonal Studies, 30*(1 & 2), 1–10.

Himelstein, S., Hastings, A., Shapiro, S., & Heery, M. (2012). A qualitative investigation of the experience of a mindfulness-based intervention with incarcerated adolescents. *Child and Adolescent Mental Health, 17*(4), 231–237.

Himelstein, S., Saul, S., & Garcia-Romeu, A. (2015). Does mindfulness meditation increase effectiveness of substance abuse treatment with incarcerated youth? A pilot randomized controlled trial. *Mindfulness, 6*(6), 1472–1480.

Johnson, C., Burke, C., Brinkman, S., & Wade, T. (2016). Effectiveness of a school-based mindfulness program for transdiagnostic prevention in young adolescents. *Behaviour Research and Therapy, 81*, 1–11.

Joyce, A., Etty-Leal, J., Zazryn, T., Hamilton, A., & Hassed, C. (2010). Exploring a mindfulness meditation program on the mental health of upper primary children: A pilot study. *Advances in School Mental Health Promotion, 3*(2), 17–25.

Kabat-Zinn, J. (1990). *Full catastrophe living: Using the wisdom of your body and mind to face stress, pain, and illness*. New York, NY: Delta.

Kovacs, M. (2003). *Children's depression inventory* (CDI). Toronto: Multi-Health Systems.

Kuyken, W., Weare, K., Ukoumunne, O. C., Vicary, R., Morton, N., Burnett, R., . . Huppert, F. (2013). Effectiveness of the mindfulness in schools programme: Non-randomised controlled feasibility study. *British Journal of Psychiatry, 203*, 126–131.

Lam, K. (2016). School-based cognitive mindfulness intervention for internalizing problems: Pilot study with Hong Kong elementary students. *Journal of Child and Family Studies, 25*, 3293–3308.

Lau, N.-S., & Hue, M.-T. (2011). Preliminary outcomes of a mindfulness- based programme for Hong Kong adolescents in schools: Well-being, stress and depressive symptoms. *International Journal of Children's Spirituality, 16*(4), 315–330.

Lu, R., Zhou, Y., Wu, Q., Peng, X., Dong, J., Zhu, Z., & Xu, W. (2019). The effects of mindfulness training on suicide ideation among left-behind children in China: A randomized controlled trial. *Child: Care, Health, and Development, 45*(3), 371–379.

Mendelson, T., Greenberg, M. T., Dariotis, J. K., Feagans Gould, L., Rhodas, B. L., & Lead, P. J. (2010). Feasibility and preliminary outcomes of a school-based mindfulness intervention for urban youth. *Journal of Abnormal Child Psychology, 38*(7), 985–994.

National Institute for Health and Care Excellence. (2019). *Depression in children and young people: Identification and management*. NICE Guidelines. Available from: www.nice.org.uk/guidance/ng134/chapter/Recommendations-step-3-managing-mild-depression.

Parker, A. E., Kupersmidt, J. B., Mathis, E. T., Scull, T. M., & Sims, C. (2014). The impact of mindfulness education on elementary school students: Evaluation of the master mind programme. *Advances in School Mental Health Promotion*, 7(3), 184–204.

Patton, K. A., Connor, J. P., Sheffield, J., Wood, A., & Gullo, M. J. (2019). Additive effectiveness of mindfulness meditation to a school-based brief cognitive—behavioral alcohol intervention for adolescents. *Journal of Consulting and Clinical Psychology, 87*(5), 407–421.

Pbert, L., Druker, S., Crawford, S., Frisard, C., Trivedi, M., Osganian, S. K., & Brewer, J. (2020). Feasibility of a smartphone app with mindfulness training for adolescent smoking cessation: Craving to Quit (C2Q)-Teen. *Mindfulness, 11*, 720–733.

Raes, F., Griffith, J. W., van der Gucht, K., & Williams, J. M. G. (2014). School-based prevention and reduction of depression in adolescents: A cluster-randomized controlled trial of a mindfulness group program. *Mindfulness, 5*, 477–486.

Santa Maria, D., Cuccaro, P., Bender, K., Cron, S., Fine, M., & Sibinga, E. (2020). Feasibility of a mindfulness-based intervention with sheltered youth experiencing homelessness. *Journal of Child and Family Studies, 29*, 261–272.

Scott, K., Lewis, C. C., & Marti, C. N. (2019). Trajectories of symptom change in the treatment for adolescents with depression study. *Journal of the American Academy of Child and Adolescent Psychiatry, 58*, 319–328.

Segal, Z. V., Williams, J. M. G., & Teasdale, J. D. (2002). *Mindfulness-based cognitive therapy for depression*. New York, NY: Guilford Press.

Semple, R. J., & Lee, J. (2011). *Mindfulness-based cognitive therapy for anxious children: A manual for treating childhood anxiety*. Oakland, CA: New Harbinger Publications.

Semple, R. J., Lee, J., Rosa, D., & Miller, L. F. (2010). A randomised trial of mindfulness-based cognitive therapy for children: Promoting mindful attention to enhance social-emotional resiliency in children. *Journal of Child and Family Studies, 19*, 218–229.

Semple, R. J., Reid, E. F. G., & Miller, L. (2005). Treating anxiety with mindfulness: An open trial of mindfulness training for anxious children. *Journal of Cognitive Psychotherapy: An International Quarterly, 19*(4), 379–392.

Sibinga, E. M. S., Perry-Parrish, C., Chung, S.-E., Johnson, S. B., Smith, M., &Ellen, J. M. (2013). School-based mindfulness instruction for urban male youth: A small randomized controlled trial. *Preventive Medicine, 57*, 799–801.

Sibinga, E. M. S., Webb, L., Ghazarian, S. R., & Ellen, J. M. (2016). School-based mindfulness instruction: An RCT. *Pediatrics, 137*(1), Article e20152532.

Singh, N. N., Chan, J., Karazsia, B. T., McPherson, C. L., & Jackman, M. M. (2017a). Telehealth training of teachers to teach a mindfulness-based procedure for self-management of aggressive behavior to students with intellectual and developmental disabilities. *International Journal of Developmental Disabilities, 63*(4), 195–203.

Singh, N. N., Lancioni, G. E., Joy, S. D., Winton, A. S., Sabaawi, M., Wahler, R. G., & Singh, J. (2007). Adolescents with conduct disorder can be mindful of their aggressive behavior. *Journal of Emotional and Behavioral Disorders, 15*(1), 56–63.

Singh, N. N., Lancioni, G. E., Karazsia, B. T., Myers, R. E., Kim, E., Chan, J., . . Janson, M. (2019). Surfing the Urge: An informal mindfulness practice for the self-management of aggression by adolescents with autism spectrum disorder. *Journal of Contextual Behavioral Science, 12*, 170–177.

Singh, N. N., Lancioni, G. E., Manikam, R., Winton, A. S., Singh, A. N., Singh, J., & Singh, A. D. (2011a). A mindfulness-based strategy for self-management of aggressive behavior in adolescents with autism. *Research in Autism Spectrum Disorders, 5*(3), 1153–1158.

Singh, N. N., Lancioni, G. E., Myers, R. M., Karazsia, B. T., Courtney, T. M., & Nugent, K. (2017b). A mindfulness-based intervention for self-management of verbal and physical aggression by adolescents with Prader-Willi syndrome. *Developmental Neurorehabilitation, 20*(5), 253–260.

Singh, N. N., Lancioni, G. E., Myers, R. M., Karazsia, B. T., McPherson, C. L., Jackman, M. M., . . Thompson, T. (2018). Effects of SOBER breathing space on aggression in children with autism spectrum disorder and collateral effects on parental use of physical restraints. *Advances in Neurodevelopmental Disorders, 2*, 362–374.

Singh, N. N., Lancioni, G. E., Singh, A. D., Winton, A. S., Singh, A. N., & Singh, J. (2011b). Adolescents with Asperger syndrome can use a mindfulness-based strategy to control their aggressive behavior. *Research in Autism Spectrum Disorders, 5*(3), 1103–1109.

van de Weijer-Bergsma, E., Formsma, A. R., Bruin, E. I., & Bögels, S. M. (2012). The effectiveness of mindfulness training on behavioral problems and attentional functioning in adolescents with ADHD. *Journal of Child and Family Studies, 21*(5), 775–787.

van de Weijer-Bergsma, E., Langenberg, G., Brandsma, R., Oort, F. J., & Bögels, S. M. (2014). The effectiveness of a school-based mindfulness training as a programme to prevent stress in elementary school children. *Mindfulness, 5*, 238–248.

van der Oord, S., Bögels, S. M., & Peijnenburg, D. (2012). The effectiveness of mindfulness training for children with ADHD and mindful parenting for their parents. *Journal of Child and Family Studies, 21*, 139–147.

van Vliet, K. J., Foskett, A. J., Williams, J. L., Singhal, A., Dolcos, F., & Vohra, S. (2017). Impact of a mindfulness-based stress reduction program from the perspective of adolescents with serious mental health concerns. *Child and Adolescent Mental Health, 22*(1), 16–22.

Vickery, C., & Dorjee, D. (2016). Mindfulness training in primary schools decreases negative affect and increases meta-cognition in children. *Frontiers in Psychology, 6*, 2025.

Visser, S. N., Danielson, M. L., Bitsko, R. H., Perou, R., & Blumberg, S. J. (2013). Convergent validity of parent-reported attention-deficit/hyperactivity disorder diagnosis: A cross-study comparison. *JAMA Pediatrics, 167*(7), 674–675.

Weersing, V. R., Jeffreys, M., Do, M. T., Schwartz, K. T., & Bolano, C. (2017). Evidence base update of psychosocial treatments for child and adolescent depression. *Journal of Clinical Child & Adolescent Psychology*, *46*, 11–43.

White, L. S. (2012). Reducing stress in school-age girls through mindful yoga. *Journal of Pediatric Health Care*, *26*(1), 45–56.

Wolraich, M. L., Hagan, J. F., Allan, C., Chan, E., Davison, D., Earls, M., . . Zurhellen, W. (2019). Clinical practice guideline for the diagnosis, evaluation, and treatment of attention-deficit/hyperactivity disorder in children and adolescents. *Pediatrics*, *144*(4), Article e20192528.

Part III

Practice

Chapter 8

Teaching mindfulness to children

Monica M. Jackman

Introduction

With the rise of contemplative practices in schools, the early studies focused more on yoga than on meditation with children (Erwin & Robinson, 2016). The reported benefits for the children in these studies included enhanced focus and attention, self-regulation, and social-emotional learning. Although these studies suffered from methodological limitations and their findings should be interpreted with caution, what is clear is that young children can learn contemplative practices, including mindful yoga and basic meditation practices (Greenberg & Harris, 2012; Razza et al., 2015).

More recent studies, some better controlled than others, have shown that children can learn a number of mindfulness practices. A small series of studies showed that the MindUP™ (Hawn Foundation, 2011) curriculum can be successfully taught to children and adolescents. For example, Schonert-Reichl et al. (2015) used the program in a randomized controlled trial with fourth- and fifth-graders (age range: 9 to 12 years). Thierry et al. (2016) used it with preschool children (mean age: 4.56 years), and Thierry et al. (2018) used a shorter version of the program with pre-kindergarten children. At its core, MindUp is a social-emotional learning program that incorporates mindfulness practices. Thierry et al. (2016) used the 15-lesson version of the MindUp curriculum, which is divided into four units. Unit 1 ("Quieting the Mind, Sharpening the Focus") includes three lessons: about the brain; introduction to mindfulness; and focusing our awareness. Unit 2 ("Our Senses") includes six lessons: mindful listening; mindful seeing; mindful smelling; mindful tasting; mindful movement I; and mindful movement II. Unit 3 ("Practical Applications: Building Blocks to Critical Thinking and Problem Solving") includes three lessons: perspective taking; learning optimism; and happy experiences. Unit 4 ("Mindful of Ourselves in the World") includes three lessons: gratitude; acts of kindness; and mindful actions in our community. As the contents suggest, MindUP has numerous mindfulness-based practices, and research indicates that even preschool children can learn them.

Flook et al. (2010) described the use of an eight-week InnerKids program with second- and third-grade children (i.e., 7- to 9-year-olds). The program is delivered through age-appropriate games and activities that

> (a) are targeted toward increasing a child/teen's capacity for present moment and felt-sense awareness of inner experience (his or her own experience), outer experience (other people's experience) and both together without blending the two; and (b) promote kindness, compassion, balance, and teamwork.
>
> (p. 84)

InnerKids is a multisession program presented in four sections: Section 1—awareness of inner experience, focusing on breath; Section 2: Awareness of inner experiences, focusing on sense impressions; Section 3: Awareness of inner and outer experience focusing on thoughts and emotions; Section 4: Awareness of inner and outer experience without blending the two together, focusing on interconnection and service. Each section includes awareness and kindness practices and takes one to four sessions to complete. While the program includes a large number of activities, children are able to learn and use them proficiently.

In a randomized controlled trial, Flook et al. (2015) evaluated the effects of a 12-week Kindness Curriculum (KC) with preschool children in a public school setting. The most recent version of KC (Healthy Minds Innovations, 2017) consists of 24 lessons presented under eight themes: Theme 1: Mindful bodies and planting seeds of kindness; Theme 2: I feel emotions on the inside; Theme 3: How I feel on the inside shows on the outside; Theme 4: Taking care of strong emotions on the inside and outside; Theme 5: Calming and working out problems; Theme 6: Gratitude; Theme 7: All people depend on each other and the earth; and Theme 8: Gratitude and caring for our world. This curriculum includes a wealth of different mindfulness-based activities that children can learn in a step-by-step manner. This well-documented practical curriculum offers teachers all the tools they need to teach mindfulness to preschool children.

In another randomized controlled trial, Zelazo et al. (2018) evaluated the effects of the Mindfulness Plus Reflection program. This program was delivered by trained teachers to preschool children (47 to 63 months old) at two schools serving low-income families. The preschoolers received the training during 30 daily small group sessions over six weeks in their classrooms. The 14 mindfulness exercises included: Lesson 1: Getting to know you, getting to know your breath; Lesson 2: The breath in my body; Lesson 3: Introduction to body scan, sound in space; Lesson 4: Body scan and mindfulness journals; Lesson 5: Mindfulness movement and deep body scan; Lesson 6: Deep body scan and mindfulness journals, Cheerios box; Lesson 7: Mindful seeing; Lesson 8: Mindful hearing, egg carton game; Lesson 9: Mindful touch, "What's behind my back?" game; Lesson 10: Mindful smelling and mindful journal blank pages; Lesson 11: Mindful taste; Lesson 12: Interconnectedness book, *Who Put the Cookies in the Cookie Jar?*; Lesson 13: Baking soda in water and *You Are Not Your Thoughts* book; and Lesson 14: Snow globe/glitter ball activity. This study showed that the preschool children could master a wide range of mindfulness activities.

Clearly, there is strong evidence that children can be taught mindfulness-based programs and exercises to enhance their well-being and quality of life. However, mindfulness programs such as the ones discussed here typically teach practices in a structured, sequenced, manualized approach, at a specific time, with distinct designated content for each lesson. In addition, many of these lessons are either language rich and didactic in nature or experiential and decontextualized in that they are practiced at the time of teaching, rather than in response to real-time academic, interpersonal, environmental, and social challenges. Given the disparity, inequity and inequality prevalent in the educational environment due to factors such as poverty, systematic racism, and ableism, there are many children who may miss out the benefits of traditional mindfulness-based programs due to differences in language skills, executive function, history of or ongoing trauma, and learning styles. In this chapter, I present the conceptual framework and details of a comprehensive mindfulness-based social-emotional learning program for preschool children aged 3 to 5 years and elementary children aged 5 to 12 years as an exemplar for teaching mindfulness to children in an inclusive, contextualized occupation-based format, with scaffolding and variation to accommodate differences in learning, attention, self-regulation, culture, and language.

The OpenMind© (OM) programs

The OpenMind Preschool program and the OpenMind Elementary programs utilize different formats but follow the same conceptual foundations. The OM programs' dual-process approach teaches both foundational skills and top-down practices to prepare young minds for learning, to support self-regulation and self-regulated learning, and to grow prosocial behaviors that will result in downstream benefits to the culture at large.

The following five basic conceptual practice foundations underpin the OM programs at both the preschool and elementary levels: (1) mindfulness training for teachers to facilitate embodying and modeling of mindfulness and to enhance authenticity of teaching; (2) bottom-up practices and practice variations to build self-regulation, executive function, and engagement that are integrated into the rhythm of life to build healthy habits and to allow for organic contextualized learning experiences; (3) planned practices and lessons in response to arising individual and classroom needs and challenges and/or anchored to academic content; (4) scaffolding and modification of practices and lessons to promote learning and mindful engagement; and

(5) a five-part process for transforming challenging behaviors into opportunities for learning, growth, autonomy, and agency and creating a prosocial classroom environment.

Conceptual foundations

The key conceptual foundations of mindfulness and social-emotional learning (SEL) are inextricably linked in the OM programs. The Collaborative for Academic Social and Emotional Learning (2013) defines SEL as having five competencies: self-awareness, self-management, social awareness, relationship management, and responsible decision making. The Center on the Social and Emotional Foundations for Early Learning lists the following six skills as competencies that promote school and community success in young children: confidence, ability to develop relationships, concentration and task persistence, effective communication of emotions, ability to pay attention and listen to instructions, and problem solving (Santos et al., 2012).

Mindfulness is an ethical way of being that has five parts: attention, awareness, being present, nonjudgment, and open-hearted intention and attitude. These five parts work together to support social-emotional learning, engagement, and quality of life. Review of the literature shows alignment between operational definitions of social-emotional learning and mindfulness.

Foundation 1: OM teacher meditation practice

To effectively teach the OM practices to children, it is essential that teachers and caregivers practice mindfulness authentically. Young children engage in observational learning, and when adults embody mindful engagement, they provide modeling and examples of the practices in action. In addition, by working to maintain a mindful presence, the teacher creates a milieu of nonjudgmental safety and connection, which further serves to foster relationship building. For ease of readability, the term "teacher" in this section will refer to any adult who is helping and supporting a child and may include a teacher, therapist, mentor, caregiver, or family member.

Positive teacher and child relationships and teacher responsiveness to the social and emotional needs of a child have predicted academic success in kindergarten and resulted in improved academic achievement. The classroom environment can be stressful and overwhelming at times, and when teachers are able to use mindfulness practices to demonstrate an engaged presence, self-regulation, positive attitude and prosocial behaviors, children will grow just by observing these mindful responses to stress and challenges. Furthermore, when a teacher is mindfully engaged, she may be less likely to use facial expressions, vocal tone, and body language that may result in unintentional harm or emotional contagion, which is defined as "a process in which a person or group influences the emotions, or behavior of another person or group through the conscious or unconscious induction of emotion states and behavioral attitudes" (Schoenewolf, 1990, p. 50).

The OM program teacher meditation practices were designed to build executive function skills such as attention, focus, emotional control, and mental flexibility, to increase awareness, to foster appreciation of positive emotional experiences, and to establish and strengthen positive wellness habits. Collectively, these practices can help teachers to develop a state of equanimity, which is the ability to maintain stability and even-mindedness when faced with challenging situations and to not get caught up in chasing pleasure and running from pain. Having equanimity is much like being a strong tree in a violent storm; the tree can stay rooted but also can bend in the wind, knowing the storm will pass.

There are seven OM mindfulness practices, and each practice is matched to a different color of the rainbow to enable teachers to remember the different practice options by color association. The rainbow also serves as a symbol of being open to and surprised by the amazing beauty that life can offer, even in the midst of or following a storm. The seven OM meditation practices are matched to seven wellness states: (1) lovingkindness meditation (red)—loving, kind, forgiving, inclusive; (2) open monitoring meditation (orange)—present, open, nonjudgmental, flexible; (3) joy meditation (yellow)—joyful; (4) embodied meditation (green)—grounded awareness and discernment; (5) *Samatha* meditation (blue)—peaceful, calm, patient; (6) compassion meditation (indigo)—compassionate, empathetic; and (7) gratitude meditation (violet)—grateful, appreciative.

The OM teacher meditation program is unique in that its format has been designed from an occupation-based perspective, which means that it can be used in the daily rhythm of life to support engagement in occupations, i.e., meaningful daily activities. Each of the seven OM meditation practices include options for formal, informal, and pause practices. The formal mindfulness practices offer a way to build attention, concentration, focus, and awareness through meditation practiced intentionally and repeatedly from the bottom up. The informal mindfulness practices are a means to put formal mindfulness meditation practices into action by applying them in daily life. Finally, the PAUSE practices offer a way to stop in daily life, notice what is happening, choose a response that is not harmful to others or ourselves, and set an intention to build a positive habit.

Foundation 2: practice in the rhythm of life

The OpenMind programs enable an occupation-based form of teaching and experience in which lessons are delivered and practiced in the context of the classroom rhythm of life, i.e., during play, academic lessons, transitions, self-care activities, social interaction, recess, and collaborative group learning. The term *rhythm of life* also refers to the use of activities in the naturalistic context of daily life when the need or opportunity for a learning experience occurs. For example, a teacher may introduce an activity to encourage lovingkindness practice and nonjudgment if an autistic child is being excluded by peers because he looks different or engages in unique methods of self-regulation such as flapping his hands.

The occupation-based format aligns with the concept of contextual interference in that for language acquisition and motor learning, retention and generalization of skills are increased when practice schedules are random and not blocked. Random practice schedules wherein all aspects of a task are practiced with a higher level of contextual interference (i.e., interference that occurs when tasks are practiced in a natural context) may result in poorer performance during practice trials but result in better retention and better performance during transfer of task.

The Center for the Social and Emotional Foundations on Early Learning outlines five guiding principles for implementation of SEL early learning programs that include individualization, intensity, normalized and naturalistic practice, fidelity of use, and cultural sensitivity and competence. Engagement in play, consistent practice of exercises throughout the academic day, and increasing executive challenges impact the success of executive function skills programs and gains in executive function. Moreover, embedding processes into the natural rhythm of classroom life can enhance the foundational skills necessary for academic engagement and provide a context for generalization of social and emotional lessons into other areas of daily life. The OM Preschool program involves 10 daily practices that are performed during the academic day. The OM Elementary program uses the same seven formal and informal meditation practices and pause practices that are used in the OM teacher meditation program, with modifications by age and developmental and/or grade level.

Foundation 3: planned practices that meet an identified need or teach an explicit lesson

The OM programs were designed to be both flexible and structured, to allow teachers to be responsive to changing individual and group needs. Thus, in addition to regular mindfulness practices to build skills, the OM programs use structured lessons that can address present moment concerns and anchor to academic tasks such as language and literacy activities. For example, two of the primary daily practices for the OM Preschool Program are the Feelings Finder practices for emotional awareness and the Super Me practices for prosocial behaviors and self-regulation. If a teacher is noticing a problem in the classroom, such as children having difficulty sharing, that results in aggression and distress, she can use these practices either retrospectively or in the moment to teach emotional awareness, perspective taking, problem solving, and prosocial alternatives using classroom tools such as story books, puppets, and interactive visuals and objects. The OM Elementary Program uses a seven-unit format to teach each of the seven mindfulness practices, self-awareness, and self-monitoring, along with specific grade-level books and/or articles that teach the concepts and also foster language and literacy skills such as narrative retell and vocabulary.

Foundation 4: mindful engagement

The OM programs were influenced by myriad theoretical perspectives, though the conceptual model underpinning the delivery of the program is that of mindful occupational engagement. The popular connotation of the term "occupation" is that of work and vocation, yet the operational definition for human occupation includes any meaningful activity or role that occupies a person's time. Occupations are not static mechanistic tasks but are multidimensional transactions between a person, physical environment, social milieu, and cultural contexts that are constantly influenced by changing personal motivation, purpose, meaning, and values. The construct of engagement speaks to the manner in which an individual performs an occupation. Engagement may be viewed as the degree to which an individual invests herself in a particular task. The value of engagement in occupation lies not in its purpose or outcome but in the subjective experience that engagement brings (Hasselkus, 2006), much like mindfulness itself.

Mindful occupational engagement can be defined as the moment-by-moment, open-hearted awareness and nonjudgmental engagement in an activity without expectation of specific outcomes (Jackman, 2014 p. 244). Mindful engagement is a state of being which requires active presence. Participation can be passive and is typically focused on a goal-directed task or avoidance of an unpleasant consequence. Children who are engaged and feel a sense of connection in learning experience more academic success than children who are disengaged. Engagement appears to be mediated by attention and persistence. Attention can be either involuntary (e.g., captured and maintained by novelty, high-interest activities) or effortful and voluntary. The OM practices and activities were designed with the goal of creating opportunities for mindfully engaged social-emotional learning to occur by using activities that may initially capture involuntary attention as a means of then practicing effortful attention. Further, the practices provide children and teachers with a means to explore *experiential* interests—engaging in activities that one finds pleasurable and exciting—and *critical* interests—engaging in activities that give meaning to our lives. Furthermore, social competence in young children has been defined in terms of the effectiveness of a child's social interactions for the achievement of personal goals within the context of positive engagement and self-regulation. Thus, practices and lessons in the OM programs are linked to individualized and classroom goals to increase motivation and engagement.

There is a qualitative difference during observation of an individual who is participating or doing without awareness or with a goal-directed focus and an individual who is mindfully engaged. With the former, the expectation of outcome may induce stress if there is a press for time or if the outcome is not meaningful to the individual. Boredom or frustration could occur if there is a mismatch between task demands and skill or arousal level. In the process of mindful engagement, there is enjoyment and reinforcement in the act of being while invested in an activity, that is, the reward is inherent in the engagement and is not dependent on the outcome of the activity or achievement of an objective. Given that a one-size-fits all lesson presentation and sequence does not always result in engagement of children who have differences in executive function, learning, language, culture, and cognition, teachers are able to use a framework to assist in problem solving to modify practices and activities to better facilitate mindful engagement.

The acronym CREATE provides a framework for developing practice activity modifications that result in mindful engagement over forced participation or compliance. The CREATE domains are various aspects of engagement that collectively form a holistic picture of potential for meaningful quality of life experiences and can apply to both adults and children. Manipulation of these factors can empower teachers to modify and individualize OM practice activities to meet children where they are in terms of interests, motivation, and development.

C: choice, control, curiosity

Choice is central to an engagement experience, particularly in young children, who may have little opportunity for autonomy and/or difficulties in accessing preferred items and communicating wants and needs. Young children are often placed into situations in which they may feel powerless, and opportunities for leadership and control can enhance motivation and competence. Novel items or multisensory activities that are interesting to a child can promote curiosity, which has been shown to promote learning. Adding a new or interesting element (e.g., object, puppet, book) to an established practice can increase curiosity and engagement.

R: response, regret prevention, reinforcement

The practice of mindful present moment remembrance of the needs of others requires cultivation of response over reaction. When teachers are present in the space between stimulus and response, they ensure the use of the most compassionate and skillful means of responding for each child, peer, or parent, depending on the time and situation. Thus, the second "R" for this element is what we term "regret prevention." The third aspect is the provision of positive reinforcement of child effort and prosocial choices, which requires ongoing awareness and attention to child cues and behaviors.

E: environment

This factor involves an understanding of how one's environment can support engagement. This may include the physical environment (e.g., temperature, sensory properties), the social environment (e.g., presence of a classroom volunteer), the embodied context (e.g., experience of a trigger of past trauma), and the temporal context (e.g., time of day). Awareness of the impact of environment on each child requires not only context-specific present moment awareness but also a broader awareness of child patterns, habits, and trends. OM practices and activities are designed to be performed in the most appropriate environment to support learning (e.g., playground, RtI, snack area, large group circle time).

A: awareness, attention, attitude

Awareness, attention and a positive open-minded attitude are required for one to fully be present and engaged. If a child cannot shift attention to a learning activity or is not aware of important aspects of a learning task, she cannot be fully engaged in learning. An open-minded attitude requires flexibility, the willingness to adapt planned activities to meet the present moment needs of a child, and the ability to see each moment as an opportunity for growth and engagement. This applies to children as well; a teacher can model and reinforce a flexible attitude for children who are struggling with change or compromise.

T: task demands

Engagement and learning are more likely to occur when challenge and skill levels are in balance—too much challenge can induce anxiety and too little challenge can result in boredom. Similarly, supporting engagement may require careful task analysis and task modification to match a child's abilities to ensure meaningful engagement.

E: energy

Recognizing a child's energy level is important in creating an engagement experience. If a child is too tired or too excited for a planned activity, engagement in that activity may not occur. A teacher must be able to modify the activity to fit the energy level of the child or classroom and/or support the child or group to become more alert or relaxed to match the activity and allow for engagement to unfold.

Foundation 5: supporting positive behaviors

A key tenet of the OM program is the belief that children who exhibit challenging behaviors are demonstrating a lack of or deficit in skills necessary for self-regulation, emotional regulation, sensory regulation, social interaction, self-regulated learning, self-efficacy, autonomy, and/or communication. Often, these challenges can arise from disparity, inequity, and inequality caused by systemic racism, implicit bias, and ableism. For example, minority children are less likely to receive an ADHD diagnosis, and black children more likely to be diagnosed with conduct disorder than white children, even upon considerations of trauma, behavioral indicators, and criminal offending. Approximately 21% of children in the United States are living in poverty, and these children experience increased risk for developmental delays, increased stress, impaired academic achievement, and reduced measures of self-regulation.

The OM program views challenging behaviors not as an opportunity for extinction of the problem behavior, but as opportunities to learn foundational skills to promote success and quality of life. The OM program provides the 5P Process (Prepare and be Present, Process, Problem-solve, Prosocial Practice, and Positive Praise) to teachers so that they can help children when these challenging situations arise in the classroom. This process supports teachers to help a child who is struggling learn what to do instead of what not to do.

Often, when children engage in challenging behaviors, it can make adults feel uncomfortable and can result in reactions to try to make the actions and feelings stop. When children are acting aggressively or engage in hurtful or disruptive behaviors, adults may take these actions personally or see the child as deliberately ignoring rules or trying to manipulate the situation. When children exhibit challenging behaviors, adults often use ignoring, time outs, and/or punishment as a response to these behaviors. However, these consequences can send a message to the child that she is not loved and accepted when she is having a rough time or having difficult emotions. These types of consequences also do not provide a means to teach a child the skills that she is lacking so that the behaviors do not continue to occur.

The 5P process was developed to meet two primary goals: (1) to view challenging behaviors as a sign that the child is lacking or has not yet adequately developed coping, self-regulation, and/or social-emotional skills, and/or that the environment is not adequately supporting the child's needs and (2) to provide support so that the child can experience, process, and cope with difficult feelings and life challenges and solve problems as they arise.

Prepare, protect, and be present

A child in distress who is having an extreme emotional reaction cannot also use the part of the brain responsible for logical thinking and problem solving. Therefore, the first step of the 5P intervention process is to be present for the child and give the child TIME to calm down and to feel safe and connected. Strategies for helping a child to de-escalate can include but are not limited to deep breathing, offering comforting words or gestures, and giving the child time and space in a quiet and safe area. It is vital that a caregiver or teacher be aware of her own state, as a child will often follow her lead; if she can cultivate a calm state, the child is more likely to feel calm.

Process

Once the child has attained a calm state, support the processing of emotional awareness in the time prior to, during, and after the behavioral incident. Help the child to identify how others involved in the situation may have felt to facilitate perspective taking and empathy. This involves the processes of affect identification (ability to identify emotions in self and others), modulation (ability to regulate responses to input), and expression (ability to communicate emotions), which are key aspects of self-regulation and trauma-sensitive intervention.

Problem-solve

Work with the child to discuss possible ways to resolve any conflicts that contributed to or are a product of the behavioral incident. Support the child to identify alternatives to engaging in a challenging behavior (e.g., ask for help using a help signal instead of ripping up paper) and use OM visuals, materials, and/or practices as needed to help the child to learn to generalize these strategies in the academic environment. This process helps a child to feel empowered and to develop autonomy and a sense of competency.

Prosocial practice

This part of the process teaches a child that even when she makes a mistake or a hurting choice, she can do something positive to help repair the damage. This step involves supporting the child to recognize and experience the opportunity to practice compassion for those who may have been hurt in the behavioral incident.

Praise

Provide verbal praise, gratitude, and/or recognition for positive behavioral choice. Remember that the more specific the praise is, the more the child will understand what exactly worked and which behaviors were positive and beneficial to the developmental, social, or academic situation.

Format of the OM Preschool program

The OM Preschool Program is a mindfulness-based social-emotional learning program for preschool children (Jackman, 2019a). The OM Preschool program uses an occupation-based, contextual, embedded approach in which daily practices and supplemental learning activities are implemented in the rhythm of life along with explicit teaching to transform the classroom milieu and to support academic and social engagement. To aid fidelity of implementation, daily practices and supplemental learning activities have detailed instructions, case examples, environmental and developmental considerations, and practice options that build in a stepwise progressive manner. The OM Preschool Program consists of daily practice activities (Jackman, 2019a) and supplementary learning activities (Jackman, 2019b). Young children's brain development is use-dependent, and learning requires frequent repetition so that the child can experience competence and contextualized understanding. The job of a teacher requires an incredible amount of planning, energy, and time management, so activities are offered in a format that allows for integration into lesson plans and the daily classroom routine. Given that the primary occupation of preschool children is to teach through play, many of the OM preschool practices use multisensory hands-on tools, visuals, songs, stories, puppet shows, and games to teach self-regulation and promote social-emotional and academic skills that can be overlaid on common preschool play, social, and academic activities. Daily practice activities include a choice of options so that teachers can adapt these practices based on child need, interest, and motivation.

Organization

The daily practice activities and practice options are grouped according to each of the 10 daily practice activities. Practice options are ordered to progress according to developmental age and social-emotional skills. However, this order is only a suggested guide, as children are different and do not necessarily follow the same developmental trajectory for all social-emotional learning domains. The teacher is able to choose which options will work best with the children in each classroom or with each child.

Each activity description provides both information on how the activity can be used with existing lesson plans and rhythm of life learning, as well as instructions on how to set up and complete the activity in the classroom (see Figure 8.1). The sections include:

1 **Why:** A brief narrative explanation of activity purpose and application.
2 **When and where:** Lists an example or examples of the context (e.g., large group time, 1:1 following child meltdown), developmental readiness (e.g., when children are feeling fidgety), and/or related motivational factors (e.g., when children want to sing a song) in which the activity may be beneficial.
3 **How:** Lists the steps for facilitating the activity and supporting a child or children to engage in the activity.
4 **Materials:** Lists the supplies and materials needed for each activity.

Daily practice activities

The daily practice activities help children learn to be aware of themselves and others, to give attention and awareness to what is happening in the present

Attention to the Sound of the Bell

Why: This practice option provides a way for young children and children new to meditation to have the experience of single-pointed focus. The activity involves focusing and listening to the starting and stopping of a ringing bell.

When and where: Large group, small group, outside; when children have not had experience with meditation and/or have difficulty with focusing and paying attention for more than a few seconds.

How:

1. Demonstrate the sound of the bell, and how it starts ringing, and then fades to silence.
2. Ask children to focus on the sound of the bell by listening and to put a hand up when the sound starts, then lower the hand when the bell is quiet or stops making a sound. Ring the bell and model this practice.
3. Repeat this based on child interest and increase the number of repetitions as attention skills increase.
4. Variations: Ask children to raise hand when bell starts and put finger on nose when bell stops. For added difficulty, ask children to raise hand or put finger on nose when the bell stops ringing.

Materials
Bell

Social-Emotional Competence:
Listening, awareness, following directions, focus, concentration, inhibitory control

Figure 8.1 A meditation practice

moment, to enhance social-emotional competence, and to act with kindness and compassion. When teachers and children practice these activities as a part of the daily routine, they can become habits that support being mindful in daily life. To ensure that daily practices remain child-driven and not prescriptive and teacher-driven, some activities are designed to change each day and/or be performed as needed in the rhythm of life in the classroom. Other daily practice activities include multiple variations of modality (e.g., song or visual) and/or rhythm of life context (e.g., time of day, large group, outside time, following child meltdown) to ensure that they are dynamic enough to meet changing classroom needs while remaining supportive of the foundational learning practices.

When implemented consistently, the daily practice activities become woven into the daily classroom schedule and serve to build a milieu in which teachers and children notice and reinforce prosocial behaviors. In this way, the system of these practices becomes self-sustaining, as often the resulting behavioral outcomes and actions (e.g., sharing, kindness) lead to reciprocal positive acts. Collectively, the daily practices serve to nourish the development of equanimity, lovingkindness, compassion, and empathetic joy, which help to bring people closer together in spite of the human tendency to act out of self-interest. In addition, these practices foster the practices of refraining from anti-social behavioral actions such as harming others, taking from others, and using unkind or incorrect speech.

The daily practice activities include: (1) Meditation—meditation on the breath, walking meditation; (2) Lovingkindness meditation; (3) Bell exercises for present moment mindful awareness and attention; (4) Yoga postures and body awareness; (5) Gratitude and interconnectedness practice; (6) Kindness and compassion reporting; (7) Feelings Finder practices; (8) Super Me practices; (9) Are you present for me?; and (10) Soles of the Little Feet and shifting practice. These activities are designed to engage all children in the classroom. The teacher has the freedom to decide when and where to practice based on the children's needs for that day. Table 8.1 provides an overview of the types of behaviors and social-emotional skills that may increase with the implementation and integration of each daily practice into the classroom culture. These behaviors and skills serve not only to enhance learning and development but also improve quality of life. The table also lists challenging behaviors that may decrease with the use of each daily practice.

OM preschool supplemental learning activities

Teachers use the OM learning activities in the natural course of the academic day to complement and enhance the daily practices to teach children how to live more mindfully and how to act with equanimity, lovingkindness, compassion, and joy. These practices help children to build social-emotional skills that can support both personal well-being and academic success, and we have organized the activities into eight different social-emotional skill areas. Beyond helping children at an individual level, the focus of these practices is to help children learn how to help others and make the world a better place for others. Many of the activities include art, music, and movement modalities common in preschool classrooms. In addition, many of the activities are designed to support extension lessons in academic topic areas (e.g., science, phonological awareness, pre-literacy), and offer teachers an opportunity to use their teaching expertise and creativity. As with the OM daily practice activities, the OM learning activities in each section are arranged to progress in level of difficulty, so that the teacher can match an activity to a child's developmental level and interests. Given that child learning, understanding, and retention of concepts is

Table 8.1 Overview of behaviors and social-emotional skills that may increase with the implementation and integration of each daily practice into the classroom culture

Daily practice	*Quality of life indicators that may increase in children*	*Challenging behaviors or problems that may decrease in children*
Meditation (A)	Attention, focus, concentration, staying present, listening, self-control of body movements and actions	Inability to sit still, difficulty waiting, impulsivity, fidgeting, becoming easily distracted, stress
Meditation (B): Walking meditation and guided movement	Attention and awareness of body movements, calming and grounding movement input, balance, control of body movements and speed of movement, inhibitory control	Impulsive movement, fidgeting, difficulty delaying gratification, poor grading and control of force and speed of body movements
Are you present for me?	Respect for others, ability to delay gratification to get the full attention of others, understanding of "being present"	Impatience, interrupting, demanding the attention of others without respect of others' time, using difficult behaviors to request attention
Bell exercises	Awareness of classroom activities, attention to teacher instruction, self-awareness, distraction and attention shift from behavioral triggers	Decreased attention to teacher instruction, loud or unruly classroom behavior, inappropriate attention or movement seeking behaviors
Yoga postures	Attention and awareness of body movements, balance, strength, control of body movements	Stress and tension, fidgeting, difficulty staying still, poor awareness and control of body movements
Feelings Finder practices	Emotion recognition in others, emotional perspective taking, emotional awareness and identification, communication of emotion with others	Difficulty expressing emotions during times of distress, poor awareness of emotions of others, difficulty with emotional perspective taking and empathy
Super Me practices	Forgiveness, helping others, sharing and giving, listening, self-calming, conflict resolution, using kind words and kind hands, comforting others, making compromises, supporting peers, self-compassion, effort for difficult tasks, making a meaningful apology	Jealousy and envy, lying, using unkind words, arguing over toys, whining, yelling, physical aggression, selfish behavior, stealing, having prolonged temper tantrums, negative self-talk, escaping tasks that are difficult, difficulty apologizing to others or resolving conflicts

(*Continued*)

Table 8.1 (Continued)

Daily practice	*Quality of life indicators that may increase in children*	*Challenging behaviors or problems that may decrease in children*
Lovingkindness practices	Unconditional caring for others, feelings of acceptance for others, and nonjudgment of others	Envy, difficulty forgiving others, fighting, judging others, being upset when others don't comply with one's wishes
Gratitude and interconnectedness practice	Gratitude (way of living), appreciation for others, thankfulness for things received, noticing the positive aspects of life, awareness of social connection	Complaining, lack of appreciation for actions of others, not expressing thanks for things received, feelings of entitlement, greed, selfish behavior
Kindness and compassion reporting	Awareness of kind and compassionate acts of others, ability to notice positive behavioral choices	Tattling, complaining about others for adult attention, focusing on negative aspects of others
Soles of the Little Feet and shifting practices	Responding instead of reacting to emotional impulses, ability to decrease suffering from difficult emotions, shifting from difficult emotions and challenges to positive emotions	Reacting to difficult emotions with physical and/or verbal aggression, engaging in disruptive behaviors

enhanced by teaching, each section also includes an option for children to have an opportunity to lead and teach the prosocial skills and practices, that is, child-as-teacher practices. These practice options can serve as classroom and teacher helper jobs. They can also provide older children with additional opportunities to apply and embody OM practices.

The OpenMind Elementary Program

Research has demonstrated that social-emotional learning can improve performance in academic skills such as language and literacy. However, many SEL programs are provided in a decontextualized format in tandem to academic lessons. Many SEL programs are often language heavy, and may not differentiate learning for students with language disorders, specific learning disorders, autism spectrum disorders, and emotional behavioral disorders. Furthermore, scripted reading programs often serve to teach to a standardized test and may thus perpetuate racial and class inequality in the school setting (Cummins, 2007; Darling-Hammond, 2007). Traditional language and literacy programs often miss out on the opportunity to naturally teach social-emotional lessons, though diverse storybooks can provide a means to build social-emotional learning skills by engaging students in social-emotional scenarios that are relatable and emotionally engaging and serve to teach emotional vocabulary and prosocial behaviors in a story context (Doyle & Bramwell, 2006)

The OpenMind Elementary Program uses a seven-unit format to teach a series of lessons and practices that support the development of seven prosocial character traits (i.e., being kind, open, joyful, grounded, calm, compassionate, and grateful), as well as foundational practices for inhibitory control, focus, and self-monitoring. Each unit combines mindfulness-based bottom-up practices and story-based lessons to teach vocabulary, social skills, emotional awareness, narrative retell, writing, and SEL competencies in a contextualized format that includes modifications for learners of all abilities. All units also include classroom practices to provide opportunities to generalize learning during the rhythm of each school day. In addition to combining SEL and language arts skills (e.g., using emotional awareness visuals and self-referential processing to teach narrative retell, teaching tier II vocabulary words that relate to SEL concepts and activities), the program also teaches thematically linked mindfulness-based practices that can be used to build focus, attention, engagement, and learning readiness. Finally, the program includes modifications for differentiation and implementation in ESE small group lessons, therapy sessions, special education classrooms, resource rooms and general education classrooms.

Research outcomes of the OM Preschool Program

The OM program is constantly being revised based on feedback from teachers as they use the program and from researchers as they evaluate its feasibility, acceptability, and outcomes for both teachers and their students. Here I present the latest research on the OM program, including its replication in Korean preschools.

In a cluster randomized controlled trial, Jackman et al. (2019) assessed the feasibility, acceptability, and preliminary effectiveness of the OM program with 262 children, 27 teachers, and 281 parents. The children were randomly assigned by classrooms to either the experimental group (i.e., OM program) or to an active control group (i.e., comparison program). The experimental group of classrooms implemented the OM daily practices (Jackman, 2016a) and supplemental learning activities (Jackman, 2016b) embedded within the High Scope curriculum of Head Start Programs. The active control group included aspects of trust-based relational intervention and social-emotional learning interventions to control for nonspecific effects of the OM program. Teacher training time was controlled across the two groups. Both groups were in effect for a school year. The teachers reported that it was feasible for them to integrate the OM program within the school's regular curriculum, but they experienced some difficulty in finding time to undertake the required daily meditation at school due to heavy workloads. When compared to teacher ratings in the control group of classrooms, those in the OM group of classrooms indicated benefits for the children in terms of improved self-regulation, increased body and emotional awareness, improved self-calming, and increased empathy and awareness of the feelings of others. The teachers rated the OM program as very acceptable, which they would recommend to other preschool teachers. The outcome data indicated positive child outcomes for both groups, with added advantage for the children in the OM program.

Kim et al. (2019a) evaluated the feasibility and acceptability of the OM program that was translated into Korean, culturally contextualized, and implemented as the OpenMind-Korea (OM-K) program in Korean preschools. Six preschools were cluster randomized into an active experimental group (OM-K) and a control group. The teachers in the OM-K group participated in the study and completed a 34-item feasibility questionnaire and an eight-item acceptability questionnaire following implementation of the OM-K program for a school year. Furthermore, they were individually interviewed regarding their views of the OM-K program. The teachers were fluent in implementing three or four of the daily practice activities on a regular basis and the rest of the activities as much as possible. They were able to embed the OM-K activities within the Nuri Curriculum that is mandated in all Korean preschools. The teachers adapted the activities commensurate with the children's needs and space available in each classroom. The teachers rated the OM-K program as being feasible to implement within the Korean preschool system and that the program was acceptable to them. All teachers uniformly reported that they would recommend the program to other preschool teachers because of its positive effects on both the teachers and the children.

In a related study, Kim et al. (2019b) assessed the parental social validity of the OM-K program. Social validity in this context means assessing the parents' opinion of the social significance of the goals, social appropriateness of the program, and social importance of the outcomes on the teachers and children. Forty of the 47 parents who were requested to participate in the study completed the seven-item social validity questionnaire. The participants were parents of 3-, 4-, and 5-year-old children who had attended the OM-K program. Results showed that the majority of the parents were positive about the OM-K program, especially with regard to its usefulness to their children both at school and at home. They found the program to be simple and easy to use and effective for their children, with no adverse unintended effects. Furthermore, they found the program acceptable for their children and would recommend it to other parents. Together with the results reported by Kim et al. (2019a), the OM-K was acceptable to both teachers and parents of 3- to 5-year-old children.

In a randomized controlled trial, Kim et al. (2020) assessed the OM-K program on preschool children's emotion regulation, resilience, and prosocial behaviors. Two of four preschools were randomly assigned to the experimental (OM-K) group and the other two to the control group. The teachers in the experimental group implemented the OM-K program (n = 42 children), and the teachers in the control group provided instruction as usual (n = 41 children). Analysis showed teacher ratings of the children in the control group as being significantly better on all outcome variables than those in the OM-K group at the start of the study (i.e., during pretest). Although children in the OM-K group improved on all outcome variables, the children in the control condition group continued to be rated somewhat higher on all outcome variables at the first post-training assessment. However, the children in the OM-K group were rated with significantly higher scores than the children in the control group at the second and third post-training assessments. The children in the OM-K group were rated with significantly higher scores on lability/negativity, resilience, and prosocial behaviors. Although the ratings for adaptive regulation were higher for the children in the OM-K group than those in the control group, the ratings did not reach statistical significance. This study suggested that engaging preschool children in the OM-K program enhanced their emotion regulation (adaptive regulation, lability/negativity), resilience, and prosocial behaviors (helping, sharing, cooperation, and comfort to others).

In sum, there is preliminary evidence that the OM program is feasible for teachers to use in preschools with 3- to 5-year-olds, can be embedded within the regular preschool curriculum, is acceptable to teachers and parents alike, and produces positive outcomes for the children across several domains of social-emotional learning.

Conclusions

The growing body of research on contemplative and mindfulness practices for children suggest that children are not only capable of learning these practices but also demonstrate social-emotional and academic growth when they are supported to use them. There are many strong and promising programs for children that combine mindfulness and social-emotional learning. The OM programs use a dynamic dual process approach to provide children with improved bottom-up and top-down self-regulation skills by targeting both explicit teaching and regular and frequent contextualized practice of discrete skills. In addition, the OM programs include teacher meditation practice to increase modeling, nonjudgment and connection, a framework for modifying and scaffolding practices and activities to foster mindful engagement regardless of ability, needs or challenges, and a structured process for supporting children who are demonstrating challenging behaviors. The OM programs offer a method of teaching mindfulness-based practices to children so that they can experience school readiness, social-emotional competency, and improved quality of life, and so that they can pass these benefits along to others.

References

Collaborative for Academic, Social, and Emotional Learning. (2013). *Effective social and emotional learning programs: Preschool and elementary school edition*. Chicago, IL: Author.

Cummins, J. (2007). Pedagogies for the poor? Realigning reading instruction for low-income students with scientifically based reading research. *Educational Research, 36*(9), 564–572.

Darling-Hammond, L. (2007). Race, inequality and educational accountability: The irony of 'No Child Left Behind'. *Race, Ethnicity, and Education, 10*(3), 245–260.

Doyle, B. G., & Bramwell, W. (2006). Promoting emergent literacy and social—emotional learning through dialogic reading. *The Reading Teacher, 59*(6), 554–564.

Erwin, E. J., & Robinson, K. A. (2016). The joy of being: Making way for young children's natural mindfulness. *Early Child Development and Care, 186*(2), 268–286.

Flook, L., Goldberg, S. B., Pinger, L., & Davidson, R. J. (2015). Promoting prosocial behavior and self-regulatory skills in preschool children through a mindfulness-based kindness curriculum. *Developmental Psychology, 51*, 44–51.

Flook, L., Smalley, S. L., Kitil, M. J., Galla, B. M., Kaiser-Greenland, S., Locke, J., . . Kasari, C. (2010). Effects of mindful awareness practices on executive functions in elementary school children. *Journal of Applied School Psychology, 26*, 70–95.

Greenberg, M. T., & Harris, A. R. (2012). Nurturing mindfulness in children and youth: Current state of research. *Child Development Perspectives, 6*(2), 161–166.

Hasselkus, B. R. (2006). The world of everyday occupation: Real people, real lives. *American Journal of Occupational Therapy, 60*, 627–640.

Hawn Foundation. (2011). *The MindUP curriculum: Grades 6–8: Brain-focused strategies for learning—and living*. Scholastic Teaching Resources. Available from: http://thehawnfoundation.org/mindup/

Healthy Minds Innovations. (2017). *The kindness curriculum—keys to kindness and well-being*. Madison, WI: Center for Healthy Minds, University of Wisconsin-Madison.

Jackman, M. M. (2014). Mindful occupational engagement. In N. N. Singh (Ed.), *Psychology of meditation* (pp. 241–277). New York, NY: Nova Publishers.

Jackman, M. M. (2016a). *OpenMind—a mindfulness-based social emotional learning program for pre-K children: Daily practice activities*. Port St. Lucie: Little Lotus Therapy and Consulting.

Jackman, M. M. (2016b). *OpenMind—a mindfulness-based social emotional learning curriculum for pre-K children: Learning activities*. Port St. Lucie, FL: Little Lotus Therapy and Consulting.

Jackman, M. M. (2019a). *OpenMind—a mindfulness-based social emotional learning program for pre-K children: Daily practice activities* (4th ed.). Port St. Lucie: Little Lotus Therapy and Consulting.

Jackman, M. M. (2019b). *OpenMind—a mindfulness-based social emotional learning curriculum for pre-K children: Learning activities* (4th ed.). Port St. Lucie, FL: Little Lotus Therapy and Consulting.

Jackman, M. M., Nabors, L. A., McPherson, C. L., Quaid, J. D., & Singh, N. N. (2019). Feasibility, acceptability, and preliminary effectiveness of the OpenMind (OM) program for pre-school children. *Journal of Child and Family Studies, 28*, 2910–2921.

Kim, E., Jackman, M. M., Jo, S.-H., Oh, J., Ko, S.-Y., McPherson, C. L., & Singh, N. N. (2019a). Feasibility and acceptability of the mindfulness-based OpenMind-Korea (OM-K) preschool program. *Journal of Child and Family Studies, 28*, 2187–2198.

Kim, E., Jackman, M. M., Jo, S.-H., Oh, J., Ko, S.-Y., McPherson, C. L., & Singh, N. N. (2019b). Parental social validity of the mindfulness-based OpenMind-Korea (OM-K) preschool program. *Journal of Child and Family Studies, 28*, 2922–2926.

Kim, E., Jackman, M. M., Jo, S.-H., Oh, J., Ko, S.-Y., McPherson, C. L., . . Singh, N. N. (2020). Effectiveness of the mindfulness-based OpenMind-Korea (OM-K) preschool program. *Mindfulness, 11*, 1062–1072.

Razza, R. A., Bergen-Cico, D., & Raymond, K. (2015). Enhancing preschoolers' self-regulation via mindful yoga. *Journal of Child and Family Studies, 24*, 372–385.

Santos, R. M., Fettig, A., & Shaffer, L. (2012). Helping families connect early literacy with social emotional development. *Young Children, 67*(2), 88–93.

Schoenewolf, G. (1990). Emotional contagion: Behavioral induction in individuals and groups. *Modern Psychoanalysis, 15*, 49–61.

Schonert-Reichl, K. A., Oberle, E., Lawlor, M. S., Abbott, D., Thomson, K., Oberlander, T. F., & Diamond, A. (2015). Enhancing cognitive and social-emotional development through a simple-to-administer mindfulness-based school program for elementary school children: A randomized controlled trial. *Developmental Psychology, 51*, 52–66.

Thierry, K. L., Bryant, H. L., Nobles, S. S., & Norris, K. S. (2016). Two-year impact of a mindfulness-based program on preschoolers' self-regulation and academic performance. *Early Education and Development, 27*(6), 805–821.

Thierry, K. L., Vincent, R. L., Bryant, H., Kinder, M. B., & Wise, C. L. (2018). A self-oriented mindfulness-based curriculum improves prekindergarten student's executive functions. *Journal of Child and Family Studies, 9*, 1443–1456.

Zelazo, P. D., Forston, J. L., Masten, A. S., & Carlson, S. M. (2018). Mindfulness plus reflection training: Effects on executive function in early childhood. *Frontiers in Psychology, 9*, 208.

Chapter 9

Teaching mindfulness to adolescents

Nirbhay N. Singh and Subhashni D. Singh Joy

Introduction

Adolescence is a period of rapid developmental changes that brings with it issues that might be unsettling for many adolescents. These may include wanting more independence from parents, peer influence and acceptance, romantic and sexual relationships, experimenting with substances, and developing social and political awareness. For others, there may be issues of adverse childhood experiences, family trauma, poverty, homelessness, out of home placements, and general neglect. In addition to the daily hassles of life, these issues can be stressful in the short-term and chronically stressful in the longer term. As with adults, stress in adolescents is often a precursor to mental health problems. Mindfulness-based interventions have been found to be helpful in ameliorating the symptoms of externalizing and internalizing problems in adolescents (see Singh & Joy, 2021 in Chapter 7 of this book). Although it is feasible to teach mindfulness practices to adolescents, the field of mindfulness with regard to adolescents is very young, and teaching methods are still in the nascent stages of development.

Mindfulness has been defined in many ways (see Ajahn Amaro & Singh, 2021 in Chapter 2 of this book), but the most commonly used research definition was proposed by Kabat-Zinn (1994, p. 4), "Paying attention in a particular way: on purpose, in the present moment, and nonjudgmentally." In the present context of how adolescents can cultivate mindfulness, Kabat-Zinn (2019) defined it as the "moment-to-moment, non-judgmental, non-reactive attending, and the awareness, insight, and potential liberation that can arise from that intentional cultivation" (p. xi). In terms of qualities of mindfulness, the aim is to teach ethically attuned mindfulness that incorporates both attention and awareness, and ethical mindedness (Ajahn Amaro & Singh, 2021).

Just as there are many definitions of mindfulness, there can be many ways of teaching mindfulness to adolescents. In this chapter, we (1) outline a selection of formal mindfulness-based programs that researchers have used to successfully teach mindfulness to adolescents and (2) describe informal single mindfulness-based practices that adolescents have used for managing specific behaviors.

Teaching formal mindfulness-based programs to adolescents

Mindfulness-based stress reduction (MBSR, Kabat-Zinn, 1990) and mindfulness-based cognitive therapy (MBCT, Segal et al., 2002) are the prototypic programs in the field of mindfulness-based programs to reduce suffering in adults. These programs provided the basis for adaptations that take into account the developmental level of adolescents and their specific needs. Given the much briefer history of using mindfulness-based programs with adolescents when compared to adults, variations of these programs are being developed and refined as new research data are coming online, and further programs are being developed and evaluated. We present a sampling of programs that have been used with adolescents.

Mindfulness-based stress reduction (MBSR)

Recent studies have shown that adolescents are fully capable of being taught the standard MBSR program, given minor modifications in session length, age-appropriate language, and choice of metaphors and examples. For example, Bennet and Dorjee (2016) taught the MBSR program to adolescents, with an average age of 17.7 years, from the local community school. The only minor modifications to the standard Center for Mindfulness authorized MBSR curriculum included adding age-appropriate vocabulary and contextualizing the discussions for local conditions. In a similar study with a larger sample size, Gouda et al. (2016) taught the standard MBSR program to adolescents with an average age of 16.2 years. These studies included a wide range of outcomes including mental health (depression, anxiety, stress), well-being, and academic attainment.

The standard MBSR program is an eight-week program, with a weekly session of 2.5 to 3.5 hours (open to adaptation for local conditions), and an all-day silent retreat between the sixth and seventh week on a weekend day. In each session, participants engage in formal (i.e., yoga, sitting and walking meditation, body scan) and informal mindfulness-based practices (i.e., mindful eating, speaking and listening, mindfulness of daily activities). There is a wide-ranging in-class discussion of various topics, such as stress, reactions and responses, skillful responses to the challenging demands of daily life, ways of taking care of self and flourishing, and enhancing well-being. The participants are given audio recordings or email/online information in each class and are expected to engage in home practice assignments. In all, the MBSR program includes 31 hours of direct instruction. The key aspects of the standard MBSR program are presented in Table 9.1, and further details can be found in the Mindfulness-Based Stress Reduction (MBSR) Authorized Curriculum Guide (Center for Mindfulness, 2017).

Table 9.1 Key components of the MBSR eight-week training program

Session 1:	There is more right with you than wrong with you a Body scan, standing yoga b Raisin-eating meditation c Body scan, mindful eating one meal this week
Session 2:	Perception and creative responding a Opening meditation, sitting meditation, standing yoga, body scan, awareness of breathing sitting meditation b Mindfulness of routine activities, yoga postures c Body scan, awareness of breathing sitting meditation
Session 3:	Pleasure and power in being present a Opening meditation, mindful lying down yoga, walking practice, closing meditation b Mindful listening and speaking c Alternate body scan with lying down yoga, sitting meditation
Session 4:	How conditioning and perception shape our experience a Opening meditation, standing yoga, sitting meditation, closing meditation b Mindful listening and speaking c Alternate body scan with lying down yoga, sitting meditation
Session 5:	Awareness of being stuck; responding rather than reacting a Opening meditation, standing yoga (few poses), sitting meditation, closing meditation b Mindful listening and speaking c Alternate sitting meditation with standing yoga and either body scan or lying down yoga
Session 6:	Working with different kinds of situations a Standing yoga, sitting meditation, closing meditation b Mindful listening and speaking c Alternate sitting meditation with body scan and/or standing or lying down yoga
All Day:	A silent retreat a Yoga b Sitting meditation c Body scan d Walking meditation e Mountain or lake meditation f Eating meditation (informally at lunch) g Lovingkindness meditation h Visual meditation followed by mindful walking, possibly outdoors, stopping and noticing one thing i Closing meditation
Session 7:	Integrating mindfulness practice into daily life a Sitting meditation: mountain, lake, or lovingkindness b Mindful listening and speaking c Practice formal sitting, yoga, walking, and/or body scan
Session 8:	Follow through practices for ever a Body scan, yoga, sitting meditation b Mindful listening and speaking c Keep up the practice and make it your own; be present in your life

Mindfulness-based cognitive therapy (MBCT)

In the earliest program for adolescents, Bögels et al. (2008) adapted MBCT (Segal et al., 2002) for the developmental level and specific difficulties of the participants who were from a community mental health center. These adolescents, with a primary diagnosis of attention deficit hyperactivity disorder, oppositional defiant disorder, conduct disorder, or autism spectrum disorder, evinced externalizing symptoms that required treatment. Given that mindfulness-based programs are purported to address attention and impulsivity problems arising from underlying deficits in information processing, Bögels et al. reasoned that mindfulness training may be effective for the externalizing problems of these adolescents. Mindfulness training was provided to the adolescents and a parallel mindful parenting training to their parents in a wait-list control design. It was expected that, when compared to the wait-list control participants, that mindfulness training for the adolescents would improve their attention, awareness, and impulsivity, reduce other externalizing symptoms, and improve the children's quality of life.

The mindfulness training was based on the eight-session MBCT program but adapted for adolescents. The structure of the program components was unchanged, with the training provided in the following sequence: body scan, mindful breathing, breathing space, mindfulness of thoughts and sounds, and sitting meditation. The key aspects of the training are presented in Table 9.2. The adolescents were provided training in small groups of seven children, with sessions lasting 1.5 hours. The adolescents received handouts in each session that described the theme of the session, instructions for practice, a CD with mindfulness exercises (body scan, mindfulness of the breath, mindfulness of

Table 9.2 Key contents of the Bögels et al. (2008) eight-session adolescent mindfulness training program

1	Raisin exercise, mindful walking outside, bringing mindfulness to routine activities, listening attentively to favorite music, mindful eating, rules of reward system
2	Body scan, mindful walking inside, pleasant event calendar, mindfulness in routine activities
3	Sitting with the breath, 3-minute breathing space, unpleasant event calendar
4	Awareness of sounds and thoughts, dealing with own impulsivity, difficult moment-breathing space answering calendar
5	Yoga I, experiencing without judging but accepting, difficult moment-breathing space answering calendar
6	Yoga II, dealing with shame, write, draw, make a list of everything you are intuition calendar
7	Trust exercises, role-plays, vulnerable moment-breathing space, honest response calendar
8	Daily mindfulness, plan for the next 2 months, process description of personal development and experiences during the training, cola and chips, stone meditation

sounds and thoughts), and home practice completion forms. These handouts were also made available to those adolescents who missed the session so that they could still engage in the home practice. In the last session, the adolescents developed their own action plans for continuing their practice in the eight weeks following the formal training. A points-based incentive system was included to enhance the adolescents' commitment to the training and regular practice. The points could be exchanged for a variety of backup reinforcers. Details of the training are presented by Bögels et al. (2008, p. 199). The same program was used in follow-up studies evaluating different outcomes (see van der Oord et al., 2012; van de Weijer-Bergsma et al., 2012).

Mindfulness-based cognitive therapy for children (MBCT-C)

In a small wait-list trial, Semple et al. (2010) evaluated the effects of MBCT-C, a manualized program designed specifically for children at the lower end of the adolescent age range (i.e., 9 to 13 years) on attention problems, symptoms of anxiety, and behavior problems. The MBCT-C is based on MBCT and aims to increase social-emotional resiliency by increasing mindful attention (Semple & Lee, 2011). The key aspects of the program are presented in Table 9.3. The goal of MBCT-C is to enhance children's awareness of their thoughts, feelings and body sensations, how these three experiences are separate but interrelated, and how they affect their perceptions of everyday life. MBCT-C is a 12-week program with a weekly 90-minute session and is provided in small group format of about eight participants and one or two mindfulness teachers (Semple & Lee, 2014). Parents are invited to be involved in the program and to participate in the home practice exercises with their children.

Integrative Contemplative Pedagogy (ICP)

The ICP was evaluated in a pilot randomized controlled trial with sixth-grade 12-year-old middle school students (Britton et al., 2014). The ICP program is designed to be embedded within the school curriculum and delivered by regular classroom teachers for six weeks. The key aspects of the program include three meditation techniques: breath awareness, awareness of thoughts, feelings, and sensations, and body sweep (i.e., paying attention to sensations in various body parts). Once the students learn these meditation techniques, they are free to choose one of the meditation techniques. Unlike other school-based programs that have focused on students with existing mental health conditions, the ICP is a public health program that is meant to be delivered to all school children. The effects of the ICP on the students who received the training were compared to those in an active control condition who did not receive the training. To control for nonspecific effects associated with the delivery of the

Table 9.3 Key components of the MBCT-C 12-week training program

Session 1:	Being on automatic pilot	
	a	Getting to know you, discovering awareness in a cup, what mindfulness means to me, taking three mindful breaths
	b	Mindful breathing lying down, mindful breathing sitting up, living with awareness
Session 2:	Being mindful is simple, but it is not easy!	
	a	Taking three mindful breaths, raisin mindfulness, mindfully moooving slooowly, taking three mindfulness breaths
	b	Living with awareness, mindful breathing, mindful eating
Session 3:	Who am I?	
	a	Taking three mindful breaths, mindfulness of the body, Hey, I have thoughts, feelings, and body sensations! Listening to the sounds of silence taking three mindful breaths
	b	Mindful breathing, mindfulness of the body, pleasant events
Session 4:	A taste of mindfulness	
	a	Introduction to three-minute breathing space, opening to one orange, mindful yoga movements, three-minute breathing space
	b	Three-minute breathing space, mindful yoga movements, tasting fruits
Session 5:	Music to our ears	
	a	Three-minute breathing space, do you hear what I hear, mindfulness of the body, three-minute breathing space
	b	Three-minute breathing space, mindfulness of the body, mindful listening
Session 6:	Sound expressions	
	a	Three-minute breathing space, sounding out emotions—mindfully, mindful yoga movements, three-minute breathing space
	b	Three-minute breathing space, mindful yoga movements, unpleasant sounds
Session 7:	Practice looking	
	a	Three-minute breathing space, visualizing with clarity, mindful yoga movements, seeing what is in the mind's eye, three-minute breathing space
	b	Three-minute breathing space, seeing the little details, stressful events
Session 8:	Strengthening the muscle of attention	
	a	Three-minute breathing space, seeing through illusions, moving mindfully, seeing what is not there, three-minute breathing space
	b	Three-minute breathing space, choosing to be aware, seeing five new things
Session 9:	Touching the world with mindfulness	
	a	Three-minute breathing space, being in touch, mindfulness of the body, three-minute breathing space
	b	Three-minute breathing space, mindfulness of the body, mindful touching

(*Continued*)

Table 9.3 (Continued)

Session 10:	What the nose knows a Three-minute breathing space, judging stinks! Mindful yoga movements, three-minute breathing space b Three-minute breathing space, mindful yoga movement, mindful smelling
Session 11:	Life is not a rehearsal a Three-minute breathing space, thoughts are not facts, feelings are not facts either, raisin mindfulness, mindfulness is. . ., three-minute breathing space b Three-minute breathing space, letter to myself
Session 12:	Living with presence, compassion, and awareness a Three minute breathing space, exploring everyday mindfulness, three-minute breathing space
Three-month follow-up	

ICP program, the students in the active control condition collaborated in the building of a life-sized Egyptian sarcophagus. When compared to the control condition, the effects of the ICP program were predicted to show greater improvements in internalizing problems (e.g., anxiety- and depression-related symptoms) and externalizing problems (i.e., problem behaviors and acting out). Other expected positive effects of participating in the ICP program included decreased attention problems, lower ratings of suicidality, enhanced attention, present-focus, awareness, acceptance, and more flexible coping styles.

Group Mindfulness Therapy (GMT)

The GMT was designed as a school-based program for young adolescents with anxiety, stress, and attention problems (McCarthy et al., 2014), and its effectiveness was evaluated in a small study with 12- to 13-year old middle school students (Crowley et al., 2018). This is a 10-week program that is delivered in 60-minute sessions after school and includes in-session and home practices. The key aspects of the program include present moment awareness, mindful breathing, walking, and eating, body scan, and loving kindness practices. These components of the program were selected from four other programs including MBSR (Kabat-Zinn, 1990), Mindful Schools (Mindful Schools, 2012), MindUP™ (Hawn Foundation, 2011); and MBCT-C (Semple & Lee, 2011).

Mindfulness in Schools Programme (MiSP)

The MiSP was developed as a universal school-based program for adolescents, and its effectiveness was evaluated in a very large nonrandomized feasibility study in 12 schools (Kuyken et al., 2013). The program is intended to help all students, but especially those who are stressed and experience subclinical mental health problems. It is designed to be embedded within a school curriculum and taught by regular schoolteachers. The program is based on MBSR, MBCT, and a lineage of contemplative mindfulness traditions (Goldstein & Kornfield, 1987) and was developed iteratively over four years with input from 200 teachers who used the MiSP curriculum with over 2,000 adolescent participants. The program explicitly teaches skills and attitudes and has mindfulness practices that are short and adapted specifically for adolescents. The instructions are age appropriate, interactive, experiential, and lively, and the program comes with teaching accessories appropriate for this age group (e.g., CD and MP3 audio files with mindfulness exercises).

Learning to Breathe (L2B)

The L2B is a well-designed research-based program for adolescents that facilitates the development of emotion regulation and stress-management skills (Broderick, 2013). BREATHE is an acronym: B—listen to your *B*ody; R—*R*eflections (thoughts) are just thoughts; E—surf the waves of your *E*motions; A—Attend to the inside and the outside; T—try *T*enderness—take it as it is; H—practice *H*ealthy habits of mind; and E—gain the inner edge, be *E*mpowered. The curriculum was informed by mindfulness-based and other programs, including MBSR and MBCT, acceptance and commitment therapy (ACT, Hayes et al., 1999), and dialectical behavior therapy (DBT, Linehan, 1993). Furthermore, L2B was designed to specifically address two major domains of social-emotional learning (SEL) competences—self-awareness and self-management—as advanced by CASEL (2011). The goals of the program include to (1) provide universal, developmentally appropriate mindfulness instruction that fosters mental health and wellness, (2) enhance capacity for emotion regulation, (3) strengthen attention and support academic performance, (4) expand the repertoire of skills for stress management, and (5) help students integrate mindfulness into everyday life (Broderick, 2013, p. 12). The curriculum comes in two formats, one for younger (i.e., fifth- to eighth- or ninth-grade) and the other for older (i.e., eighth- or ninth- to twelfth-grade) adolescents, with both being presented in exquisite detail in an easy-to-read and inviting manner.

MYmind

A preliminary version of the MYmind program was used by Bögels et al. (2008) with adolescents with externalizing disorders. Revised versions of the MYmind programs were used in later studies with children and adolescents with ADHD (van der Oord et al., 2012; van de Weijer-Bergsma et al., 2012) and replicated by other research groups (e.g., Haydicky et al., 2015; Zhang et al., 2017). The final version of the program is for children and adolescents with ADHD and their parents (Bögels, in preparation). This eight-week program with 90-minute sessions is presented in parallel for adolescents and their parents. There is a booster session eight weeks following the last training session. The adolescents have home practice for about 15 minutes. The program for adolescents includes a variety of components including sitting and walking meditation, body scan, yoga, breathing space, and a number of exercises and activities. The key aspects of the program are presented by de Bruin et al. (2021) in Chapter 5 of this book (see Table 5.2).

In sum, this sampling of mindfulness-based programs for adolescents show that a broad range of mindfulness-based practices have been used, sometimes together with social-emotional learning components and positive reinforcement principles. These programs are multi-component, often embedded in standard school curriculum, and often taught by regular schoolteachers to ensure long-term sustainability. There is a certain commonality in these programs, but this is to be expected given that most have relied on MBSR and/or MBCT as the foundational programs from which to pick and choose their components, depending on the focus of the adapted programs. To this, some have added other components, such as lovingkindness, that increase the likelihood of wider beneficial effects of these programs on the adolescents. The current pilot, feasibility, and initial outcome studies indicate that the adolescent participants were able to master and use these practices.

Teaching informal single mindfulness-based practices to adolescents

Formal mindfulness-based programs provide adolescents with a relatively comprehensive set of practices directed at different aspects of their life. These practices can reduce their suffering in specific areas if that is the intent, but they can also be used as an approach to public health in helping them to develop a healthy lifestyle. Occasionally, however, some of the issues that adolescents face overwhelm them, and they might need a default mindfulness-based practice to keep these issues under control. We present three such practices that have proven useful to adolescents.

Soles of the Feet (SoF)

The SoF practice was first developed for an adolescent who wanted to control his own aggressive behavior. SoF required the adolescent to learn a simple sequence of steps—at the first awareness of a negative emotion arising, pause, and shift your attention from the emotionally arousing situation to a neutral part of your body, the soles of the feet (see Table 9.4 for key aspects of the SoF procedure). Once the adolescent learned to use the SoF practice with fluency at the first indication of emotional arousal, he was able to manage his aggressive behavior. The SoF is a mindfulness-based practice that is portable, easy to use, and enables self-management of socially undesirable behavior. It enables

Table 9.4 Key training steps for the Soles of the Feet program for anger

1	If you are standing, stand in a natural rather than an aggressive posture, with the soles of your feet flat on the floor.
2	If you are sitting, sit comfortably with the soles of your feet flat on the floor.
3	Breathe naturally and do nothing.
4	Cast your mind back to an incident that made you very angry. Stay with the anger.
5	You are feeling angry, and angry thoughts are flowing through your mind. Let them flow naturally, without restriction. Stay with the anger. Your body may show signs of anger (e.g., rapid breathing).
6	Now, shift all your attention fully to the soles of your feet.
7	Slowly, move your toes, feel your shoes covering your feet, feel the texture of your socks, the curve of your arch, and the heels of your feet against the back of your shoes. If you do not have shoes on, feel the floor or carpet with the soles of your feet.
8	Keep breathing naturally and focus on the soles of your feet until you feel calm.
9	Practice this mindfulness exercise until you can use it wherever you are and whenever an incident occurs that may otherwise lead to you being verbally or physically aggressive.
10	Remember that once you are calm, you can walk away from the incident or situation with a smile on your face because you controlled your anger. Alternatively, if you need to, you can respond mindfully to the incident or situation with a calm and clear mind without verbal threats or physical aggression.

the adolescent to shift from an automatic reaction to an internal (e.g., a negative thought, remembrance of a past negative event) or an external event (e.g., a hurtful comment) to a mindful response. Once the adolescent moves their attention to the soles of the feet, it provides a safe space within which to discern possible skillful and unskillful responses and to respond mindfully with a skillful response. With practice, the adolescent develops skillful inhibitory responses to emotionally negative arousal situations.

Although the SoF was originally developed for self-management of anger and aggression, it has been used widely for fostering self-management of a broad range of emotions, thoughts, feelings, perceptions, and negative events. Research using single-subject experimental designs and a randomized controlled trial have provided empirical support for this practice. For example, in two related papers, adolescents with ASD taught to use SoF were able to self-manage their aggressive behavior and maintain the behavioral gains for up to four years during the follow-up period (Singh et al., 2011a, 2011b). Ahemaitijiang et al. (2020) reported that adolescents were able to use SoF for controlling their destructive behaviors. Felver et al. (2014, 2017) showed that SoF can be successfully used in school settings for the self-management of disruptive behavior and for increasing academic engagement. With regard to school-based training, programmatic details for using SoF with individual students or with the whole class as a preventive program are presented in Felver and Singh (2020). Griffith et al. (2019) reported benefits of SoF that included the participants being able to better handle anger without it resulting in aggression, enhanced positive mood, and increased sociability.

SOBER Breathing Space

Given that no evidence-based program works well for all individuals who need it, other programs need to be researched as viable alternatives. Two such programs have shown initial promise—SOBER Breathing Space and Surfing the Urge. SOBER is an acronym: S = Stop, O = Observe, B = Breathe, E = Expand, and R = Respond. SOBER Breathing Space has been used as part of the Mindfulness-Based Relapse Prevention (MBRP) program for addictive behaviors (Bowen et al. 2011), and it can be used as an informal practice to respond mindfully to emotionally arousing situations that might trigger an automatic physical and/or verbal aggression. For example, Singh et al. (2018) taught this informal mindfulness-based practice to young adolescents for managing their verbal and physical aggression. When used for anger and aggression management, at the first indication of rising anger the adolescents learn to *stop* and be aware of what is happening in that moment, *observe* the physical sensations and emotional changes in the body as a result of the rising anger, *breathe* by deliberately bringing attention to the breath, *expand* their awareness of the situation and discern unskillful (reactive) and skillful (mindful) response, and then *respond* mindfully. The key aspects of the program are presented in Table 9.5. Although usually used in the context of addiction treatment, this informal mindfulness-based practice could be used in other high-risk situations that might trigger an almost automatic response with negative outcomes. At its most basic level, SOBER Breathing Space is an effective way of rapidly but positively regulating one's emotions, thoughts, feelings, and desires.

Surfing the Urge

Surfing the Urge provides another alternative to SoF for adolescents to manage their automatic negative reactions in emotionally arousing situations. It is an informal mindfulness-based practice that was first used in the context of substance abuse to produce behavior change through enhanced self-control. Urges are the impulse to engage in a behavior such as drinking alcohol or using illicit drugs that may be initially felt as a physical sensation in the body (Marlatt & Gordon, 1985). These urges may arise repeatedly, like waves, increase in intensity, peak, and then slowly dissolve or dissipate of their own accord if the individual does not engage with the urges. In Surfing the Urge, adolescents learn to use breath like a surfboard to ride out the waves of urges to be reactive to rising anger by simply observing each urge with an open, equanimous, and curious attitude,

Table 9.5 Key training steps for the SOBER Breathing Space practice for anger

Preliminaries

1 Occasionally you will find some situations, interactions, thoughts, or feelings upsetting enough to cause anger or aggression.
2 While you cannot control events from happening in your lives, you have a choice in terms of how you respond to the rising anger and aggression.
3 Having a personal meditation practice will help you to achieve equanimity—a calmness and stability of mind that will enable you to respond mindfully as events unfold in your life.
4 Furthermore, a few minutes of daily meditation practice will enhance your ability to use informal mindfulness practices, such as SOBER, throughout the day.

SOBER Breathing Space Practice

1 Stop—Stop whatever you are doing at the first instance you feel anger arising, or at the first thought of being verbally or physically aggressive.
2 Observe—Observe the changing sensations in your mind and body. Pay close attention to the thoughts, feelings, emotions, and physical changes that accompany the rising anger or aggression.
3 Breathe—Redirect your attention to your breath and take a few breaths until your attention is centered on your breath.
4 Expand—Expand your awareness and examine the possible consequences of being angry or aggressive. How would it make you feel when you are angry? When you hurt someone's feelings through verbal aggression? When you see that your physical aggression has caused pain to the other person? How would you feel if you were in the other person's shoes?
5 Response—Respond mindfully to the situation instead of reacting mindlessly. Remind yourself that how you respond is your choice and yours alone. You have the choice to respond mindfully or continue with your old habit of being verbally or physically aggressive.

Strengthening the Practice

1 Use SOBER Breathing Space to create a little behavioral distance between the trigger that makes you angry and/or aggressive and your habitual conditioned response.
2 Practice using the SOBER Breathing Space every time anger arises and every time you have thoughts of verbal or physical aggression.
3 It may take a little while, but the results will arise with practice. It is just like building muscles at the gym; nothing happens overnight.
4 There will be times, especially during the early stages of using this practice, when you may forget to use it in time and be angry or aggressive. Have compassion for yourself, set your intention to do better next time, and then get on with life.

without self-judgment, and with nonattachment to the urge. Much like an extinction burst, there may be an initial increase in the occurrence of the urges, but repeated engagement in the practice results in overcoming the urges. Mindful attention to the urge, without engaging in escape or avoidance, provides an

Table 9.6 Key training steps for Surfing the Urge practice for anger

Preliminaries

1. An urge is an impulse to engage in habitual (often addictive) behavior, like drinking, using substances, speeding in your car, or reflexively reacting to upsetting situations with verbal or physical aggression.
2. An urge begins with a transient thought or feeling that arises slowly, grows fast, peaks in intensity, and then dissipates of its own accord.
3. If you mentally engage with an urge, hold a dialogue with it, try to eliminate it by distraction, or try to suppress it, means you are "feeding" it, and the urge will grow bigger and faster.
4. Giving in to the urge will serve to strengthen it and make it even more difficult to curb it in future.
5. If at all possible, learn mindfulness meditation with a focus on the breath. This will increase your awareness of the earliest signs of an urge arising in your mind and body.
6. A few minutes of daily meditation practice will provide you with stability of mind that will enhance your ability to use informal mindfulness practices, such as Surfing the Urge, throughout the day.

Surfing the Urge practice

1. At all times, be mindful of arising urges.
2. When you detect an urge arising, focus on places in your body where the urge is present—dryness of the mouth, anticipatory salivation, sensations in the abdomen, tightness or heaviness in the chest—and notice its intensity.
3. Be present for the urge—observe it with nonjudgmental awareness, cradle it without attachment, and remember that it is transient.
4. Bring your attention to your breath, without changing the flow, speed, or length of each breath.
5. Use your breath as a surfboard to ride the urge as it flows through you—arising, gaining strength, peaking in intensity, and then dissolving. Surf the urge for a minute or two.
6. Shift your attention back to the places in your body where the urge was initially present and observe the transformation taking place—reduction of the feelings and sensations associated with the urge.
7. Return to the breath and observe the urge until it is fully dissolved.
8. Show gratitude to yourself for being present for the urge without giving in to it. Smile and mentally note that you responded according to your intentions and did not react to the urge by going back to your old habits.

Strengthening the practice

1. Use Surfing the Urge each time an urge arises.
2. Be consistent in your practice, but should the urge get the better of you, smile, and reset your intention to practice again and again with each new urge.
3. To strengthen your practice in the early stages of learning to use Surfing the Urge, set aside a regular time to practice. Close your eyes, recreate the scene the last time you engaged in verbal or physical aggression, and go through Surfing the Urge steps from the time you noticed the arising urge to engage in a verbal or physical response to the situation until it dissipates.

alternative context for experiencing the negative private event, thereby decreasing the magnitude of the conditioned stimulus and eventually eliminating it (Levin et al., 2013). Singh et al. (2019) reported a study in which adolescents with ASD were able to successfully use Surfing the Urge to self-manage their verbal and physical aggression and had their prescribed medications for aggression discontinued because of lack of need following mindfulness training. The key training steps of Surfing the Urge practice are presented in Table 9.6.

In sum, the emerging literature on informal mindfulness-based programs for managing negative emotional states is suggestive of their effectiveness. The adolescents in these studies were able to learn and use SoF, SOBER Breathing Space, and Surfing the Urge and maintain the behavioral gains during the follow-up periods, with the longest being four years. The key issue in this context is that adolescents found the single informal mindfulness-based practices to be acceptable, easy to learn, and effective.

Conclusions

Teaching mindfulness to adolescents is a relatively new area of training when compared to adults. However, much progress has been made even in the short period since the first studies were published on the effects of mindfulness-based training with adolescents. Two streams of training have been evident. First, many programs have been customized for adolescents based on adult mindfulness-based training programs, with MBSR and MBCT providing the foundation for developing such programs. The diversity of the programs for adolescents in terms of content is remarkable, with programs focusing on a mix of mindfulness content, developmental concerns and age appropriateness, motivation for engagement, quality of life issues, mental health concerns, and prevention based on a public health model of training. Second, there is emerging a small group of informal mindfulness-based practices that focus on specific issues, such as anger, aggression, disruptive, and destructive behaviors of adolescents. Adolescents appear to be comfortable with these single mindfulness practices because it enables them to exercise self-determination, an important developmental issue for adolescents. Given the current knowledge in this field, teaching mindfulness to adolescents is mainly an art, because there are too many known and unknown variables involved to make it a science.

References

Ahemaitijiang, N., Hu, X., Yang, X., & Han, Z. H. (2020). Effects of meditation on the soles of the feet on aggressive and destructive behaviors of Chinese adolescents with autism spectrum disorders. *Mindfulness*, *11*, 230–240.

Amaro, A., & Singh, N. N. (2021). Mindfulness: Definitions, attributes, and mechanisms. In N. N. Singh & S. D. Singh Joy (Eds.), *Mindfulness-based interventions with children and adolescents: Research and practice*. London, UK: Routledge.

Bennet, K., & Dorjee, D. (2016). The impact of a mindfulness-based stress reduction course (MBSR) on well-being and academic attainment of sixth-form students. *Mindfulness*, *7*, 105–114.

Bögels, S. M. (in preparation). MYmind mindfulness voor kinderen en adolescenten met ADHD en hun ouders: Trainershandleiding [*MYmind mindfulness for children and adolescents with ADHD and their parents: Manual for professionals*]. Houten, the Netherlands: Lannoo Campus.

Bögels, S. M., Hoogstad, B., van Dun, L., de Schutter, S., & Restifo, K. (2008). Mindfulness training for adolescents with externalizing disorders and their parents. *Behavioural and Cognitive Psychotherapy*, *36*(2), 193–209.

Bowen, S., Chawla, N., & Marlatt, G. A. (2011). *Mindfulness-based relapse prevention for addictive behaviors: A clinician's guide*. New York, NY: Guilford Press.

Britton, W. B., Lepp, N. E., Niles, H. F., Rocha, T., Fisher, N. E., & Gold, J. S. (2014). A randomized controlled pilot trial of classroom-based mindfulness meditation compared to an active control condition in sixth-grade children. *Journal of School Psychology*, *52*, 263–278.

Broderick, P. C. (2013). *Learning to breathe: A mindfulness curriculum for adolescents to cultivate emotion regulation, attention, and performance*. Oakland, CA: New Harbinger Publications.

CASEL. (2011). *What is SEL? Skill competencies*. Chicago, IL: Collaborative for Academic, Social, and Emotional Learning.

Center for Mindfulness. (2017). *Mindfulness-based stress reduction (MBSR) authorized curriculum guide*. Worcester, MA: University of Massachusetts Medical School.

Crowley, M. J., Nicholls, S. S., McCarthy, D., Greatorex, K., Wu, J., & Mayes, L. C. (2018). Innovations in practice: Group mindfulness for adolescent anxiety—results of an open trial. *Child and Adolescent Mental Health*, *23*(2), 130–133.

de Bruin, E. I., Meppelink, R., & Bögels, S. M. (2021). Mindfulness in attention deficit hyperactivity disorder. In N. N. Singh & S. D. Singh Joy (Eds.), *Mindfulness-based interventions with children and adolescents: Research and practice*. London, UK: Routledge.

Felver, J. C., Felver, S. L., Margolis, K. L., Ravitch, N. K., Romer, N., & Horner, R. H. (2017). Effectiveness and social validity of the Soles of the Feet mindfulness-based intervention with special education students. *Contemporary School Psychology*, *21*, 358–368.

Felver, J. C., Frank, J. L., & McEachern, A. D. (2014). Effectiveness, acceptability, and feasibility of the Soles of the Feet mindfulness-based intervention with elementary school students. *Mindfulness*, *5*, 589–597.

Felver, J. C., & Singh, N. N. (2020). *Mindfulness in the classroom: An evidence-based program to reduce disruptive behavior and increase academic engagement*. Oakland, CA: New Harbinger Publications.

Goldstein, J., & Kornfield, J. (1987). *Seeking the heart of wisdom*. Boston, MA: Shambhala Publications.

Gouda, S., Luong, M. T., Schmidt, S., & Bauer, J. (2016). Students and teachers benefit from mindfulness-based stress reduction in a school-embedded pilot study. *Frontiers in Psychology*, *7*, 590.

Griffith, G. M., Hastings, R. P., Williams, J., Jones, R. S. P., Roberts, J., Crane, R. S., . . Edwards, R. T. (2019). Mixed experiences of a mindfulness-informed intervention: Voices from people with intellectual disabilities, their supporters, and therapists. *Mindfulness*, *10*, 1828–1841.

Hawn Foundation. (2011). *The MindUP curriculum: Grades 6–8: Brain-focused strategies for learning—and living*. Scholastic Teaching Resources. Available from: http://thehawnfoundation.org/mindup/

Haydicky, J., Shecter, C., Wiener, J., & Ducharme, J. M. (2015). Evaluation of MBCT for adolescents with ADHD and their parents: Impact on individual and family functioning. *Journal of Child and Family Studies, 24*(1), 76–94.

Hayes, S. C., Strosahl, K. D., & Wilson, K. G. (1999). *Acceptance and commitment therapy: An experiential approach to behavior change*. New York, NY: Guilford Press.

Kabat-Zinn, J. (1990). *Full catastrophe living: Using the wisdom of your body and mind to face stress, pain, and illness*. New York, NY: Delta.

Kabat-Zinn, J. (1994). *Wherever you go, there you are: Mindfulness meditation in everyday life*. New York, NY: Hyperion.

Kabat-Zinn, J. (2019). Seeds of a necessary global renaissance in the making: The refining of psychology's understanding of the nature of mind, self, and embodiment through the lens of mindfulness and its origins at a key inflection point for the species. *Current Opinion in Psychology, 28*, xi–xvii.

Kuyken, W., Weare, K., Ukoumunne, O. C., Vicary, R., Morton, N., Burnett, R., . . . Huppert, F. (2013). Effectiveness of the mindfulness in schools programme: Non-randomised controlled feasibility study. *The British Journal of Psychiatry, 203*, 126–131.

Levin, M. E., Hayes, S. C., & Vilardaga, R. (2013). Acceptance and commitment therapy: Applying an iterative translational research strategy in behavior analysis. In G. J. Madden, W. V. Dube, T. D. Hackenberg, G. P. Hanley, & K. A. Lattal (Eds.), *APA handbook of behavior analysis* (Vol. 2, pp. 455–479). Washington, DC: American Psychological Association.

Linehan, M. (1993). *Cognitive-behavioral treatment of borderline personality disorder*. New York, NY: Guilford Press.

Marlatt, G. A., & Gordon, J. R. (1985). *Relapse prevention: Maintenance strategies in the treatment of addictive behaviors*. New York, NY: Guilford Press.

McCarthy, D., Nicholls, S., & Crowley, M. J. (2014). *Group mindfulness therapy (GMT) for anxiety*. New Haven, CT: Yale Child Study Center.

Mindful Schools. (2012). *Mindful schools curriculum*. Available from: www.mindfulschools.org/

Segal, Z. V., Williams, J. M., G., & Teasdale, J. D. (2002). *Mindfulness-based cognitive therapy for depression*. New York, NY: Guilford Press.

Semple, R. J., & Lee, J. (2011). *Mindfulness-based cognitive therapy for anxious children: A manual for treating childhood anxiety*. Oakland, CA: New Harbinger Publications.

Semple, R. J., & Lee, J. (2014). Mindfulness-based cognitive therapy for children. In R. A. Baer (Ed.), *Mindfulness-based treatment approaches: Clinician's guide to evidence base and applications* (pp. 161–188). Waltham, MA: Academic Press.

Semple, R. J., Lee, J., Rosa, D., & Miller, L. F. (2010). A randomised trial of mindfulness-based cognitive therapy for children: Promoting mindful attention to enhance social-emotional resiliency in children. *Journal of Child Family Studies, 19*, 218–229.

Singh, N. N., & Joy, S. D. S. (2021). Mindfulness in mental health. In N. N. Singh & S. D. Singh Joy (Eds.), *Mindfulness-based interventions with children and adolescents: Research and practice*. London, UK: Routledge.

Singh, N. N., Lancioni, G. E., Karazsia, B. T., Myers, R. E., Kim, E., Chan, J., . . Janson, M. (2019). Surfing the Urge: An informal mindfulness practice for the self-management of aggression by adolescents with autism spectrum disorder. *Journal of Contextual Behavioral Science, 12*, 170–177.

Singh, N. N., Lancioni, G. E., Manikam, R., Winton, A. S., Singh, A. N., Singh, J., & Singh, A. D. (2011a). A mindfulness-based strategy for self-management of aggressive behavior in adolescents with autism. *Research in Autism Spectrum Disorders, 5*(3), 1153–1158.

Singh, N. N., Lancioni, G. E., Myers, R. M., Karazsia, B. T., McPherson, C. L., Jackman, M. M., . . Thompson, T. (2018). Effects of SOBER breathing space on aggression in children with autism spectrum disorder and collateral effects on parental use of physical restraints. *Advances in Neurodevelopmental Disorders, 2*, 362–374.

Singh, N. N., Lancioni, G. E., Singh, A. D., Winton, A. S., Singh, A. N., & Singh, J. (2011b). Adolescents with Asperger syndrome can use a mindfulness-based strategy to control their aggressive behavior. *Research in Autism Spectrum Disorders, 5*(3), 1103–1109.

van de Weijer-Bergsma, E., Formsma, A. R., Bruin, E. I., & Bögels, S. M. (2012). The effectiveness of mindfulness training on behavioral problems and attentional functioning in adolescents with ADHD. *Journal of Child and Family Studies, 21*(5), 775–787.

van der Oord, S., Bögels, S. M., & Peijnenburg, D. (2012). The effectiveness of mindfulness training for children with ADHD and mindful parenting for their parents. *Journal of Child and Family Studies, 21*, 139–147.

Zhang, D., Chan, S. K. C., Lo, H. H. M., Chan, C. Y. H., Chan, J. C. Y., Ting, K. T., . . Wong, S. Y. S. (2017). Mindfulness-based intervention for Chinese children with ADHD and their parents: A pilot mixed-method study. *Mindfulness, 8*, 859–872.

Chapter 10

Teaching mindfulness to parents, caregivers, and teachers

Nirbhay N. Singh, Giulio E. Lancioni, and Rachel E. Myers

Introduction

Children's transactions with their environment, broadly defined, can influence protective factors for typical development and/or risk factors for atypical development (Sameroff, 1986; Singh & Singh, 2001). Children's development is a function of "the interplay between child and context across time, in which the state of one affects the next state of the other in a continuous dynamic process" (Sameroff, 1993, p. 6). This transactional process influences not only brain development but also psychological functioning of children as they engage in bidirectional interactions with their physical, social, and emotional environments. For example, in the context of a birth complication, a new mother may experience anxiety that negatively affects the temperament of the child, resulting in avoidance from the mother, and eventually leading to a language delay due to a lack of incidental teaching by the mother (Sameroff & Fiese, 2000, p. 142). In an alternative ecological scenario, an experienced or more confident mother may not be anxious due to birth complications, which positively affects the temperament of the child, resulting in a loving and close relationship with the mother and eventually leading to neurotypical development.

Transactional or bidirectional processes between parents and children involve mutual and reciprocal exchanges that result in an interrelated series of observable behavioral changes in both parents and children (Bronfenbrenner & Morris, 2006). Over time, these reciprocal behavioral exchanges between parents and children may result in what has been called "positive" and "negative" feedback loops (Sameroff & Mackenzie, 2003) or as "vicious" versus "virtuous" cycles (Lerner, 1982). For example, in Patterson's (1982) classic coercive family model, a child's aggressive behavior may lead to progressively less effective parental response (e.g., verbal reprimands, restraints, physical punishment) to reduce the rate of the child's behavior, eventually leading to increased likelihood of more aggressive behavior in the future. Alternatively, when parents find the child's behavior highly aversive and want to avoid it, they may temporarily terminate the behavior by giving in to the child's demands, only to find that this contributes to later antisocial behavior and conduct problems (Dishion et al., 1992). These bidirectional parent-child interactions are examples of vicious cycles. Parents responding in an effective way that leads to reductions in the child's aggressive behavior over time would be an example of a virtuous cycle. More specifically, an example of a virtuous cycle would be when a parent teaches the child a socially acceptable, functionally equivalent response as an alternative to physical aggression. This bidirectional model of parent-child interactions suggests that interventions can be directed at the parent level, the child level, or both to change from a vicious to a virtuous cycle.

Correlational and longitudinal studies have indicated that parental mindfulness may have bidirectional linkages to a number of child behaviors. For example, Parent et al. (2010) found that lower levels of parental mindfulness were associated with higher levels of parental depressive symptoms, which in turn were related to more negative parenting behaviors. Furthermore, higher levels of parental depressive symptoms were associated with higher levels of child internalizing problems, and higher levels of positive parenting were associated with lower levels of child externalizing problems. In a more recent study, Han et al. (2021) found that Chinese parents' dispositional mindfulness was indirectly associated with child internalizing and externalizing behaviors. Other studies have reported that mindful parenting is associated with better parent-child communication (Lippold et al., 2015, 2021). Campbell et al. (2017) reported that higher levels of parental mindfulness are associated with lower levels of parental stress, which in turn are associated with enhanced parental attunement and responsiveness to the child's needs. Zhang et al. (2019) found that parental dispositional mindfulness was associated with higher levels of mindful parenting, which in turn facilitated parent-child attachment that was associated with the children's lower emotional negativity. What these studies suggest is that parental mindfulness is directly associated with positive child outcomes.

Understanding parent-child transactional processes enables mindfulness interventions to be directed at either the parent or the child. Of particular interest is that intervening only with the parents and enhancing their trait mindfulness may lead to more positive outcomes not only for themselves but also for their children. Correlational and longitudinal studies have suggested various pathways by which these positive outcomes may be achieved. Another way of looking at the effects of intervening only with parents is within the cascades framework in which the interventions produce specific changes in parents, which in turn produce changes in their children's behavior through complex multiple pathways (Masten & Cicchetti, 2010). In behavioral terms, "spill over" effects may provide a more parsimonious explanation. Children perceive positive changes in their parents' behavior due to mindfulness intervention, which in turn differentially affects parent-child interactions, leading to enhanced reinforcement value of parent-child transactions, thus enhancing socially appropriate behavior. While the mechanism of cascading or spill over effects of parental mindfulness on child behavior remains to be fully established, in the ecological transactional model of behavior change, intervening with the child's parents produces changes in the children's behavior. That is, the bidirectional interactions between parents and children, professional caregivers (referred to as just "caregivers" hereafter) and their clients, and teachers and their students can be changed by manipulating the mindfulness levels of the adults.

In the context of mindfulness-based interventions, the earliest demonstration of this bidirectional effect involved enhancing the mindfulness of caregivers and assessing its effects on nonverbal individuals with profound physical, medical, and intellectual disabilities (Singh et al., 2004). Baseline measures of happiness of these individuals were recorded via behavioral observation while being provided leisure activities individually by one of six caregivers. Then three caregivers were provided training in mindfulness, with the other three remaining as yoked controls. Behavioral observations of happiness displayed by the individuals were recorded for 16 weeks following caregivers being trained in mindfulness. Results showed that the levels of happiness displayed by the individuals when provided leisure activities by the caregivers trained in mindfulness was significantly higher when compared to the control caregivers. This study suggested that a virtuous bidirectional transaction can be established by providing training only to the caregivers. One of the implications of this finding was that it may be more efficient to intervene with caregivers because effects of the training may cascade to those in their care, thereby maximizing overall effects of training a single person.

This chapter presents an overview of mindfulness-based programs that have been used to teach mindfulness to parents, caregivers, and teachers that have produced cascading or spill over effects on children and adolescents. The importance of this literature is that it provides research-based evidence for mindfulness-based programs that can be used not only with children and adolescents with academic, social, and clinical problems but also as public health programs that may preempt or lessen the arising of such problems in children and adolescents generally. We present an overview of mindfulness-based programs from studies in which teaching mindfulness to parents, caregivers, and teachers changed the behavior of children and adolescents. The emphasis is less on the studies than on the *programs* used in these studies.

Teaching mindfulness to parents

Parent training programs have been effective in reducing typically developing children's behavioral problems. The underlying rationale for parenting programs is that enhancing parenting skills and focusing on parent-child interactions will have positive effects on their children. Given that child behavior problems exacerbate parenting stress and mindfulness-based programs attenuate stress, mindful parenting programs have been developed that focus on stress reduction in parents, thereby changing the nature of parent-child interactions (Bögels & Restifo, 2014; Dykens et al., 2014; Neece, 2014; Singh et al., 2006b). Mindful parenting programs are designed for training parents and, naturally, most studies have reported the effects of such training on parents. However, if mindful parenting changes bidirectional parent-child interactions, it would be expected that enhancing parent mindfulness would also change the behavior of their children. If this is the case, then what kinds of mindful parenting programs produce such effects?

In a multiple baseline experimental design study, Singh et al. (2006b) provided customized 12-session mindfulness-based training to three parents of children with autism spectrum disorder (ASD). Each session was for two hours and held once a week. Behavioral observation measures of the children's behavior were recorded during the 80-week study. When compared to baseline observations, changes in the children's aggression, noncompliance, and self-injury decreased following mindfulness training of the parents. Given the experimental design, the bidirectional changes in the children's behavior can be attributed to parent mindfulness training. The key aspects of the 12-week mindfulness program are presented in Table 10.1. Singh et al. (2007) replicated this study with four parents of children with intellectual and developmental disabilities using the same 12-week mindfulness-based training program. Event recording and behavioral observation were used to collect data on two child behaviors—physical aggression (i.e., hitting, biting, kicking, slapping, pushing, and shoving) and social interaction with siblings (i.e., positive, negative, or neutral). Commensurate with mindfulness training of the parents, the children's physical aggression decreased to near-zero levels. Concomitantly, when compared to baseline levels, there were minimal changes in the children's positive social interaction with their siblings, but there were significant reductions in negative social interactions with siblings and significant increases in neutral social interactions (i.e., the children played by themselves without interacting with their siblings). In a subsequent study, parents of children with attention deficit hyperactivity disorder were provided the same 12-week mindfulness-based training, and similar cascading effects of their training was evident on the children's compliance (Singh et al., 2010b).

In another study, parents were referred for training in mindful parenting because of their child's and/or their own psychopathology, or because of parent-child relationship problems (Bögels et al., 2014). In a wait-list design study, the parents participated in an eight-week mindful parenting program, with a follow-up session eight weeks after termination of the training. The key aspects of the eight-week mindfulness program are presented in Table 10.2. Results showed that parent-rated internalizing and externalizing psychopathology of the children showed statistically significant improvements both at the termination of parent mindfulness training and at the eight-week follow-up. These are important findings of the cascading effects of mindful parenting because no clinical intervention was provided for the children's mental health issues, and the training was relatively short (24 hours spread over eight weeks). Meppelink et al. (2016) essentially replicated this study with a multisite training program.

Table 10.1 Outline of the 12-session mindfulness staff training program (Singh et al., 2006b)

1 General introduction to mindfulness parent training program
   - a Discussion of mother-child positive and negative interactions
   - b Discussion of parent and/or child training programs that mother has previously participated in
   - c Mother's experiences with previous parent training programs
   - d Discussion of mother's expected outcomes from a parent training program
   - e Discussion of the aims of the mindfulness parent training program
   - f Review of program requirements: reading, meditation practice, application of mindfulness, and data collection
   - g Maintaining a practice journal
   - h Set home practice tasks

2 Knowing your mind
   - a Interactive review of homework
   - b Review of mindfulness and mindlessness
   - c Identification of instances of mindfulness and mindlessness during mother-child interactions
   - d Basic meditation techniques for sitting and walking meditation
   - e Meditation practice on observing your mind
   - f Discussion of practice on observing your mind and its applications in mother-child interactions
   - g Set homework practice tasks

3 Focused attention
   - a Interactive review of homework
   - b Review of focused attention
   - c Breathing as focused attention or awareness
   - d Meditation practice on breathing
   - e Discussion of practice on breathing and its applications in mother-child interactions
   - f Set home practice tasks

4 Focused attention on arousal states
   - a Interactive review of homework
   - b Review of arousal states that precede and follow mother-child interactions
   - c Meditation practice on arousal
   - d Discussion of practice on arousal and its applications in mother-child interactions
   - e Set home practice tasks

5 Being in the present moment
   - a Interactive review of homework
   - b Review of being in the present moment in the midst of chaos
   - c Meditation practice on being in the present moment
   - d Discussion of practice on being in the present moment and its applications in mother-child interactions
   - e Set home practice tasks

(*Continued*)

Table 10.1 (Continued)

6 Beginner's mind
- a Interactive review of homework
- b Review of premature cognitive commitment; bounded vs. unbounded reality
- c Meditation practice on beginner's mind
- d Discussion of practice on beginner's mind and its applications in mother-child interactions
- e Set home practice tasks

7 Being one with your child
- a Interactive review of homework
- b Review of being in the "zone" or having a "peak experience;" being one with your child
- c Meditation practice on being your child
- d Discussion of practice on being your child and its applications in mother-child interactions
- e Set home practice tasks

8 Nonjudgmental acceptance
- a Interactive review of homework
- b Review of acceptance and nonjudging; nonjudgmental acceptance of your child
- c Meditation practice on nonjudgmental acceptance
- d Discussion of practice on nonjudgmental acceptance and its applications in mother-child interactions
- e Set home practice tasks

9 Letting go
- a Interactive review of homework
- b Review of doing one's part and letting go of everything else
- c Meditation practice on letting go
- d Discussion of practice on letting go and its applications in mother-child interactions
- e Set home practice tasks

10 Lovingkindness
- a Interactive review of homework
- b Review of acting with compassion
- c Meditation practice on lovingkindness
- d Discussion of practice on lovingkindness and its applications in mother-child interactions
- e Set home practice tasks

11 Problem solving
- a Interactive review of homework
- b Review the nature of problems and solutions
- c Meditation practice on problem solving
- d Discussion of practice on problem solving and its applications in mother-child interactions
- e Set home practice tasks

12. Using mindfulness in daily interactions
    a Interactive review of homework; data collection
    b Putting it all together; review of meditation exercises and applications
    c Meeting mother's expectations; mother-child interactions then vs. now
    d Discussion on mindfulness in daily interactions
    e Plans for follow-up, keeping in touch, and long-term practice

The basic program was as presented in Table 10.2, plus at least a one hour of meditation practice a day. No clinical services were provided to the children as a part of this study. Parent ratings indicated statistically significant reductions in the children's psychopathology at the end of the mindfulness parenting program and at the eight-week follow-up. This study provided added support for the cascading effects of mindfulness training of parents reported by Bögels et al. (2014) for children with serious mental health issues.

Given that mindfulness-based stress reduction (MBSR; Kabat-Zinn, 1990) is the seminal mindfulness program, which spawned most others that followed, the question arises whether the effects of teaching MBSR to parents would cascade to their children in the absence of direct intervention with the children. In a wait-list control study, Neece (2014) provided MBSR training to parents of young children with developmental delays. The key aspects of the eight-week MBSR program are presented in Table 10.3. To assess the cascading effects of mindfulness training on the children's behavior, the parents rated their children's behavior problems on the Child Behavior Checklist (Achenbach, 2000) before and following MBSR training. Results showed a cascading effect of parental MBSR training on the children's behavior problems (i.e., attention problems and symptoms of attention deficit hyperactivity disorder). Variations of the Neece (2014) study data were reanalyzed with different sample sizes and additional measures (Lewallen & Neece, 2015; Roberts & Neece, 2015) and showed similar findings. For example, as secondary informants, teachers noted improvements in the children's self-control, communication, responsibility, and cooperation. Both mothers and teachers also reported improvements in the children's empathy and engagement.

In follow-up studies, a second wave of data was collected on MBSR training with parents of young children with developmental delays (Chan & Neece, 2018a, 2018b; Neece et al., 2019) and combined with the data collected by Neece (2014) for further analyses with a larger data set. Chan and Neece (2018a) reported reductions in the children's inattention and withdrawn behaviors that were maintained during the six-month follow-up period. When the data were grouped by ethnicity, it neatly fell into two groups—Latino and non-Latino

Table 10.2 Outline of the eight-session mindful parenting program, with an eight-week follow-up (Bögels et al., 2014)

1 Automatic pilot versus nonreactive parenting, awareness of each moment, perceiving with a "fresh" view
   a Getting to know each other
   b Rationale
   c Raisin exercise
   d Body scan

2 Beginners mind parenting, perception vs. interpretation, obstacles to practice
   a Body scan
   b Interactive review of homework
   c Exploration of obstacles to practice
   d Attitudinal foundation of mindfulness
   e Seeing your child with beginner's mind
   f 10-minute sitting meditation on the breath

3 Watching the body during parenting stress, mindful seeing
   a Exercise seeing with a "fresh" view
   b. 20-minute sitting meditation with focus on breath and body sensations
   c Interactive review of homework (meditation exercises and pleasant event calendar)
   d Yoga practice (lying) with theme of limits
   e 3-minute breathing space

4 Responding vs. reacting to parenting stress
   a 30-minute sitting meditation with awareness of breath, body, and sounds
   b Interactive review of homework
   c Discussing negative events
   d 3-minute breathing space
   e 3-minute coping space; flight-fight-freeze dance demonstration
   f Yoga practice (sitting and standing) with theme of balance

5 Recognizing patterns, responding with acceptance to self and child
   a 40-minute sitting meditation with awareness of breath, body, sounds, and thoughts
   b Interactive review of homework
   c Discussing stressful interactions with child; experiential practice of accepting emotions of parent and child
   d 3-minute coping space using the most difficult behavior of your child, interactive discussion of parent-child patterns

6 Dealing with difficult emotions
   a 40-minute sitting meditation with awareness of breath
   b Body, sounds, and thoughts
   c Choiceless awareness; interactive review of homework
   d Discussing stressful situations with partner/child
   e Experiential awareness of automatic reactions from parents' own childhood
   f Walking meditation; meditation practice of mindfulness applied to a stressful parenting event
   g 3-minute coping space, allowing emotions to be there, "doors"

7 Rupture and repair; acceptance and limits
   a 40-minute sitting meditation with awareness of breath, body, sounds, and thoughts and choiceless awareness
   b Interactive review of homework
   c Rupture and repair exercise for parent-child conflicts; awareness of limits

8 What has been learned and the future
   a Body scan, review of homework, meditation on goals and hopes, evaluation of personal process via symbolic objects and process description
   b Make plans for continuing mindful parenting practice for the next eight weeks, and bring intention to them

9 Follow-up meeting (eight weeks after session 8)
   a Sitting meditation
   b Discussion of home practice in the past eight weeks
   c Setting intentions for the coming eight months
   d Mountain meditation
   e Stone meditation
   f Individual feedback on the assessment results
   g Final questions or help needed

parents (Neece et al., 2019). As expected, the child data showed the same overall outcomes as in the Chan and Neece (2018a) study, given that the same data were analyzed. However, a comparative analysis of the child data grouped by ethnicity indicated lower levels of parent-ratings of behavior problems following MBSR training of Latino parents when compared to the children of the non-Latino parents. Overall, this set of interrelated studies showed that training on the MBSR program also results in the cascading of parental mindfulness to their children with developmental delays, and it does so regardless of ethnicity.

In a series of three studies, mothers of children with ASD were given training in a specific mindfulness-based program, Mindfulness-Based Positive Behavior Support (MBPBS), a multicomponent personal transformation program that seamlessly braids two evidence-based approaches (see Singh et al. 2020a). The key aspects of the seven-day MBPBS program are presented in Table 10.4. In a proof-of-concept study, mothers of adolescents with ASD participated in an eight-week MBPBS program (Singh et al., 2014). Although no training was provided to the adolescents, their problem behaviors decreased and compliance behaviors increased commensurate with mindfulness training of the mothers. The second study addressed whether mindfulness training was equally effective for mothers of children with ASD vs. mothers of children with intellectual disability (Singh et al., 2019). Both groups of mothers participated in a three-day version of the seven-day MBPBS training, but no training was provided to their children. The children of both groups of mothers showed significant reductions in aggressive and disruptive behaviors and increases in compliance

Table 10.3 Key components of the MBSR eight-week training program

Session 1:	There is more right with you than wrong with you a Body scan, standing yoga b Raisin-eating meditation c Body scan, mindful eating one meal this week
Session 2:	Perception and creative responding a Opening meditation, sitting meditation, standing yoga, body scan, awareness of breathing sitting meditation b Mindfulness of routine activities, yoga postures c Body scan, awareness of breathing sitting meditation
Session 3:	Pleasure and power in being present a Opening meditation, mindful lying down yoga, walking practice, closing meditation b Mindful listening and speaking c Alternate body scan with lying down yoga, sitting meditation
Session 4:	How conditioning and perception shape our experience a Opening meditation, standing yoga, sitting meditation, closing meditation b Mindful listening and speaking c Alternate body scan with lying down yoga, sitting meditation
Session 5:	Awareness of being stuck; responding rather than reacting a Opening meditation, standing yoga (few poses), sitting meditation, closing meditation b Mindful listening and speaking c Alternate sitting meditation with standing yoga and either body scan or lying down yoga
Session 6:	Working with kinds of situations a Standing yoga, sitting meditation, closing meditation b Mindful listening and speaking c Alternate sitting meditation with body scan and/or standing or lying down yoga
All Day:	A silent retreat a Yoga b Sitting meditation c Body scan d Walking meditation e Mountain or lake meditation f Eating meditation (informally at lunch) g Lovingkindness meditation h Visual meditation followed by mindful walking, possibly outdoors, stopping and noticing one thing i Closing meditation
Session 7:	Integrating mindfulness practice into daily life a Sitting meditation: mountain, lake, or lovingkindness b Mindful listening and speaking c Practice formal sitting, yoga, walking and/or body scan
Session 8:	Follow through practices for ever a Body scan, yoga, sitting meditation b Mindful listening and speaking c Keep up the practice and make it your own; be present in your life

Table 10.4 Outline of the seven-day MBPBS program (Singh et al., 2014)

Day 1: Introduction to the MBPBS program (first one-day training; Week 1)
- a *Samatha* meditation
- b *Kinhin* meditation
- c *Vipassanā* meditation
- d Five hindrances—sensory desire, ill will, sloth and torpor, restlessness and remorse, and doubt
- e Daily logs and journaling
- f Home meditation practice (Weeks 1–4)

Day 2: The Four Immeasurables (first day of five-day intensive training; Week 5)
- a Review of meditation practice
- b Introduction to the Four Immeasurables (*Brahmavihara*: *metta*—lovingkindness; *karuna*—compassion; *mudita*—empathetic joy; *upekkha*—equanimity)
- c Equanimity meditation
- d Beginner's mind
- e Applications to PBS practice

Day 3: Being in the present moment
- a Review of Day 2 instructions and practices
- b Further instructions on the Four Immeasurables
- c Equanimity meditation
- d Lovingkindness meditation
- e Being in the present moment
- f Applications to PBS practice

Day 4: The Three Poisons
- a Review of Days 2 and 3 instructions and practices
- b Further instructions on the Four Immeasurables
- c Equanimity meditation
- d Lovingkindness meditation
- e Compassion meditation
- f The Three Poisons—attachment, anger, and ignorance
- g Applications to PBS practice

Day 5: Attachment and anger—*shenpa* and compassionate abiding meditations
- a Review of Days 2 to 4 instructions and practices
- b Further instructions on the Four Immeasurables
- c Equanimity meditation
- d Lovingkindness meditation
- e Compassion meditation
- f Joy meditation
- g Attachment and anger—*shenpa* and compassionate abiding meditations
- h Applications to PBS practice

Day 6: Attachment and anger—meditation on the soles of the feet
- a Review of Days 2 to 5 instructions and practices
- b Review and practice *Samatha*, *Kinhin* and *Vipassanā* meditations
- c Review of the Four Immeasurables
- d Practice equanimity, lovingkindness, compassion, and joy meditations

(*Continued*)

Table 10.4 (Continued)

	e	Attachment and anger—meditation on the soles of the feet
	f	Review of applications to PBS practice
	g	Review of the MBPBS training program
	h	Continue to implement MBPBS program (Weeks 6–10)
Day 7:		Review and moving forward (second one-day training; last day of Week 10)
	a	Review of the meditation instructions and practices (daily logs)
	b	Review and practice *Samatha, Kinhin* and *Vipassanā* meditations
	c	Review of the Four Immeasurables
	d	Practice equanimity, lovingkindness, compassion, and joy meditations
	e	Emotion regulation and anger—meditation on the soles of the feet
	f	Instructions for practicing three ethical precepts—refrain from (a) harming living creatures, (b) taking that which is not given, and (c) incorrect speech
	g	Applications to PBS practice
	h	Review of the seven-day MBPBS training program

commensurate with their mothers' training in MBPBS. This study suggested that mothers' training in mindfulness cascades to their children regardless of whether the children have ASD or intellectual disability. The third study was designed to assess the differential contribution of the MBPBS program and its components, PBS and mindfulness, in a three-arm randomized controlled design, with a 10-week pre-treatment control condition and a three-year post-training follow-up (Singh et al., 2021). Mothers of children with ASD were trained in the full MBPBS program, mindfulness alone, and PBS alone. Their children did not receive any additional training as a part of this study. The results clearly showed differential cascading effects of mothers' training on their children's behavior. Statistically significant reductions in the children's aggressive behavior and increases in their compliance behaviors were most pronounced for those children whose mothers were trained in the full MBPBS program, followed by mindfulness training alone, and lastly PBS alone. Changes in child outcomes were maintained during the three-year follow-up period, suggesting lasting differential effects of training in each of the training conditions.

In sum, the emerging data on the cascading effects of parental training in mindfulness on their children is suggestive of the potential of this approach. The cascading effects are evident regardless of the nature of the mindfulness training provided to the parents, the nature of the psychopathology of the parents and children, the age of the children, or the cognitive, social, and behavioral variables measured.

Teaching mindfulness to caregivers

Extant studies of mindfulness training for caregivers have included those who provided services to adults with intellectual and developmental disabilities.

While acknowledging that with age comes experiential knowledge, generally it is the level of functioning and not age that is correlated with learning in this population. Thus, given the paucity of studies with children and adolescents, we have included studies of caregivers of adults with intellectual and developmental disabilities. These studies show that enhanced caregiver mindfulness positively cascades to their clients. For example, Singh et al. (2006a) reported that group home residents' mastery of learning objectives significantly increased commensurate with caregivers participating in a five-day mindfulness-based training (see Table 10.5 for key aspects of this program). In a follow-up study, Singh et al. (2009) reported that staff and peer injuries caused by aggressive behavior of the residents were eliminated after caregivers attended a 12-week mindfulness training program. Furthermore, caregivers virtually eliminated their use of physical restraints with the residents by the end of the study—a key finding that was replicated by Brooker et al. (2014) with a different set of mindfulness training components.

The effects of the seven-day MBPBS program (see Table 10.4) were evaluated in a series of studies on caregivers and the people they provided services to. In the first study, caregivers from community group homes participated in the MBPBS program within a multiple-baseline design and were reported to show clinically and statistically significant reductions in the use of verbal redirection and elimination of the use of physical restraints for aggressive behavior by the residents (Singh et al., 2015). The elimination of aggressive behavior by the residents, in turn, eliminated all staff and peer injuries. These findings were essentially replicated in a larger proof-of-concept quasi-experimental design study (Singh et al., 2016b). This study was followed by a randomized controlled trial (RCT) of caregiver training in MBPBS against a training-as-usual (TAU) condition (Singh et al., 2016a). The caregivers were from a large congregate care facility for residents who functioned at the severe and profound levels of intellectual and developmental disabilities. In addition to caregiver and agency variables, of interest was the cascading effects of caregiver mindfulness on the aggressive behavior of the residents. Results showed significant reductions in the residents' aggressive behavior, which in turn eliminated caregiver turnover due to injury and stress. In addition, reductions in the residents' aggressive behavior also resulted in significant reductions in 1:1 staffing that was needed for the safety and protection of caregivers and peers from the residents who were aggressive.

In the most recent study in this series, Singh et al. (2020b) evaluated the effectiveness of caregiver training in MBPBS and positive behavior support (PBS) in a RCT. Given that PBS alone is an evidence-based intervention that caregivers typically use to manage residents with challenging behavior, this was a head-to-head comparative assessment of two active interventions in a 40-week RCT. Although both interventions were effective with regard to caregiver, resident, and agency variables, MBPBS produced significantly superior effects than PBS alone. In the context of cascading effects of caregiver mindfulness, the results

Table 10.5 Outline of the five-day staff mindfulness training program (Singh et al., 2006a)

1 Concepts of mindfulness and mindlessness
  a Philosophical differences between behavioral staff training and mindfulness staff training; external vs. internal contingencies
  b Focus on how to change one's own behavior so that it may positively affect others
  c Holistic, ecological and transactional perspectives
  d Introduction to mindfulness in everyday life: open to new information; being able to see old information in new ways; having an awareness of multiple perspectives; avoiding premature cognitive commitment; understanding mindfulness and mindlessness; appreciating the positive aspects of mindlessness
  e Introduction to meditation postures (sitting and walking); mindful breathing and the conscious returning of attention to the breath when the mind wanders away; objective viewing of the mind
  f Mindfulness exercises and home practice
2 Mindfulness in wisdom traditions
  a Hindu and Buddhist wisdom traditions
  b Practice sitting and walking meditation
  c Mindfulness exercises and home practice
3 Understanding and using various methods to enhance mindfulness
  a Nonjudging; patience and perseverance; a beginner's mind; trust; non-striving; acceptance; letting go; doing without a focus on personal reward
  b Practice sitting and walking meditation
  c Mindfulness exercises and home practice
4 Understanding and using various methods to enhance mindfulness (continued)
  a Active observation of oneself, other, and the "problem"; accepting life as it is; knowing and experiencing "I am not my thoughts"; being compassionate; listening with calm attention; seeing through other's eyes; engaging in loving kindness; being in the present moment
  b Practice sitting and walking meditation
  c Mindfulness exercises and home practice
5 Work and play as mindfulness practice (putting it all together in daily life)
  a Applications of mindfulness in family life, at work and during play; overcoming history of mindless work behaviors and feeling the spirit within; experiencing the present moment; being loving, kind, compassionate and interacting with wisdom as a way of life
  b Practice sitting and walking meditation
  c Mindfulness exercises and home practice

essentially replicated and confirmed previous findings—greater reduction in the residents' aggressive behavior resulted in significantly reduced caregiver and peer injuries, which in turn reduced the need for 1:1 staffing for residents who were physically aggressive.

These studies indicate that the effects of training caregivers in mindfulness cascades to and improves the quality of life of those in their care. A tangential question arises regarding the cascading effects of mindfulness training of caregivers: do the cascading effects spill over to the family members of the caregivers trained in mindfulness? The short answer is that it appears to do so. Singh et al. (2004) provided mindfulness training to caregivers and observed its cascading effects on nonverbal individuals with profound physical, medical, and intellectual disabilities. The key aspects of the seven-session mindfulness training program are presented in Table 10.6. In a subsidiary study, Singh et al. (2010a) collected data on the interactions of these caregivers with their children at home with the aim of capturing generalization of the cascading effects of their mindfulness training. The target behavior was noncompliance with the caregiver's (i.e., their mother's) requests. Results showed that regardless of the different ages of the children and the baseline levels of their noncompliance, there was a significant decrease in the children's noncompliance commensurate with the mothers' training in mindfulness. The outcome of this study hinted at the much wider effects of mindfulness training beyond the person being trained.

In sum, these studies were uniformly consistent in suggesting that mindfulness training for caregivers leads to a cascading effect on the people they provide services to, resulting in improvements in their learning and maladaptive behaviors, which in turn positively transact with other variables, such as 1:1 staffing, caregiver and peer injuries inflicted by individuals who are aggressive, and caregiver turnover. These downstream positive changes flow from mindfulness training of caregivers.

Teaching mindfulness to teachers

Many studies have investigated the effects of mindfulness-based programs for teachers on various aspects of teacher well-being, including psychological stress and burnout and teaching practices (Hwang et al., 2017). However, almost all of the studies on teaching mindfulness to teachers measured the effects on teacher variables only but did not include measures of child behaviors (e.g., academic, social, mental health) that may have been affected by enhanced mindfulness of the teachers. In terms of transactional analysis, mindfulness training for teachers should change bidirectional teacher-student interactions. In a test of this concept, Singh et al. (2013) reported a study in which teachers engaged in a mindfulness program and the effects of the training were measured in terms of changes in their preschool students' behavior. When compared to baseline, behavioral observations showed statistically significant changes in the students' socially unacceptable behaviors, compliance with teacher requests, and social interactions with peers following mindfulness training of their teachers. The teachers had participated in an eight-week mindfulness program that included basic meditations, instructions on the Four Immeasurables (i.e., the *Brahmaviharas*), the Three Poisons (i.e., attachment, anger, and ignorance), beginner's mind, and being in the present moment. The key aspects of the customized mindfulness program are presented in Table 10.7.

Table 10.6 Outline of the seven-session mindfulness training (Singh et al., 2004)

Session 1:	Pretraining a Review and discussion of quality of life b Happiness as a major indicator of quality of life c Measuring and increasing happiness in individuals with profound multiple disabilities d What is mindfulness? e Mindfulness as a mediator of happiness in others f Reading assignment: *Peace Is Every Step*
Session 2:	Knowing your mind a Update and discussion from Session 1 b Discussion of mindfulness and mindlessness c Identification of instances of mindfulness and mindlessness when interacting with people at work; outcomes of each type of behavior d Meditation exercise on observing your mind e Instructions on basic meditation techniques for sitting and walking meditation f Discussion: any activity with the mind properly focused can be a meditation
Session 3:	Appreciating oneness of everything a Update and discussion from Session 2 b Discussion of diversity, duality, non-duality and oneness c Meditation exercise on emptiness; single pointed meditation on an object d Discussion: developing a disciplined meditation practice; journaling
Session 4:	Being in the present moment a Update and discussion from Session 3 b Discussion: being in the moment in the midst of chaos; c Applications when working with individuals with profound multiple disabilities d Meditation exercise on being in the present moment e Discussion: living in the silence between thoughts
Session 5:	Beginner's mind a Update and discussion from Session 4 b Discussion: premature cognitive commitment; bounded vs. unbounded reality c Meditation exercise on the beginner's mind d Discussion: responding with our hearts rather than with our minds; doing what is right rather than what is correct
Session 6:	Being the activity a Update and discussion from Session 5 b Discussion: being in the "zone" or having a "peak experience" c Meditation exercise on being the activity d Discussion: putting it all together and practicing mindfulness on a daily basis

Session 7:	Review and wrap-up	
	a	Update and discussion from Session 6
	b	Review of mindfulness training course and arrangements for individual follow-up
	c	Discussion: disciplined practice of mindfulness in daily life

Table 10.7 Outline of mindfulness training program for teachers (Singh et al., 2013)

Pretraining:	Introduction to the mindfulness training program	
	a	What is mindfulness?
	b	Everyday mindfulness
	c	Mindful teaching
	d	Mindfulness in the classroom
	e	Discussion of course requirements
	f	Home practice: Complete course requirements
Week 1:	Basic meditations	
	a	Review of pretraining and collection of consent forms
	b	Discussion of mindfulness and mindlessness in the classroom
	c	Instructions on body scan
	d	Basic meditations—calm abiding and walking meditation
	e	Discussion: applications of body scan, calm abiding and walking meditation
	f	Home practice: journaling and meditation practice
Week 2:	Developing awareness	
	a	Review of Week 1 and home practice
	b	Difficult situations as opportunities for practice
	c	Instructions on developing awareness
	d	Meditation on observation of thoughts
	e	Discussion: applications of observation of thoughts in the classroom and daily life; breathing in, breathing out
	f	Home practice: journaling and meditation practice
Week 3:	Beginner's mind	
	a	Review of Week 2 and home practice
	b	Premature cognitive commitment and confirmation bias
	c	Developing awareness in the classroom
	d	Meditation on the beginner's mind
	e	Discussion: applications of beginner's mind in the classroom and daily life
	f	Home practice: journaling and meditation practice
Week 4:	Being in the present moment	
	a	Review of Week 3 and home practice
	b	You are where your mind is
	c	Being in the present moment in the midst of chaos
	d	Meditation on being in the present moment

(Continued)

Table 10.7 (Continued)

	e	Discussion: applications of being in the present moment in the classroom and daily life
	f	Home practice: journaling and meditation practice
Week 5:		The Four Immeasurables
	a	Review of Week 4 and home practice
	b	Lovingkindness and compassion
	c	Instructions on the Four Immeasurables
	d	Meditation on loving kindness and compassion
	e	Discussion: applications of loving kindness and compassion in the classroom and daily life
	f	Home practice: journaling and meditation practice
Week 6:		The Four Immeasurables
	a	Review of Week 5 and home practice
	b	Joy and equanimity
	c	Instruction on the Four Immeasurables
	d	Meditation on equanimity
	e	Discussion: Applications of equanimity in the classroom and daily life
	f	Home practice: journaling and meditation practice
Week 7:		The Three Poisons
	a	Review of Week 6 and home practice
	b	Attachment, anger, and ignorance
	c	Getting "hooked"
	d	Meditation on *shenpa*
	e	Discussion: applications of *shenpa* in the classroom and daily life
	f	Home practice: journaling and meditation practice
Week 8:		Review and wrap-up
	a	Review of Week 7 and home practice
	b	Putting it all together
	c	A *Sangha* of teachers
	d	Discussion: Disciplined practice of mindfulness in teaching and daily life
	e	Review of mindfulness training course and arrangements for individual follow-up interviews
	f	Post-course interviews

In a large cluster randomized study involving 185 teachers across 20 schools, Hwang et al. (2019a, 2019b) evaluated the effects of an eight-week mindfulness-based program on teacher well-being. In addition to measures of teacher well-being, the teachers rated the quality of their relationship with their students, and the students rated their sense of relatedness to their teachers (Hwang et al., 2019a). Furthermore, the teachers' verbal interactions with their students were rated by independent observers (Hwang et al., 2019b). These additional measures provide subjective (teacher and student self-ratings) and objective

Table 10.8 Weekly intervention topics, objectives, and activities (Hwang et al., 2019a)

Week 1:	Introduction mindfulness
	a Body, breath, being
	b Progressive muscle relaxation into mindfulness of body and breath
	c Quality of mind: relaxation
Week 2:	Coming to senses
	a Previously learned activities
	b Common practice problems
	c Mindful yoga/walking mindfulness of sounds
	d The senses, presence, and mental well-being
	e Quality of mindfulness: presence
	f Mindful eating
Week 3:	Noticing reactions
	a Previously learned activities
	b Mind in the jar
	c Feelings: when do they affect stress reactivity?
	d Noticing reactions
	e Breathing in, breathing out
	f How to continue
Week 4:	Who's the boss? Me or my thoughts?
	a Previously learned activities
	b Defining and identifying thoughts
	c How thoughts affect stress reactivity
	d Metaphors for thoughts
	e Mindfulness of thoughts
	f Remembering kindness
	g How to continue
Week 5:	Developing emotional intelligence
	a Previously learned activities
	b What are emotions?
	c What do I notice, in body and mind, when I feel stressed?
	d We are not our thoughts and emotions
	e R.A.I.N
	f What is my emotional timeline?
Week 6:	Being a friend to myself
	a Previously learned activities
	b Being a friend to myself
	c Love for myself and others
	d What nourishes and depletes me?
	e Mindful listening
	f Quality of mind: kindness
Week 7:	Emotional intelligence in action
	a Previously learned activities
	b Introducing empathy, compassion and emotional intelligence
	c Mindful yoga into love for myself and others
	d Emotional intelligence
	e Role-play with emotions
	f Just like me

(Continued)

Table 10.8 (Continued)

Week 8:	Continuing in awareness	
	a	Previously learned activities
	b	Quality of mind: spacious
	c	Mindful stretching into simply being
	d	Self-review and mindful listening
	e	Cultivating gratitude
	f	How to continue

(behavioral observations) data on teacher-student transactions that can be used to infer the cascading effects of enhanced teacher mindfulness on the students. Results indicated no significant change in teacher ratings of teacher-student relationship, but there was a significant change in student ratings of their sense of connectedness to their teachers. The behavioral observations showed significant positive changes in teacher-student verbal transactions, and these changes were maintained during the five-month post training follow-up. The key aspects of the mindfulness program used in this study are presented in Table 10.8.

In sum, although the literature is somewhat meager, research suggests that positive bidirectional teacher-student changes occur commensurate with mindfulness training of teachers. Providing mindfulness training to teachers may be more efficient than implementing individualized behavior change programs with individual students.

Conclusion

Based on transactional models of adult-child interactions, studies on teaching mindfulness to parents, caregivers, and teachers suggest that child and adult interactions are linked in ongoing reciprocal ways. When parents, caregivers, and teachers are provided mindfulness training, personal transformation takes place, and it cascades on the children and adolescents in their care. The cascading effects of adult mindfulness can be measured behaviorally by observing well-defined behaviors of the children (e.g., aggression, physical disruption, compliance with parental requests, social interactions). These effects are evident irrespective of the nature and length of the mindfulness programs, the psychopathological status of the adults and the children, the age of the children and adolescents, and the nature of the child variables being measured. Although this is an emerging area of mindfulness research, with limited extant data, the significance of the findings cannot be overstated. Clinically, it means that teaching mindfulness to a few adults can change the behavior of a much larger population of children and adolescents without programming specific intervention(s) for them.

References

Achenbach, T. M. (2000). *Manual for the child behavior checklist 1.5–5*. Burlington, VT: University of Vermont, Department of Psychiatry.

Bögels, S. M., Hellemans, J., van Deursen, S., Römer, M., & van der Meulen, R. (2014). Mindful parenting in mental health care: Effects on parental and child psychopathology, parental stress, parenting, co-parenting, and marital functioning. *Mindfulness, 5*, 536–551.

Bögels, S. M., & Restifo, K. (2014). *Mindful parenting: A guide for mental health practitioners*. New York, NY: Springer.

Bronfenbrenner, U., & Morris, P. A. (2006). The bioecological model of human development. In R. M. Lerner & W. Damon (Eds.), *Handbook of child psychology: Vol. 1. Theoretical models of human development* (6th ed., pp. 793–828). Hoboken, NJ: Wiley.

Brooker, J. E., Webber, L., Julian, J., Shawyer, F., Graham, A. L., Chan, J., & Meadows, G. (2014). Mindfulness-based training shows promise in assisting staff to reduce their use of restrictive interventions in residential services. *Mindfulness, 5*, 598–603.

Campbell, K., Thoburn, J. W., & Leonard, H. D. (2017). The mediating effects of stress on the relationship between mindfulness and parental responses. *Couple and Family Psychology: Research and Practice, 6*(1), 48–59.

Chan, N., & Neece, C. L. (2018a). Mindfulness-based stress reduction for parents of children with developmental delays: A follow-up study. *Evidence-Based Practice in Child and Adolescent Mental Health, 3*(1), 16–29.

Chan, N., & Neece, C. L. (2018b). Parenting stress and emotion dysregulation among children with developmental delays: The role of parenting behaviors. *Journal of Child and Family Studies, 27*, 4071–4082.

Dishion, T. J., Patterson, G. R., & Kavanagh, K. A. (1992). An experimental test of the coercion model: Linking theory, measurement, and intervention. In J. McCord & R. E. Tremblay (Eds.), *Preventing antisocial behavior: Interventions from birth through adolescence* (pp. 253–282). New York, NY: Guilford Press.

Dykens, E. M., Fisher, M. H., Taylor, J. L., Lambert, W., & Miodrag, N. (2014). Reducing distress in mothers of children with autism and other disabilities: A randomized trial. *Pediatrics, 134*, 454–463.

Han, Z. R., Ahemaitijiang, N., Yan, J., Hu, X., Parent, J., Dale, C., . . Singh, N. N. (2021). Parent mindfulness, parenting, and child psychopathology in China. *Mindfulness, 12*(1), Advance of Print.

Hwang, Y.-S., Bartlett, B., Greben, M., & Hand, K. (2017). A systematic review of mindfulness interventions for in-service teachers: A tool to enhance teacher wellbeing and performance. *Teaching and Teacher Education, 64*, 26–42.

Hwang, Y.-S., Goldstein, H., Medvedev, O. N., Singh, N. N., Noh, J.-E., & Hand, K. (2019a). Mindfulness-based intervention for educators: Effects of a school-based cluster randomized controlled study. *Mindfulness, 10*, 1417–1436.

Hwang, Y.-S., Noh, J.-E., Medvedev, O. N., & Singh, N. N. (2019b). Effects of a mindfulness-based program for teachers on teacher wellbeing and person-centered teaching practices. *Mindfulness, 10*, 2385–2402.

Kabat-Zinn, J. (1990). *Full catastrophe living: Using the wisdom of your body and mind to face stress, pain, and illness*. New York, NY: Delta.

Lerner, R. M. (1982). Children and adolescents as producers of their own development. *Developmental Review, 2*, 342–370.

Lewallen, A. C., & Neece, C. L. (2015). Improved social skills in children with developmental delays after parent participation in MBSR: The role of parent-child relational factors. *Journal of Child and Family Studies, 24*, 3117–3129.
Lippold, M. A., Duncan, L. G., Coatsworth, J. D., Nix, R. L., & Greenberg, M. G. (2015). Understanding how mindful parenting may promote mother-youth communication. *The Journal of Youth and Adolescence, 44*, 1663–1673.
Lippold, M. A., Jensen, T. M., Duncan, L. G., Nix, R. L., Coatsworth, J. D., & Greenberg, M. T. (2021). Mindful parenting, parenting cognitions, and parent-youth communication: Bidirectional linkages and mediation processes. *Mindfulness, 12*(1), Advance of Print.
Masten, A. S., & Cicchetti, D. (2010). Developmental cascades. *Development Psychopathology, 22*, 491–495.
Meppelink, R., de Bruin, E. I., Wanders-Mulder, F. H., Vennik, C. J., & Bögels, S. M. (2016). Mindful parenting training in child psychiatric settings: Heightened parental mindfulness reduces parents' and children's psychopathology. *Mindfulness, 7*, 680–689.
Neece, C. L. (2014). Mindfulness-based stress reduction for parents of young children with developmental delays: Implications for parental mental health and child behavior problems. *Journal of Applied Research on Intellectual Disabilities, 27*(2), 174–186.
Neece, C. L., Chan, N., Klein, K., Roberts, L., & Fenning, R. M. (2019). Mindfulness-based stress reduction for parents of children with developmental delays: Understanding the experiences of Latino families. *Mindfulness, 10*, 1017–1030.
Parent, J., Garai, E., Forehand, R., Roland, E., Champion, J. E., Haker, K., . . Compas, B. E. (2010). Parent mindfulness and child outcome: The roles of parent depressive symptoms and parenting. *Mindfulness, 1*, 254–264.
Patterson, G. R. (1982). *Coercive family processes*. Eugene, OR: Castalia.
Roberts, L. R., & Neece, C. L. (2015). Feasibility of mindfulness-based stress reduction intervention for parents of children with developmental delays. *Issues in Mental Health Nursing, 36*, 592–602.
Sameroff, A. J. (1986). Environmental context of child development. *Journal of Pediatrics, 109*, 192–200.
Sameroff, A. J. (1993). Models of development and developmental risk. In C. H. Zeanah, Jr. (Ed.), *Handbook of infant mental health* (pp. 3–13). New York, NY: Guilford Press.
Sameroff, A. J., & Fiese, B. H. (2000). Transactional regulation: The developmental ecology of early intervention. In J. P. Shonkoff & S. J. Meisels (Eds.), *Handbook of early intervention* (pp. 135–159). Cambridge, UK: Cambridge University Press.
Sameroff, A. J., & MacKenzie, M. J. (2003). Research strategies for capturing transactional models of development: The limits of the possible. *Development and Psychopathology, 15*, 613–640.
Singh, N. N., Lancioni, G. E., Chan, J., McPherson, C. L., & Jackman, M. M. (2020a). Mindfulness-based positive behavior support. In I. Ivtzan (Ed.), *Handbook of mindfulness-based programs: Mindfulness interventions from education to health and therapy* (pp. 42–52). London, UK: Routledge.
Singh, N. N., Lancioni, G. E., Karazsia, B. T., Chan, J., & Winton, A. S. W. (2016a). Effectiveness of caregiver training in mindfulness-based positive behavior support (MBPBS): A randomized controlled trial. *Frontiers in Psychology, 7*, 1549.
Singh, N. N., Lancioni, G. E., Karazsia, B. T., & Myers, R. E. (2016b). Caregiver training in mindfulness-based positive behavior support (MBPBS): Effects on caregivers and adults with intellectual and developmental disabilities. *Frontiers in Psychology, 7*, 98.

Singh, N. N., Lancioni, G. E., Karazsia, B. T., Myers, R. E., Hwang, Y.-S., & Anālayo, B. (2019). Effects of mindfulness-based positive behavior support (MBPBS) training are equally beneficial for mothers and their children with autism spectrum disorder or with intellectual disabilities. *Frontiers in Psychology, 10*, 385.

Singh, N. N., Lancioni, G. E., Karazsia, B. T., Myers, R. E., Winton, A. A. W., Latham, L. L., & Nugent, K. (2015). Effects of training staff in MBPBS on the use of physical restraints, staff stress and turnover, staff and peer injuries, and cost effectiveness in developmental disabilities. *Mindfulness, 6*, 926–937.

Singh, N. N., Lancioni, G. E., Medvedev, O. N., Hwang, Y.-S., & Myers, R. E. (2021). A component analysis of the mindfulness-based positive behavior support (MBPBS) program for mindful parenting by mothers of children with autism spectrum disorder. *Mindfulness, 12*(1), Advance of Print.

Singh, N. N., Lancioni, G. E., Medvedev, O. N., Myers, R. E., Chan, J., McPherson, C. L., . . Kim, E. (2020b). Comparative effectiveness of caregiver training in mindfulness-based positive behavior support (MBPBS) and positive behavior support (PBS) in a randomized controlled trial. *Mindfulness, 11*, 99–111.

Singh, N. N., Lancioni, G. E., Winton, A. S. W., Curtis, W. J., Wahler, R. G., Sabaawi, M., . . McAleavey, K. (2006a). Mindful staff increase learning and reduce aggression in adults with developmental disabilities. *Research in Developmental Disabilities, 27*, 545–558.

Singh, N. N., Lancioni, G. E., Winton, A. S. W., Fisher, B. C., Wahler, R. G., McAleavey, K., . . Sabaawi, M. (2006b). Mindful parenting decreases aggression, noncompliance, and self-injury in children with autism. *Journal of Emotional and Behavioral Disorders, 14*, 169–177.

Singh, N. N., Lancioni, G. E., Winton, A. S. W., Karazsia, B. T., Myers, R. E., Latham, L. L., & Singh, J. (2014). Mindfulness-based positive behavior support (MBPBS) for mothers of adolescents with autism spectrum disorder: Effects on adolescents' behavior and parental stress. *Mindfulness, 5*, 646–657.

Singh, N. N., Lancioni, G. E., Winton, A. S. W., Karazsia, B. T., & Singh, J. (2013). Mindfulness training for teachers changes the behavior of their preschool children. *Research in Human Development, 10*(3), 211–233.

Singh, N. N., Lancioni, G. E., Winton, A. S. W., Singh, A. N., Adkins, A. D., & Singh, J. (2009). Mindful staff can reduce the use of physical restraints when providing care to individuals with intellectual disabilities. *Journal of Applied Research in Intellectual Disabilities, 22*, 194–202.

Singh, N. N., Lancioni, G. E., Winton, A. S. W., Singh, J., Curtis, W. J., Wahler, R. G., & McAleavey, K. M. (2007). Mindful parenting decreases aggression and increases social behavior in children with developmental disabilities. *Behavior Modification, 31*(6), 749–771.

Singh, N. N., Lancioni, G. E., Winton, A. S. W., Singh, J., Singh, A. N., Adkins, A. D., & Wahler, R. G. (2010a). Training in mindful caregiving transfers to parent-child interactions. *Journal of Child and Family Studies, 19*, 167–174.

Singh, N. N., Lancioni, G. E., Winton, A. S. W., Wahler, R. G., Singh, J., & Sage, M. (2004). Mindful caregiving increases happiness among individuals with profound multiple disabilities. *Research in Developmental Disabilities, 25*, 207–218.

Singh, N. N., Singh, A. N., Lancioni, G. E., Singh, J., Winton, A. S. W., & Adkins, A. D. (2010b). Mindfulness training for parents and their children with ADHD increases the children's compliance. *Journal of Child and Family Studies, 19*, 157–166.

Singh, N. N., & Singh, D. S. (2001). Developmental considerations in treatment. In H. Orvaschel, J. Faust, & M. Hersen (Eds.), *Handbook of conceptualization and treatment of child psychopathology* (pp. 9–38). New York, NY: Pergamon.

Zhang, W., Wang, M., & Ying, L. (2019). Parent mindfulness and preschool children's emotion regulation: The role of mindful parenting and secure parent-child attachment. *Mindfulness, 10*, 2481–2491.

Index

Page numbers in **bold** refer to tables.